A MUSICAL MEMOIR: REFLECTIONS ON LIFE, DEATH, AND AMERICAN CULTURE, 1942-2022

VOLUME 2

B. Lee Cooper

Project Editor: Frank W. Hoffmann

Paw Paw Press

2023

Lee and Jill Cooper

AUDIO IMAGES OF AMERICAN CULTURE, 1965-2008	209
1965 - A Revolutionary Year in Popular Music?	211
The Black Civil Rights Struggle	215
The Women's Movement	225
The Vietnam War Experience	235
The Republic of Rock	239
The Lunar Landing	243
John Fogerty	247
Launching The Rock & Roll Hall of Fame	277
Splitting the BILLBOARD Pop Music Charts, 1955-1989	281
Technology	285
ADULTHOOD, MARRIAGE, FAMILY LIFE, AND EXAMINING MUSIC	335
Baby Boomers	337
Cats	341
Christmas Songs and Holiday Celebrations	343
Health and Happiness	347
One-Hit Wonders	351
Record Store Days	357
Romance	361
Spiritual Ideas and Religious Imagery	383
Wedding Bells	393
"White Christmas" - and "Unchained Melody"	397
RECORDING GIANTS AND PERFORMING HEROES	401
Chuck Berry	403
Solomon Burke	409
Ray Charles	413
Sam Cooke	417
Aretha Franklin	421
Jerry Lee Lewis	425
Jerry Lee Lewis and Elvis Presley	429
Little Richard	433
Keb' Mo'	437
Roy Orbison	439
Jimmy Reed	443
Marty Robbins	447
Nina Simone	451
Jackie Wilson	455
KEY INFLUENCES IN MUSIC ANALYSIS	457
Larry Birnbaum	459
Ken Burns	463
Mark Duffett	467
Peter Guralnick	471

TABLE OF CONTENTS

FOREWORD	7
"Still Life" - A Poem	9
INTRODUCTION	11
AUDIO IMAGES OF AMERICAN CULTURE, 1942-1964	39
World War II	41
Atomic Weaponry	45
Korean Conflict	51
Teenagers & Teen Culture	55
Disc Jockeys	87
The Elvis Presley Phenomenon	89
The Birth of Loud	93
Sputnik - October 4, 1957	97
The Day the Music Died - February 3, 1959	99
The Berlin Wall & The Cold War	103
The Beatles and Beatlemania	105
CHILDHOOD, FAMILY LIFE, AND LEARNING OPPORTUNITIES	107
An Age of Political Incorrectness	109
Baseball Players	111
Characters from TV and Feature Films	119
Classic Cars and Car Songs	127
Dance Styles on "American Bandstand" and "Soul Train"	131
Familiar Figures from Children's Literature	139
"Forbidden Planet" and Other Sci-Fi Films	147
"The Girl Can't Help It!"	153
Novelty Recordings	155
Public Schooling and Personal Learning	157
Rockin' Movie Soundtracks	167
Teasing, Tempting, and Sexually Suggestive Tunes	169
Teenage Telephone Communications	173
TV Westerns and Singing Cowboys	175
FAVORED MUSICAL GENRES AND PERFORMING STYLES	177
Blue-Eyed Soul Songs	179
Blues Records	187
Doo-Wop Vocal Harmony Discs	189
Instrumental Records	195
Rhythm & Blues Records	199
Rockabilly Music	203
Soul Music	207

David Hajdu	473
Jack Hamilton	477
James Sullivan	481
Steve Sullivan	485
AUDIO IMAGES OF AMERICAN CULTURE, 2009-2022	489
Personal Memoirs by Musicians	491
The Presidency of Barack Obama - Part One	497
The Presidency of Barack Obama - Part Two	501
The Decline of Protest Songs within American Popular Music	505
The Great Wall of American Music	511
Celebrating Audio Joys of Yesteryear - Christmas Songs	515
Celebrating Audio Joys of Yesteryear - Halloween and Horror Tunes	519
ACKNOWLEDGING PERSONAL MORTALITY	523
Tribute Recordings as Lyrical Eulogies	525
Aging and Death	531
Obituary - Kathleen M. Cooper (1921-2008)	537
Obituary - Charles A. Cooper (1920-2009)	539
A Health Crisis and MemoryCare Assistance	541
Obituary - Jill E. Cooper (1942-2022)	543
Death and Dying	545
APPENDICES	
Professional Resume of B. Lee Cooper	549
A Chronological Profile of Books and Articles by B. Lee Cooper, 1971-2016	567
OLLI Classes at UNC-Asheville Taken by Jill and Lee Cooper (2008-1018)	591
A Course Outline for "America in Transition, "1945-1975" (2016)	597
A Course Outline for "Persistent Themes in Popular Music" (2015)	605
Popular Music Research, Ltd. Membership List (2019)	613
PRINT RESOURCES ON POPULAR MUSIC	621
Author/Editor Profiles	635
The Paw Paw Press	637

Beach Boys

ADULTHOOD, MARRIAGE, FAMILY LIFE, AND EXAMINING MUSIC

Stevie Wonder

BABY BOOMERS

BABY BOOMER ROCK 'N' ROLL FANS: THE MUSIC NEVER ENDS
Joseph A. Kotarba
Lanham, Maryland: Scarecrow Press, 2013

Texas State University sociologist Joseph A. Kotarba attempts to demonstrate how Baby Boomers, Americans born between 1945 and 1964, were initiated into a distinctive rock 'n' roll culture during their adolescence and have continued to use this rock 'n' roll idiom to master daily challenges during their adulthood. He contends that rock 'n' roll music has served and continues to function as a meaningful reference in shaping Boomer identifies as lovers, parents, believers, political actors, and social adaptors. Kotarba mixes anecdotal, experiential, and research-based evidence to support his thesis. Initially, he posits that technological advancements, ranging from CD recordings and MP3 players to Pandora playlists and radio/TV channels offering 24/7 access to "Classic Rock", create an uninterrupted audio lifeline for Boomers. Expanding on this soundtrack-of-your-life idea, Kotarba reflects on his male, middle class, Catholic, Chicagoan background in respect to constructing his own lyric-based understanding of women. He identifies five key songs that have guided his thinking - "Runaround Sue", "Sweet Thing", "Come Saturday Morning", "Why", and "I Knew I Loved You". He then explains how these particular tunes have shaped his understanding and interactions with the female gender. Rejecting some popular numbers like "Under My Thumb", Kotarba asserts, "I never liked songs that were overtly mean or degrading to women." (p. 26) Over the following nine chapters the author cites examples of Boomers making sense of intimate relationships (a single Queen tune is referenced), songs and performances assisting in parenting (any tune by Madonna will reportedly generate mother-daughter bonding), artist preferences shaping or defining political orientations (from The Beach Boys influencing John McCain to Stevie Wonder creating meaning for Barack Obama), songs impacting spiritual journeys (from "Astral Weeks" to "The Joshua Tree"), songs encouraging sociability (several unspecified tunes reportedly favored by Houston Blues Society members), and songs that address the aging process (any New Age recording). The brief text concludes with a five-page, single-spaced list of "References" and a single-page "Index".

In a book sub-titled "The Music Never Ends", it is inconceivable that Kotarba underplays direct references to specific recordings. That is, while he speculates that a vast array of memorable songs are suitable lyrical guides to confront complex personal development issues (especially among audio-driven Boomers), he fails to provide the necessary research-based causal links between specific recordings and the modified judgments, informed decisions, and altered behaviors that he claims to exist. Humorously, Kotarba's bare-bones "Index" lists only six songs. The author's use of the generic term "rock 'n' roll" to depict the diverse musical listening universe of Baby Boomers is also monumentally misleading. Undeniably, the music of Elvis Presley, Little Richard, and Buddy Holly does constitute a small portion of the rock 'n' roll roots for some Boomers. But a much more complex mix of lyrics, rhythms, instrumentations, and artists fills the total Baby Boomer playlist. From The Beatles to Fleetwood Mac, from Johnny Cash to Dolly Parton, from Aretha Franklin to John Fogerty, from Led Zeppelin to Bonnie Raitt, Boomer sounds include blues, country, pop, rock, and soul. Described in a more accurate, neutral, research fashion, it's "popular music" rather than the more narrow rock 'n' roll designation.

Regrettably, there are several other serious problems with this study. First, Kotarba is too self-referential in ascribing his own beliefs about music to the general Baby Boomer population. This overly-personalized perspective, which is anathema to all cultural anthropologists and to most sociologists as well, leads the author into lengthy literary digressions not only about his favorite songs about women (pp. 26-34), but also concerning his personal admiration for little-known spiritual singer John Michael Talbot (pp. 59-62), a recent musical epiphany aboard an international airline flight (pp. 67-71), and his experiences guiding the "Blues-N-Kids" musical project in Houston, Texas (pp. 78-87). Clearly, this much mental meandering in a slim 143-page text is counter-productive. Second, Kotarba's "Reference" section is overloaded with antique sociological studies and more than 25 citations to the author's own previously published commentaries. What is glaringly absent are citations related directly to the book's topic. Where are the scholarly volumes related to cross-generational analysis (William Strauss and Neil Howe, GENERATIONS (1991) and THE FOURTH TURNING (1997), for instance), to Baby Boomer opinion surveys (Rex Weiner and Deanne Stillman, WOODSTOCK CENSUS (1979), perhaps), to the timing of musical taste acquisition (David Hajdu's thought-provoking May 24, 2011 NEW YORK TIMES article "Forever Young" as an example), to the evolution of U. S. recorded music styles (Phillip Ennis, THE SEVENTH STREAM (1992) fills that bill), to changes in American popular culture (George Lipsitz, TIME PASSAGES (1990) is relevant), and, finally, to contemporary fan cultures (Daniel Cavicchi, TRAMPS LIKE US (1998) and Erika Doss, ELVIS CULTURE (2004) are worth consulting)? This lack of current scholarship renders many of Kotarba's observations and generalizations questionable at best. Finally, the editors at Scarecrow Press are to be faulted for allowing this volume to be printed with several paragraphs of identical commentary repeated verbatim (pp. 38/42 and 74-75/121-122). Likewise, the throw-away "Index" is a sign of careless proofreading as well as disdain for serious readers.

This book is not totally without merit. Kotarba is fully justified in seeking to explore the distinctive role of recorded music in the lives of Baby Boomers. However, his hypothesis needs to be tested by examining the reactions of various age groups to hundreds and hundreds of popular recordings. Specifically, one might begin by assessing individual and group responses to recordings presenting themes about military conflicts (from "Fortunate Son" to "War"), about social perfectionism (from "Imagine" to "Simple Song Of Freedom"), about materialism (from "Mr. Businessman" to "It's Money That Matters"), and so on. Of course, Kotarba must then be able to link such John Lennon, Ray Stevens, and Randy Newman tunes to changing aspirations, beliefs, and behaviors among senior Baby Boomers in these surveys. In addition, he must also demonstrate that pre-Baby Boomers and members of Generation X are somehow less influenced by their distinctive adolescent musical experiences. As published, though, BABY BOOMER

ROCK 'N' ROLL FANS is a seriously flawed, under-researched, self-indulgent compendium of speculations about generational musical preferences and the personal effects of fandom.

(This commentary was originally published as B. Lee Cooper. "Review of BABY BOOMER ROCK 'N' ROLL FANS by Joseph A. Kotarba," POPULAR MUSIC AND SOCIETY, 37:3 (July 2014): 381-383.)

Fleetwood Mac in 1969

CATS

FELINE GROOVY: 24 PURRFECT TRACKS FOR KOOL KATS
Various Artists
CD, Ace Records Ace CDCHD 1168, 2008

This theme-directed grouping of 24 tunes salutes cats imagery in American recordings between 1955 and 1966. Ace compiler and felineophile Vicki Fox offers no explanation about either the narrow chronological window for song selection or the process by which the particular numbers were chosen. Among the two dozen tracks presented, rarities abound. Seldom encountered cuts include: "Cleo" by Rene Hall, "Kitty Kat" by Paul Ott, "El Pussy Cat" by Mongo Santamaria, "Love Kitten" by Noreen Corcoran, and "Top Cat Theme Song" by The Top Cat Orchestra and Chorus. The latter is a 55-second performance taken from a 1962 Little Golden Record. The more familiar releases featured on this CD are: "What's New Pussycat?" by Tom Jones, "Leave My Kitten Alone" by Little Willie John, "Three Cool Cats" by The Coasters, and "Tom Cat" by The Rooftop Singers. The unusual mix of R&B, country, jazz, and folk recordings is distinctive and the campy illustrations scattered throughout the liner notes are fanciful.

Despite the breadth of musical styles, though, one wishes that the compiler had been less narrow in time frame and more expansive in her presentation of cat-related recordings. This is not to suggest absurd extrapolation, such as the random inclusion of tunes issued by Kitty & The Haywoods, The Pussy Cat Dolls, Cat Stevens, Little Charlie & The Nightcats, Faster Pussycat, or even the very catty Eartha Kitt. Nor is it a request for an examination of the profane uses of feline-related descriptors by 2 Live Crew, Missy "Misdemeanor" Elliott, Funkdoobiest, Queen Pen, Luke, or The 5th Ward Boyz. Finally, no exploration of recordings like "Pussy Willow" (1982) by Jethro Tull, "Pussywillows, Cattails" (1969) by Gordon Lightfoot, the numerous cat house numbers by ZZ Top, or even "Pussy Galore's Flying Circus" (1966) by Roland Shaw are being sought. In reality, of course, cats, kittens, and all sorts of fascinating metaphorical feline images have dominated both song titles and recorded lyrics to a much greater degree than is even hinted at in FELINE GROOVY.

How many lives (and incarnations) do audio cats have in American recordings released over the past 90 years? Let's count. First, piano salutes like "Kitten on The Keys" extend from Zez Confrey (1921) to Roger Williams (1964) and beyond. Second, the 1949 novelty number "Pussy Cat Song (Nyow! Nyot! Nyow)" as hit recording material for a multitude of singers such as Patty Andrews, Bob Crosby, Perry Como, Joy Nichols & Benny Lee, and Jo Stafford & Gordon MacRae. Third, feline-oriented songs have appeared in many motion picture soundtracks, including WHAT'S NEW PUSSYCAT ("Pussycats On Parade" - 1965), THE GREAT GATSBY ("Kitten on The Keys" - 1974), VICTOR/VICTORIA ("Cat and Mouse" - 1982), PRIVATE PARTS ("Cat Scratch Fever" - 1997), and DETROIT ROCK CITY ("Cat Scratch Fever" - 1999).

Fourth, television viewers have experienced salutes to felines via THE MICKEY MOUSE CLUB's "Pussy Cat Polka" (1975) and the frequently-aired commercial championing "Meow Mix Cat Food" (1989). Fifth, the volatility of felines is illustrated in songs like "Bear Cat" (1953) by Rufus Thomas, "Cat Scratch Fever" (1977) by Ted Nugent, and "Kittens Got Claws" (1989) by Whitesnake. Sixth, the haunting sounds of cat creatures of the night are captured in "Black Cat Moan" (1973) by Beck, Bogart & Appice, "Black Cat Moan" (1990) by John Mayall, "Pussycat Moan" (1991) by Katie Webster, and "Pussycat Meow" (1992) by Dee-lite.

Seventh, literary references to cats inform recordings such as "Puss 'N' Boots" 1973) by The New York Dolls, "Puss 'N' Boots" (1984) by Adam Ant, and "Puss 'N' Boots . These Boots (Are Made for Walkin'") (1989) by Kon Kan. Eighth, the tune "Cat's in The Cradle" has been reliable recording material for such diverse male artists as Harry Chapin (1974), The Compton Brothers (1975), Ugly Kid Joe (1993), and Ricky Skaggs (1996). Finally, the 1954 observation by Big Joe Turner in "Shake, Rattle, and Roll" that a jilted boyfriend is like a one-eyed cat peeping in a seafood store still constitutes one of the best lines in R&B lyric history. As Salty Dog noted in his 1990 ode to the number of feline lives - "Cat's Got Nine"!

FELINE GROOVY provides an interesting but overly constrained perspective on an important lyrical subject. This collection substitutes artistic obscurity for the broader opportunity to explore the comedy, tragedy, excitement, novelty, and astounding frequency of feline imagery in 20th century American music. Nevertheless, if a black cat crosses your path, run to your local record shop and purchase this CD. It's a sure antidote against bad luck - or a personal CATastrophy.

(This commentary was originally published as B. Lee Cooper. "Review of FELINE GROOVY: 24 PURRFECT TRACKS FOR KOOL KATS by Various Artists," POPULAR MUSIC AND SOCIETY, 33 (October 2010): 566-567.)

CHRISTMAS SONGS AND HOLIDAY CEKEBRATIONS

SLEIGH RIDES, JINGLE BELLS, AND SILENT NIGHTS: A CULTURAL HISTORY OF AMERICAN CHRISTMAS SONGS
Ronald D. Lankford, Jr.
Gainesville: University Press of Florida, 2013

Holiday hits abound. From Black Friday, the first Christmas shopping day following Thanksgiving, until December 26th, American airwaves are glutted with Yuletide music. "Silent Night" joins the playlist with "Run, Run Rudolph"; "Away in The Manger" often follows a rendition of "Jingle Bell Rock". Not surprisingly, the singers of these tunes are as diverse as the holiday songs themselves. Gene Autry, Perry Como, Ella Fitzgerald, Burl Ives, and Mel Torme represent traditional Christmas music artistry. Meanwhile, Alabama, Big Bad Voodoo Daddy, Harry Connick, Jr., the Eagles, Toby Keith, Kathy Mattea, Brian Setzer, Bruce Springsteen, and Vanessa Williams offer more contemporary interpretations of old and new holiday numbers. The 1982 duet of "Peace on Earth/Little Drummer Boy" performed by Bing Crosby and David Bowie symbolically bridged the generation gap in holiday harmonizing. Of course, there are some Christmas recordings that defy analysis related to artistic style. Such holiday classics include: "The Chipmunk Song" by The Chipmunks [Alvin, Simon, and Theodore], "Christmas Dragnet" by Stan Freberg, with Daws Butler, "Do They Know It's Christmas?" by Band Aid, "Five Pound Box Of Money" by Pearl Bailey, "Jingle Bells" by The Singing Dogs, "Redneck 12 Days Of Christmas" by Jeff Foxworthy, "Santa Baby" by Eartha Kitt, "Santa Claus Is Watching You" by Ray Stevens, and "The Twelve Gifts Of Christmas" by Allan Sherman. Christmas recordings are undeniably deep-seated within American popular culture. Yet there are very few scholarly studies that have attempted to assess the meaning of holiday music within modern U.S. history.

Ronald D. Lankford, Jr. examines the emergence of popular Christmas recordings during the 1940s along with the rampant expansion of chart-topping holiday hits during the following two decades. The audio bookends for his study are Bing Crosby's "White Christmas" (1942) and Elmo and Patsy's "Grandma Got Run Over by A Reindeer" (1979). While he references several holiday songs issued prior to Crosby's monster hit, including religious hymns ("Ave Maria"), traditional carols ("God Rest Ye Merry Gentlemen"), and pop tunes ("Jingle Bells", "Jolly Old St. Nicholas", and "Up on The House Top"), Lankford focuses his research on recordings created during the historical period from the beginning of World War II to the fall of Saigon. Specifically, Lankford explains his approach by noting, "Beneath the familiar melodies and words, Christmas songs reveal a portrait of the American psyche past and present, wishing simultaneously to embrace nostalgia, commerce, charity, carnival, romance, and travesty (p. 7)."

Christmas music ostensibly provides the audio background for the annual Christian celebration of the birth of Jesus in Bethlehem. But the American holiday soundscape crafted between 1940 and 1970 added other heroes, other places, and other values.

Lyrical images of the Blessed Virgin, the manger scene, the Wise Men, and even the Holy Child were joined by audio tributes to the nuclear family and their home, to children and their desires for overwhelming piles of gifts beneath well-decorated Christmas trees, and to fictional characters like Santa Claus and Rudolph the Red-Nosed Reindeer. In addition, modern Christmas tunes also expressed anxiety about overwhelming holiday expenses, loneliness among single adults during the extended Yuletide period, and anger among those who object to the commercialism, hypocrisy, and foolishness that dominates the lengthy Christmas season. Obviously, Lankford's study is not just an extension of the longstanding "sacred vs. secular" holiday debate. Nor is it another put-Christ-back-into-Christmas diatribe. The author identifies numerous contradictions, conflicts, and misconceptions that underlie American approaches to December 25th activities.

SLEIGH RIDES, JINGLE BELLS, AND SILENT NIGHTS offers extensive illustrations of Christmas recordings, a thorough print bibliography of popular culture writings and holiday-related resources, and a succinct seven-chapter analysis of America's obsession with Yuletide-related ideas, events, and music. The initial chapter of the text offers an overview of American Christmas music from colonial times up to the Second World War. It also plumbs the distinctive form of idealism featured in "White Christmas", "The Christmas Song (Chestnuts Roasting On An Open Fire)", and "I'll Be Home for Christmas". Chapter Two explores nostalgia, both real and imaginary, transmitted via the classic recordings of Bing Crosby, Nat King Cole, and Perry Como. Chapter Three investigates the growing centrality of Santa Claus in both regional and national holiday advertising. Lankford assesses the Jolly Old Elf from Haddon Sundblom's inventive Coca-Cola advertisements and through the numerous child-centered holiday tunes that came to define Kris Kringle. Chapter Four examines the increase in holiday romance topics and playful sexuality themes featured on recordings like "Winter Wonderland", "Let It Snow! Let It Snow! Let It Snow!", and "Baby, It's Cold Outside". Chapter Five dwells on the underside of Yuletide festivities. Lankford studies audio responses to hard times during the holidays, with specific references to loneliness, joblessness, lost love, and alienation from common social expectations. Recordings emblematic of these feelings are "Please Come Home for Christmas", "Will Santy Come to Shanty Town", "Hard Candy Christmas", "Christmas In Prison", "Blue Christmas", and "Pretty Paper". Chapter Six confronts recordings that express comical or satirical perspectives about Christmas traditions. Here Lankford explores a range of releases, including "I Saw Mommy Kissing Santa Claus", "Nuttin' for Christmas", "Green Chritma", "Daddy's Drinking Up Our Christmas", "Yingle Bells", and "Grandma Got Run Over by A Reindeer". In the concluding chapter, Lankford summarizes his earlier assertions about the paradoxical nature of holiday values featured in America's Christmas recordings. He also observes that holiday hits are encoded with mythic (though often vague and imprecise) ideals of home-and-family and democracy-and-equality. Finally, Lankford shows how Christmas recordings stitch together a smorgasbord of ideas about children, gifts, love, Santa Claus, and snowy weather while down-playing religious doctrine and the Bethlehem Story.

Lankford's scholarly investigation follows Christmas recordings from their 19th century seasonal novelty status into the golden age of popular holiday hits following the Second World War. But during the late '70s and '80s he describes a systemic collapse of public interest concerning most Yuletide tunes. The author reminds his readers that the chart-topping years of Christmas recordings coincided with the homecoming of American soldiers in 1945, the heightened wedding rates / birth rates and the lower divorce rates during the '40s and '50s, the emphasis on family unit solidarity and the centrality of residential life, the growth of the U.S. economy into the late '60s, and the enlargement of the post-war middle class with its growing disposable income. When the convergence of these demographic and economic circumstances began to erode after 1963, Christmas music idealism suddenly seemed antique and irrelevant. A less homogenous American populace, being challenged economically and feeling politically disoriented, didn't totally abandon Christmas though. Churches still held candle-light services; hymns were sung; Christmas dinners were hosted; charitable donations were made; and Christmas trees were still surrounded by gifts. But the holiday music that echoed throughout cavernous malls and over radio stations was no longer of primary interest.

Perhaps the only weakness in Lankford's perceptive analysis is his over-emphasis on country tunes to demonstrate attitudes about hard times and holiday blues. He probably should have relied more heavily on R&B recordings to illustrate the lyrical frequency of loneliness, alcoholism, and broken romantic relationships. Examples of African-American commentaries on these topics are available in "Christmas Blues" by Larry Darnell, "Empty Stocking Blues" by Floyd Dixon, with Johnny Moore's Three Blazers, "How I Hate To See Xmas Come Around" by Jimmy Witherspoon, "(It's Gonna Be A) Lonely Christmas" by the Orioles, "Just A Lonely Christmas" by the Moonglows, "Lonesome Christmas" by Lowell Fulson, "Santa's Messin' With The Kid" by Eddie C. Campbell, and "Sonny Boy's Christmas Blues" by Sonny Boy Williamson. Beyond this minor criticism, though, Lankford's study is superb. It is meticulous and loaded with keen insights and well-supported conclusions.

(This commentary was originally published as B. Lee Cooper. "Review of SLEIGH RIDES, JINGLE BELLS, AND SILENT NIGHTS: A CULTURAL HISTORY OF AMERICAN CHRISTMAS SONGS by Ronald D. Lankford, Jr.," ROCK MUSIC STUDIES, 1:3 (October 2014): 299-300.)

The Moonglows

HEALTH AND HAPPINESS

DESTINATION HEALTH: DOC FEELGOOD'S ROCK THERAPY
Various Artists
CD, Bear Family BCD 17524, 2020

Medical imagery has been a staple within recorded song lyrics since 1890. It's manifestations vary greatly, of course. Sometimes audio commentaries relate to direct contacts with doctors and nurses within hospital settings. Think of recordings like "I Don't Want To Get Well (I'm In Love With A Beautiful Nurse)" (1918), "Just Dropped In (To See What Condition My Condition Was In)" (1968), "Michael Casey As A Physician" (1891), "Terrible Operation Blues" (1930), and "Transfusion" (1956). Formal appointments and personal visits with physicians often stem from personal worry about particular symptoms. Such problems arise from "Allergies" (1983), "Chills And Fever" (1961), an "Itchy Twitchy Feeling" (1958), being "Paralyzed" (1957), contacting "Poison Ivy" (1959), or fearing the onset of "Scarlet Fever" (1983).

Many times, though, lyrical references to medical personnel or individual health needs are less involved with treatable maladies and more related to romantic issues. Illustrations of these emotionally-informed audio concerns occur in recordings like "Addicted To Love" (1986), "Bad Case Of Loving You (Doctor, Doctor)" (1979), "Doctor Feelgood" (1967), "Doctor's Orders" (1982), "Dr. Rock And Roll" (1980), "Good Lovin'" (1966), and "You're My Remedy." Of course, there are also numerous tunes that attribute mental and physical wellness to either a mutal loving relationship or to the more questionable practice of self-medication. Audio examples of these assertions are found in "Back On My Feet Again" (1968), "Found A Cure" (1979), "I Don't Need No Doctor" (1966), "Love Potion No. 9" (1959), "The Pill" (1975), "Rolaids, Doan's Pills, and Preparation H" (1980), and "Mothers Little Helper." Finally, high humor can be found in medically-related numbers such as "Jeremiah Peabody's Poly Unsaturated Quick Dissolving Fast Acting Plasant Tasting Green and Purple Pills" (1961), "Like A Surgeon" (1985), and "They're Coming To Take Me Away, Ha-Haaa!" (1966). This array of recordings demonstrates the prevalence of healthcare topics and medical imagery scattered throughout 20th century music. Strangely, though, not one of the aforementioned songs is anthologized in the 2020 Bear Family compendium DESTINATION HEALTH: DOC FEELGOOD'S ROCK THERAPY.

DESTINATION HEALTH illustrates a good compilation idea gone awry. The assembly of this thematic CD constitutes audio bungling at best and sonic malfeasance at worst. Project coordinator Nico Feuerbach and liner notes writer Bill Dahl have taken a potentially fascinating topic with an extensive, diverse recording heritage and mismanaged both the compilation itself and the accompanying discographic description work as well. The 30 recordings cobbled together for DESTINATION HEALTH are generally second-rate performances by little-known artists. Dahl devotes an extensive number of pages to explaining the minor league backgrounds of these strange performers. But who cares? Examples of vocal and instrumental mediocrity abound.

Just listen to Benn Joe Zeppa on "Doctor Doctor" (1959), Dennis Bell on "Quarantine" (1961), Macy Skipper on "Bop Pills" (1985), Joey Nepote on "Doctor, Doctor, Doctor" (1960), Noro Morales on "Vitamina" (1959), and Homer "Zeke" Clemons on "Operation Blues No. 2" (1950).

Worse yet, Feuerbach and Dahl elect to ignore noteworthy performances of fascinating health-related tunes by well-recognized stars. Instead, they substitute sub-par versions of well-known numbers. For example, DESTINATION HEALTH features Herbert Hunter singing "Doctor Feel-Good" (1962) rather than the original recording by Dr. Feelgood and The Interns. The collection highlights The Knockouts performing "Fever" (1961) rather than featuring either Little Willie John or Peggy Lee. And it champions Sonny Burgess wailing "Feelin' Good" instead of Little Junior Parker. Finally, the organizers of DESTINATION HEALTH even choose weak recordings by prominent artists when more appropriate tunes by the same singers are readily available. The most stunning example of this sonic malpractice is the anthologizing of the derivative "Tu-Ber-Cu-Lucas and The Sinus Blues" (1959) by Huey "Piano" Smith and The Clowns instead of his two high-charting tunes "Rockin' Pneumonia And The Boogie Woogie Flu" (1957) and "High Blood Pressure" (1958).

Is there anything of value hidden in DESTINATION HEALTH? Drawing from a recording pool than spans 1939 to 1985, Feuerbach and Dahl do manage to unearth a few interesting, unfamiliar recordings with fascinating medical connections. For instance, Woody Herman's Orchestra greets "Doctor Jazz" (1939) and Louis Jordan introduces "Rock Doc" (1957). These two physicians turn out to be dancing fools. Little Willie Littlefield's "Drinkin' Hadacol" (1949) and Bo Diddley's "Pills" (1961) are laughable tributes to the practice of self-medication. The McGuire Sisters, Ebe Sneezer [a.k.a. John D. Loudermilk] and The Epidemics, and Lonnie Miley suffer through bouts of "Achoo-Cha-Cha (Gesundheit)" (1958), "Asiatic Flu" (1957), and "Satellite Fever - Asiatic Flu" (1958). And from a psychiatric perspective, The Mysterions, Their Singing Bodies, and Big Jay McNeely explore "Amnesia" (1959), "Diagnosis -- Neurosis" (1965), and "Psycho Serenade" (1959). Finally, Johnny Burnette and Doctor Ross happily agree that no amount of "Rock Therapy" (1956) will ever diminish the dancing zeal associated with "The Boogie Disease" (1954).

Amidst the 2020 Coronavirus pandemic, playful recorded material about healthcare would seem to be just what the doctor ordered. While DESTINATION HEALTH is a poor prescription for audio enjoyment, a second compilation opinion might prove to be helpful. Public spirits might be lifted via tunes that praise old-time TV physicians like Dr. Ben Casey or "Marcus Welby, M.D." (1970). It might also be beneficial to recall more relaxed times when no face masks were required and self-medication was as easy as securing "Kicks" (1966), riding a "Magic Bus" (1968), or receiving guidance from "Mr. Tambourine Man" (1965). Likewise, battling the COVID-19 scourge makes other problems like being "Fit or Fat - Fat As I Am" (1985) or displaying "Skinny Legs And All" (1967) seem tolerable. Bear Family compilers Feuerbach and Dahl need to reformultate their audio diagnosis after they perform a final autopsy on their DOA disc. To get contemporary listeners "Feeling Alright" (1969) and to eliminate chances of future

"Hurt" (1961) or "Pain" (1971), the next incarnation of DESTINATION HEALTH should be headlined by "I Feel Good" (1956), "Little Fine Healthy Thing" (2003), "Physical" (1982), and "Work That Body" (1982). A friendly chat with "The Doctor" (1989), accompanied by the smooth singing Doobie Brothers, would be advisable, too.

The Doobie Brothers

ONE-HIT WONDERS

ALLEY OOP: 30 ONE-HIT WONDERS - U.S. POP!
Various Artists
CD, Jasmine JASCD 901, 2014

CHILLS & FEVER: 30 ONE-HIT WONDERS - U.S. RHYTHM & BLUES
Various Artists
CD, Jasmine JASCD 902, 2014

HERE COMES SUMMER: 30 ONE-HIT WONDERS - U.K. POP!
Various Artists
CD, Jasmine JASCD 900, 2014

YOU'RE THE REASON: 30 ONE-HIT WONDERS - U.S. COUNTRY & WESTERN
Various Artists
CD, Jasmine JASCD 903, 2014

ONE-HIT WONDERS OF THE 50S & 60S
Various Artists
3 CD, Golden Stars GSS 5688, 2011

ONE-HIT WONDERS 2
Various Artists
2 CD, Time-Life Music R696-16, 2001

ONE-HIT WONDERS
Various Artists
3 CD, Goldies GLD 25420-1/2/3, 2000

ONE-HIT WONDERS
Various Artists
2 CD, Time-Life Music R696-05, 1999

THE ONE & ONLY: 21 ONE-HIT WONDERS
Various Artists
CD, Crimson MIDCD 052, 1999

RCA'S GREATEST ONE-HIT WONDERS
Various Artists
CD, RCA 66881-2, 1996

ONE-HIT WONDERS
Various Artists
2CD, E. M. I. (Germany) 2CD 686-7-98766-2, 1992

Utilizing a literary metaphor, one notes that the record-related descriptor "One-Hit Wonder" is less a RED BADGE OF COURAGE and more of a SCARLET LETTER. No, this single hit artist designation does not suggest a serious moral lapse. However, it does imply that a performer was a one-trick pony. It triggers perceptions about limited musical talent, limited song production skills, and even limited energy as a professional artist. Issuing a single hit recording, but never duplicating that feat again, amounts to failure by omission. Disc jockeys, music critics, rock journalists, and even pop music fans wield the one-hit wonder sword with vengeance. It is so deeply ingrained within commercial recording industry parlance that in 1998 Chicago-based record collector Wayne Jancik issued an entire volume titled THE BILLBOARD BOOK OF ONE-HIT WONDERS. Single hit artists are frequently bound together within this non-musical category of under-accomplishment. Upon closer examination, though, the world of one-hit wonder recordings is much too diverse and complex to be blanketed by the simple fiction of personal artistic laxity. Over the past three decades, hundreds of songs by one-hit wonders have been anthologized and successfully marketed to contemporary CD buyers. Note the eleven releases listed above. The rich variety of tunes presented in these retrospective compilations suggests that there may be several logical justifications for the high incidence of single hit artists. The following commentary cites a multiplicity of reasons for the existence of the one-hit wonder phenomenon within American popular music.

One-hit wonders have dotted the U.S. musical landscape since the initial commercial circulation of sound recordings. Prior to World War II, single hits were the fate of many highly talented performers. These individuals included legendary pop composer Harold Arlen ("Let's Fall in Love" - 1936), 8-year-old movie sensation Bobby Breen ("Let's Sing Again" - 1936), glamorous film star Joan Crawford ("It's All So New to Me" - 1939), and prominent stage comedian Jimmy Durante ("Inke Dinka Doo" - 1934). By the early 1950s, of course, BILLBOARD and CASH BOX had refined the weekly, monthly, and yearly music chart rankings of commercial recordings throughout America. Over the following five decades these two hit-charting magazines calculated the individual rankings of particular songs within the weekly top 100 best-selling releases. Thus, between 1950 and 1999, the reality of being a one-hit wonder was statistically quantified and publicly reported. Even during the 21st century, there are numerous examples of single-hit recording stars. Illustrations include Atlanta-born rapper Lil' Joe ("Who U Been Wit" - 2002), female singer-songwriter Bonnie McKee ("American Girl" - 2013), and Brooklyn-born singer/actress Jeanie Ortega ("Crowded" - 2006). But the primary locus of one-hit wonder scolding occurred during the second-half of the 20th century. Not surprisingly, the eleven CD compilations listed above feature songs that were released after 1950, ranging from the single hits by The Chords ("Sh-Boom" - 1954) and Joan Weber ("Let Me Go Lover" - 1954) to the isolated pop novelties by Carl Douglas ("Kung Fu Fighting" - 1974) and Toni Basil ("Mickey" - 1982).

Why are there so many one-hit wonder artists? What professional circumstances, personal issues, or social/political situations hinder certain singers from attaining a second or a third hit recording? Undeniably, music chart competition among all recording artists is incredibly fierce. Likewise, competition among record companies to help their own artists achieve "Top 10" BILLBOARD and CASH BOX listings is a cut-throat system as well. And the record-buying public remains amazingly fickle and unpredictable concerning their purchases of pop songs. It's extremely rare for an artist to establish a comfortable sonic niche that will guarantee public acceptance of song-after-song.

But there are several understandable reasons why so many performers are able to achieve only one isolated hit. First, some recorded tunes are idiosyncratic items, produced as either an answer song or a cover recording. Such novelty releases tend to be ephemeral at best. For example, Jeanne Black ("He'll Have to Stay" - 1960) responded successfully to Jim Reeves' "He'll Have to Go." But after that she never issued another hit. And Bonnie Lou ("Daddy-O" - 1955) saw her first hit song successfully covered by The Fontane Sisters - and she never charted a tune again. Second, mortality and youthful recording age can also dramatically impact potential pop chart longevity. The Big Bopper ("Chantilly Lace" - 1958) died in an airplane crash on February 3, 1959 and never had the opportunity to repeat his initial "Top 10" recording performance. And 9-year-old Ricky Zahnd ("(I'm Gettin') Nuttin' for Christmas" - 1955) and 14-year-old Laurie London ("He's Got the Whole World in His Hands" - 1958) were child performers who achieved singular youthful hits, but never re-entered the music charts as adults. Third, the dissolution of a singing duo or the false attribution of a performing artist's name will inevitably inhibit future hit-making possibilities. Jan & Arnie ("Jennie Lee" - 1958) simply split up after their first charted hit. In more complex circumstances, though, rockabilly performer Bill Parsons ("The All-American Boy" - 1958) was wrongly-listed as the lead vocalist on the hit recording actually performed by Bobby Bare; The Marathons ("Peanut Butter" - 1961) was a pseudonym temporarily adopted by The Vibrations; and The Hollywood Argyles ("Alley-Oop" - 1960) were a fictitious group manufactured by clever singer-songwriter and producer Gary Paxton. Fourth, new television programs often promote their specific theme songs or issue general cast recordings to increase viewer interest. These tunes tend to be singular recording experiences with few follow-up song options. This was the case for Joan Weber ("Let Me Go Lover" - 1954) as well as for Heights ("How Do You Talk to An Angel" - 1992).

Fifth, lyrical uniqueness and artist ethnicity may prompt one-hit wonder status. The foreign language hit recordings by Domenico Modugno ("Nel Blu Dipinto Di Blu (Volare)" - 1958) and The Singing Nun ("Dominique" - 1963) were unique audio events. Likewise, the spooky Halloween classic manufactured by John Zacherle ("Dinner with Drac" - 1958) was pre-destined to shiver alone on the music charts. Sixth, most recorded political commentary exists as a singular audio time capsule of social protest, with little chance of extended music chart shelf life or successful audio duplication. Examples abound. Among the best illustrations from the Vietnam War era are hits by Byron MacGregor ("The Americans" - 1974), Barry McGuire ("Eve of Destruction" - 1965), and SSgt. Barry Sadler ("The Ballad of the Green Berets" - 1966). Seventh, instrumental recordings frequently become one-time hits for previously unknown regional or international artists. This situation occurred with tunes by The Chantay's ("Pipeline" -

1963), Jorgen Ingmann ("Apache" - 1961), and Kokomo ("Asia Minor" - 1961). Eighth, dance trend recordings are often amazingly hot chart items. But they face speedy cooling factors driven by the appearance of new dance styles and new dance numbers. Performers who experienced this type of brief dance-related hit recording fame include Billy Joe & The Checkmates ("Percolator (Twist)" - 1962), Lou Bega ("Mambo No. 5 (A Little Bit of...)" - 1999), and Los Del Rio ("Macarena" - 1995). Finally, most novelty recordings are instantly funny, but remarkably fragile in terms of both chart longevity and repeatable recording success. Among the best one-hit wonders within this comedy category are Larry Groce ("Junk Food Junkie" - 1976), Larry Verne ("Mr. Custer" - 1960), Barry Gordon ("Nuttin' For Christmas" - 1955), and Nervous Norvus ("Transfusion" - 1956).

The eleven CD anthologies listed above provide extensive illustrations of recordings that achieved high-level U.S. music chart placements between 1950 and 1999. Nevertheless, the artists represented within these collections were unable to produce a second, a third, or a fourth major hit. Regrettably, the numerous anthology compilers offer no consistent definitional standard for either a hit recording or a successful follow-up release. That is, some compilers accept a "Top 40" ranking for a song to be labeled a hit, while others acknowledge only a "Top 10" listing for legitimate hit status. Similarly, there is absolutely no agreement among the various compilers about how many lesser-ranked (but still charted) recordings constitute an escape from the one-hit wonder category. For instance, it's difficult to accept the label one-hit wonder for Texas-born R&B songstress Barbara Lynn ("You'll Lose a Good Thing"—1962) because she not only scored a No. 8 hit during the early '60s, but she also charted eleven other songs during her successful decade-long recording career. These definitional flaws create confusion. Actually, the only clear agreement among these compilers is found in the identification of early '50s vocal groups who achieved one lone charted tune. These one-hit wonder ensembles include The Penguins ("Earth Angel (Will You Be Mine)" - 1955), The Silhouettes ("Get a Job" - 1958), The Monotones ("Book of Love" - 1958), and The Danleers ("One Summer Night" - 1958). One main point remains valid, though. There are numerous legitimate reasons for limited pop hit success. Being a one-hit wonder is actually the sign of a rare professional achievement. The odds of a young vocalist or an aspiring instrumentalist creating a "Top 10"-ranked song are considerably less than those of a golfer sinking a hole-in-one or a bowler rolling a perfect 300 game. Thus, singers and instrumentalists should be hailed rather than ridiculed for hitting national music chart heights with a single recording.

Works Cited

Jancik, Wayne. THE BILLBOARD BOOK OF ONE-HIT WONDERS (Revised Edition). NewYork: Billboard Books, 1998.

(This commentary was originally published as B. Lee Cooper. "One-Hit Wonders," in AIN'T THAT PECULIAR: ANSWER SONGS, NOVELTY NUMBERS, ONE-HIT WONDERS, AND MORE, edited by B. Lee Cooper and Frank W. Hoffmann (Lexington, Kentucky: Paw Paw Press, 2020): 197-200.)

Gary Paxton, the guiding force behind The Hollywood Argyles

RECORD STORE DAYS

RECORD STORE DAYS: FROM VINYL TO DIGITAL AND BACK AGAIN
Gary Calamar and Phil Gallo
New York: Sterling Publishing, 2009

In the beginning was the record store, more like a modern-day temple with its attendant priesthood and initiates, a holy repository of the culture's most sacred beats and rhymes. By comparison, the Internet is a clean room in a hospital - it lacks the funk and feeling of a place with floors and ceilings and racks full of soul-stirring goodness.

--David Was and Don Was of Was (Not Was) (pp. 222-223)

If you're into Picasso and you go to a museum, you could buy a nice print or a postcard, but you know it's nothing like the original. An MP3 is like a postcard that's a vague facsimile of a painting.

--Marc Weinstein, Co-owner of Amoeba Music (p. 183)

RECORD STORE DAYS chronicles the commercial distribution of sound recordings over the past century. Through informative vintage photographs, thoughtful commentaries from entrepreneurs who established disc dens of varying sizes, and heartfelt testimonials from contemporary musicians and record collectors about their audio epiphanies in disc shops across America, Gary Calamar and Phil Gallo craft a delightful overview of record store culture. While recent liquidation sales and closings of Tower Records, Wherehouse Records, and the Virgin Megastores are documented with sadness and the negative sales impacts of music downloading (MP3 and iTunes) are lamented, the authors spin a positive tale that focuses on the magic of the collecting mania among music mavens. Granted, money remains the common denominator among music marketers, disc purchasers, sales representatives, and record store owners. It is clear that from wholesale to retail, from new to used, and from legit product to bootleg discs, sound recordings have flexible financial value. Calamar and Gallo examine the variety of storefronts that have sought monetary gain through audio sales.

Initially, downtown stores that peddled pianos and sold sheet music also randomly stocked a few 78 rpm records. In 1932, however, Bernie George established the first independent record store - George's Song Shop - in Johnstown, Pennsylvania. Soon other stores emerged, including New York City's Commodore Music Shop and Hollywood's Wallichs Music City. From the 1940s to the present, the names of specific stores have illustrated the idiosyncratic nature of the dynamic record sales enterprise. Just consider Antone's Records, Bleecker Bob's Records, Criminal Records, Dolphin's of Hollywood, Ernest Tubb Record Shop, Grimey's New and Pre-Loved Music, Jazz Man Record Shop, Licorice Pizza, Oar Folkjokeopus, Record-Rama, Rhino

Records, Schoolkids Records, Times Square Records, and Wax 'N' Facts. Two stores that are especially well-profiled in this volume are John Goddard's Village Music in Mill Valley, California and Bob Koester's Jazz Record Mart in Chicago.

The general decline of record dens across the United States is attributed to several interrelated factors. First, many independent store owners have been overwhelmed by the emergence of monster music chains like Tower, Sam Goody, and Wherehouse Records. Second, even big record chain outlets lost sales on current hit CDs to giant general retailers like Barnes and Noble, Best Buy, Target, and Wal-Mart. Third, record collectors have diversified their pursuits of vinyl and compact disc treasures beyond local stores to estate sales, flea markets, and weekend swap meets. Fourth, mail order record outlets like Columbia House and BMG Music invariably undercut the prices on newly-released audio products. Finally, the younger generation of music consumers tend to consider audio recordings as disposable commodities rather than treasured caches of albums, cassettes, or CDs. In many ways, nation-wide marketing, changing technologies, and demographic shifts augur against the resuscitation of a thriving independent record store system. Of course, exceptions exist. Amoeba Music, which first opened its doors in 2001, is a booming mega-music outlet in Los Angeles and the Princeton Record Exchange, a relatively small disc swapping enterprise near the university, is still succeeding in New Jersey.

The RECORD STORE DAYS authors contend that the survival of vinyl stores and CD specialty shops is dependent upon an intentionally collaborative effort among business owners, disc buyers, and local musicians. This is why annual "Independent Record Store Days" celebrations were launched throughout America on April 17, 2008. Over the past three years local artists, major record companies, and store proprietors have used this special day to attract former disc-buying loyalists and new audio customers - and to assert the "community" ethos among all music fans. Unfortunately, today's diversity of fandom options has fractured the old magnetism of record store counterculture commercialism, embodied in concert posters, record star photos, character and album cover stand-ups, and back-catalogued vinyl. Too many other competing cultural and technological sites attract youthful attention and financial investment. Among these are computer game arcades, skateboarding parks, video game centers, comic book havens, baseball card shows, and numerous live concert venues. Even hardcore vinyl collectors have begun to shop on-line through Amazon and e-Bay.

For the general reader, RECORD STORE DAYS is a well-illustrated, carefully scripted introduction to the history of American disc sales centers. For the long-time vinyl trader or CD collector, the authors identify nationwide sources for disc searching and also provide a strong rationale about the positive impacts of music merchandising. For the popular culture scholar, this text reflects on the joys and the frustrations of pursuing a particular technologically-shifting audio product, along with the unpredictable instances of changes in taste and specific interests that can marginalize old-time objects of passion. Personally, we were awed by the number and variety of record shops highlighted throughout the text. Of course, it was strange to note that several of our favorite disc-hunting locations were omitted from discussion. We're convinced, though, that Calamar and Gallo would have enjoyed touring Cleveland's Record Rendezvous, Bowling Green's Madhatter Music, Detroit's Car City Classics, Lansing's Flat, Black, and Circular, Toledo's Boogie Records, Greenville's Horizon Records, and even Asheville's Voltage Records.

Enthusiasm for independent record shops still abounds. From Bruce Springsteen to Joe Satriani, from Ziggy Marley to Ian Gillan of Deep Purple, performing artists sincerely appreciate the personalized services rendered by geeky vinyl junkies. On the inside cover of the hardback edition of RECORD STORE DAYS, Joan Jett eloquently pleads her case: "The indie record stores are the backbone of the recorded music culture. It's where we go to network, browse around, and find new songs to love. The stores whose owners and staff live for music have spread the word about exciting new things faster and with more essence than either radio or the press. Any artist that doesn't support the wonderful Ma & Pa record stores across America is contributing to [her] own extinction."

(This commentary was originally published as B. Lee Cooper and William L. Schurk, "Review of RECORD STORE DAYS: FROM VINYL TO DIGITAL AND BACK AGAIN by Gary Calamar and Phil Gallo," POPULAR MUSIC AND SOCIETY, 34 (February 2011), pp. 125-127.)

The fabled Tower Records outlet on Hollywood's Sunset Boulevard

ROMANCE

Popular music thrives on hyperbole. Unlike most literary works, though, song lyricsutilize hyperbolic motifs as normative circumstances rather than as occasional orexceptional situations (Johnson; Schlueter; Stein; Webb). Of course, lyricists have always recognized the value of superlatives when crafting songs about romantic relationships. The handsome men and beautiful women who inhabit many popular songs warrant excessive verbal adulation. Among these elegant folks, lyrical pledges of eternal love seem quite natural. Pop singers eagerly propagate this brand of hyperbolic romantic fantasy. When describing perfect passion and pure love, recording artists willingly forsake critical evaluation and measured judgments. Similarly, they magnify the emotions of outrage and heartbreak over incidents of marital infidelity; they overstate the physical attributes and potential dangers posed by romantic rivals; they present inflated opinions about their own intellectual acuity, good looks, and sexual prowess. Naturally, these extreme songwriting and vocalizing efforts would be meaningless without an accepting cadre of record/CD-buyers and radio/TV/iPad listeners. Clearly, public opinion validates lyrical hyperbole as an acceptable standard for describing romance. Rather than ridiculing extravagant observations as babble, pipe dreams, sweet talk, or balderdash, most music listeners revel in the over-the-top compliments and outrageous self-aggrandizement found in commercial recordings. Thus, the lyricist (and composer, as well), the singer, and the audience agree to suspend reality once the music begins to play. Recordings function as an audio escape from common sense and normal situations that may seem mundane, sad, boring, or unwanted. Hyperbolic song lyrics become pretenses rather than perjury, dreams rather than deceptions, seductions rather than verbal trickery, and distortions rather than lies. Hyperbole, the act of utilizing exaggeration for effect, achieves the status of agreed-upon audio delusion among lyricists/singers/listeners.

If hyperbole is a universally acceptable descriptive device within the lyrics of sound recordings, then composers and performers are free to depict portions of the human condition in grandiose terms. Everything can become larger than life in lyrics. But which topics are most susceptible to exaggerated presentation? Since courtship and romance are dominant themes within contemporary recordings, it is predictable that hyperbolic descriptors will be particularly prominent in love songs (Cooper, "Personal Relationships"; Farber; Furia; Green; Macken, Fornatale, and Ayres; Pessen; Tawa). Three phases of romantic involvement are frequently subjected to exorbitant audio observations. First, the singer may seek to impress a loved one. Hyperbole is especially effective in proclaiming unwavering personal commitment, in affirming eternal adoration and affection, and in pledging absolute fidelity. Second, the vocalist may wish to contrast the boundless joy of being in a loving relationship with the unimaginable gloom of separation and personal isolation. Finally, the artist may sadly acknowledge that a seemingly perfect relationship is unexpectedly crumbling.

Hyperbole also functions well to capsule volatile reactions to either infidelity or to outright rejection by a loved one. Many song lyrics express the shock of discovering cheating and infidelity, the agony of a permanent separation, and the endless stream of teardrops resulting from a dissolved romantic union. Beyond these regrettable circumstances, of course, hope awaits. Songwriters and singers understand that the search for a new love offers opportunities for hyperbole to once again become an emphatic lyrical aid. Recordings frequently depict a lonesome soul conjuring a perfect mate in his or her dreams. Such rebounding romantics may also exhibit behaviors toward potential mates that are deemed crazy or foolish by their more objective long-time friends. This happens when would-be lovers describe their recent dates as splendid matches or rare catches, or when they speculate about the ecstasy of imagined sexual encounters. Clearly, there is a recognizable romantic cycle at play in the "love gained-love lost-new love pursued" system that populates popular music lyrics. And recording companies are always prepared to capitalize on this pattern.

The specific songs presented in this study were selected from a field of over 1,200 romance-oriented recordings that were issued commercially over the past century. This array of songs was initially assembled from three discographic references sources: POP MEMORIES, 1890-1954 (Record Research, 1986), TOP R&B/HIP-HOP SINGLES, 1942-2004 (Record Research, 2004), and TOP POP SINGLES, 1955-2012 (Record Research, 2013). Utilizing a content analysis approach to highlight lyrical tendencies toward hyperbole, the author winnowed the total number of romance-related songs to be examined down to 190. This paper includes nearly all of those recordings. It should be noted that beyond such linguistic tropes as "never", "always", "forever", and so on, no consideration was given to other musical elements within the romantic songs. That is, lyrics were thoroughly analyzed, but harmony, melody, and rhythm were treated as neutral elements in all recordings. No consideration was provided for particular performing artists or composers, either. However, specific singers are identified with their recordings of individual tunes throughout the study. The following pages outline the use of hyperbole in romantic recordings. This discographic investigation is presented in three sections, arranged by the following topics: (1) impressing and influencing a loved one, (2) reacting to the infidelity of or the rejection by a loved one, and (3) expressing positive feelings toward a new object of affection. While several song titles and performing artists are mentioned within the introductory texts for each section, full discographic identification – including the song title, performer, record label and number, and date of release – for each recording cited occurs at the end of the topical section. This presentation is descriptive rather than definitive. It does not strive to list every hyperbolic recording related to the three romantic topics addressed in this investigation.

Impressing And Influencing A Loved One

The Four Aces crooned "Love Is A Many-Splendored Thing" and Ira Gershwin speculated that "'S Wonderful", it's marvelous, it's awful nice, and it's paradise to be loved. While seemingly gushing, these sentiments only scratch the surface in respect to hyperbole in popular songs. Cole Porter also raved "You're The Top", The Falcons sang "You're So Fine", and Marvin Gaye and Tammi Terrell mutually acknowledged "You're

All I Need To Get By". Not to be outdone, Jackie Wilson shouted "(Your Love Keeps Lifting Me) Higher and Higher", while Ray Charles asserted "You Are My Sunshine" and Stevie Wonder declared "You Are The Sunshine Of My Life". Advancing the same hyperbolic cause, Ed Townsend unabashedly admitted that he would do anything, absolutely anything, "For Your Love". Clearly, there is no commitment too strong, no pledge too bold to secure the unrelenting romantic acceptance of a desired mate. Beyond gifts of diamonds and pearls or Cadillacs and money, Frank Sinatra offers "All Of Me" to the girl of his dreams. Etta James sighs that "At Last" her life-time lover has come along and Sammy Turner promises eternal affection in "Always". Billy Eckstine is similarly all-in-for-love when he affirms "Everything I Have Is Yours".

Ben Selvin notes the total change in his life once true love arrives. "Blue Skies" were smiling just for him. Robert Knight's claim of "Everlasting Love" is matched by The Lettermen's proclamation that "When I Fall In Love", it will be forever. Bob Braun's traditional "Till Death Do Us Part" vow pales in comparison to the "Forever And A Day" timeline suggested by Jackie Wilson and the "Now And Forever (You And Me)" statement by Anne Murray. Donna Lewis is even more emphatic in "I Love You Always Forever". Romantic hyperbole knows no temperal boundaries. While the Rockies may crumble and Gilbralter may tumble, Dinah Washington finds stability in the assertion that "Our Love Is Here To Stay". Likewise, The Flamingos offer their love until the end of time in "Mio Amore" and Robert and Johnny chant "We Belong Together" for eternity. Of course, Perry Como also pledges faithful adoration "Till The End Of Time", just as Foreigner echoes this same sentiment in "Until The End Of Time". This lyrical hyperbole is slightly more complicated, but still chronologically present, when The Casinos set a numerical limit on their romantic engagement. They sing, kiss me each morning for a million years and "Then You Can Tell Me Goodbye". In terms of topography and astronomy, recording artists invariably go to extremes to affirm the outer boundaries of their affection. Peggy Lee asks "How Deep Is The Ocean?" and how high is the sky in extolling the limitless nature of her love; Les Paul and Mary Ford chart parallel territory in "How High The Moon"; and Marvin Gaye and Tammi Terrell, a crooning couple always ready to proclaim boundless love, confirm that there "Ain't No Mountain High Enough" to keep them apart.

The discovery of being in love also unearths hyperbolic exclamations (Davis; Weisman). Frank Sinatra claims "I've Got You Under My Skin"; The Platters find "Heaven On Earth" with "Only You (And You Alone)"; The Flamingos assert "I Only Have Eyes For You"; Aretha Franklin confesses in ecstasy that "I Never Loved A Man (The Way I Love You)"; Dick Haymes and Helen Forrest agree "It Had To Be You"; and Stevie Wonder freely admits that "Signed, Sealed, Delivered I'm Yours". Whether generated by The Temptations' "My Girl" or Mary Wells' "My Guy", The Drifters are accurate when they label the eureka of love as "This Magic Moment". To quote Natalie Cole and her famous father on this subject, the beginning of a romantic relationship is "Unforgettable" in every way. These hyperbolic dimensions in love songs offer no room for doubt, no chance of failure, and no fear for future separation. Margaret Whiting outlaws the possibility of meteorological interference in her romance in "Come Rain Or Come Shine"; The Flamingos maintain an unquestionable assurance that "Lovers Never Say

Goodbye"; and The Association double-down on the value of fidelity and fortitude in "Never My Love". Superlatives reign and doubt is vanquished in songs that strive to impress and influence loved ones.

"Ain't No Mountain High Enough" (Tamla 54149)
Marvin Gaye and Tammi Terrell (1967)

"All Of Me" (Columbia 38163)
Frank Sinatra (1948)

"Always" (Big Top 3029)
Sammy Turner (1959)

"At Last" (Argo 5380)
Etta James (1961)

"Blue Skies" (Columbia 860)
Ben Selvin (1927)

"Come Rain Or Come Shine" (Capitol 247)
Margaret Whiting (1946)

"Everlasting Love" (Rising Sons 705)
Robert Knight (1967)

"Everything I Have Is Yours" (MGM 10259)
Billy Eckstine (1948)

"For Your Love" (Capitol 3926)
Ed Townsend (1958)

"Heaven On Earth" (Mercury 70893)
The Platters (1956)

"How Deep Is The Ocean?" (Columbia 36754)
Peggy Lee, with Benny Goodman and His Orchestra (1945)

"I Love You Always Forever" (Atlantic 87072)
Donna Lewis (1996)

"I Never Loved A Man (The Way I Love You)" (Atlantic 2386)
Aretha Franklin (1967)

"I Only Have Eyes For You" (End 1046)
The Flamingos (1959)

"I've Got The World On A String" (Capitol 2505)
Frank Sinatra (1953)

"It Had To Be You" (Decca 23349)
Dick Haymes and Helen Forrest (1944)

"Love Is A Many-Splendored Thing" (Decca 29625)
The Four Aces (1955)

"Lovers Never Say Goodbye" (End 1035)
The Flamingos (1959)

"Mio Amore" (End 1065)
The Flamingos (1960)

"My Girl" (Gordy 7038)
The Temptations (1965)

"My Guy" (Motown 1056)
Mary Wells (1964)

"Never My Love" (Warner Brothers 7074)
The Association (1967)

"Now And Forever (You And Me)" (Capitol 5547)
Anne Murray (1986)

"Only You (And You Alone)" (Mercury 70633)
The Platters (1955)

"Our Love Is Here To Stay" (Mercury 71812)
Dinah Washington (1961)

" 'S Wonderful" (Verve MGVS 6082-5)
Ella Fitzgerald (1959)

"Signed, Sealed, Delivered, I'm Yours" (Tamla 54196)
Stevie Wonder (1970)

"Then You Can Tell Me Goodbye" (Fraternity 977)
The Casinos (1967)

"This Magic Moment" (Atlantic 2050)
The Drifters (1960)

"Till Death Do Us Part" (Decca 31355)
Bob Braun (1962)

"Till The End Of Time" (Victor 1709)
Perry Como (1945)

"Unforgettable" (Capitol 1808)
Nat King Cole (1951)

"Unforgettable" (Elektra 64875)
Natalie Cole, with Nat King Cole (1991)

"Until The End Of Time" (Generama 53183)
Foreigner (1995)

"We Belong Together" (Old Town 1047)
Robert and Johnny (1958)

"When I Fall In Love" (Capitol 4658)
The Lettermen (1961)

"You Are My Sunshine" (ABC-Paramount 10375)
Ray Charles (1962)

"You Are The Sunshine Of My Life" (Tamla 54232)
Stevie Wonder (1973)

"You're All I Need To Get By" (Tamla 54169)
Marvin Gaye and Tammi Terrell (1968)

"You're So Fine" (Unart 2013)
The Falcons (1959)

"You're The Top" (Victor 24766)
Cole Porter (1935)

"(Your Love Keeps Lifting Me) Higher And Higher" (Brunswick 55336)
Jackie Wilson (1967)

Reacting To Infidelity Or Rejection By A Loved One

If the lyrical affirmation of love is extravagant in popular recordings, then it should not be surprising that audio responses to infidelity and cheating or to breaking up and total rejection by a loved one are similarly extreme (Gabree; Hoskyns; McLaurin and Peterson; Rogers, "Audience Attitudes; Rogers, "Country Music"). Hyperbole rules in both love and hate. For Bill Withers, there "Ain't No Sunshine" when his lover is absent. Of course, signs of romantic betrayal or love slipping away are often incremental rather than sharply defined. For instance, Elvis Presley traces the erosion of romantic trust in "Suspicious Minds"; Marvin Gaye laments in "I Heard It Through The Grapevine" that his lover was being untrue; The Sanford/Townsend Band warns about the corrosive effect of "Smoke From A Distant Fire"; and The Temptations give voice to the obvious in "(I Know) I'm Losing You". Ending a love affair or a marriage is rarely easy or neat. Exceptions to this rule are illustrated in "At This Moment" by Billy Vera and "Don't Worry" by Marty Robbins. But rationality almost never conquers the pain and anger that constitute typical reactions to losing a loved one. The Righteous Brothers sadly acknowledge "You've Lost That Lovin' Feeling"; Ray Charles laments "I Can't Stop Loving You"; Otis Redding screams "I Can't Turn You Loose"; The Drifters descend into the depths of depression in "If You Don't Come Back"; Tom Jones swears "I'll Never Fall In Love Again"; Patsy Cline confesses "I Fall To Pieces"; Bob Seger admits that "Tryin' To Live My Life Without You" is the hardest thing he'll ever do; and The Walker Brothers concede that "The Sun Ain't Gonna Shine (Anymore)".

Keeping the focus on weeping and wailing is where hyperbolic lyrics are crucial (Cooper, "Sky Is Crying"). Jimmy Ruffin asks "What Becomes Of The Brokenhearted" and Sarah Vaughan croons a "Brokenhearted Melody". Sadness approaches death as Ray Charles expresses the fear that he might "Drown In My Own Tears". Others contribute to this weeping audio montage. Johnnie Ray sings "Cry"; Bobby "Blue" Bland multiplies the feeling in "Cry Cry Cry"; The Box Tops "Cry Like A Baby"; Roy Orbison is "Crying"; Ricky Skaggs is "Crying My Heart Out Over You"; Tanya Tucker is "Down To My Last Teardrop"; Jackie Wilson's eyes are full of "Lonely Teardrops"; Guy Mitchell admits "My Heart Cries For You"; Hank Williams says "I'm So Lonesome I Could Cry"; and Jay and The Americans note that "She Cried" when he told her that he didn't love her anymore. The feeling of lost love is overwhelming. Lyrical license encourages extreme reactions such as "Heartaches" by Somethin' Smith, "Heartaches By The Number" by Guy Mitchell, "Heartbreak (It's Hurtin' Me)" by Little Willie John, and "Hurt" by Timi Yuro.

After the initial shock of separating from a romantic partner, the lyrics of popular recordings suggest a variety of options. Once again, many of these responses are extreme and are frequently vocalized in that manner. Some singers find fault with themselves, proclaiming their roles as dupes or fools; others cease crying and emerge as angry and bitter over mistreatment by a former lover (Cooper, "Wise Men"). Hyperbole flavors both reflection and rage. Aaron Neville acknowledges that "Everybody Plays The Fool" at one time or another; Connie Francis follows this same line of thought in "Everybody's Somebody's Fool". But Joe Barry recognizes that "I'm A Fool To Care" when you don't care for me. The Flamingos reflect "I Was Such A Fool (To Fall In Love With You)", while Ricky Nelson condemns himself as a "Poor Little Fool". Looking ahead toward future dating and more lasting relationships, singers tend to shift gears from the past and begin to speculate about future. But remnants of resentment linger. Bobby Bland ponders "I Pity The Fool" who falls in love with his former girlfriend. In like fashion, Charlie Rich wonders aloud "Who Will The Next Fool Be". Sanford Clark concludes that he's been "The Fool" for allowing the love of his life to escape. In anger, Julie London demands that her former lover "Cry Me A River"; Frankie Lymon shouts "Goody Goody" over the romantic misfortunes of his ex-girlfriend; and Johnny Tillotson finds irony in taunting an old flame by noting "It's Funny How Time Slips Away". In the end, though, there are three generic reactions to romantic rejection. These are capsuled in "Wisdom Of A Fool" by The Five Keys, in "These Foolish Things Remind Me Of You" by The Dominoes, and in "Stardust" by Frank Sinatra.

"Ain't No Sunshine" (Sussex 219)
Bill Withers (1971)

"At This Moment" (Rhino 74403)
Billy Vera and The Beaters (1986)

"Broken-Hearted Melody" (Mercury 71477)
Sarah Vaughan (1959)

"Cry" (Okeh 6840)
Johnnie Ray and The Four Lads (1951)

"Cry Cry Cry" (Duke 327)
Bobby "Blue" Bland (1960)

"Cry Like A Baby" (Mala 593)
The Box Tops (1968)

"Cry Me A River" (Liberty 55006)
Julie London (1955)

"Crying" (Monument 447)
Roy Orbison (1961)

"Crying My Heart Out Over You" (Epic 02692)
Ricky Skaggs (1982)

"Down To My Last Teardrop" (Liberty 57768)
Tanya Tucker (1992)

"Don't Worry" (Columbia 41922)
Marty Robbins (1961)

"Drown In My Own Tears" (Atlantic 1085)
Ray Charles (1956)

"Everybody Plays The Fool" (A & M 1563)
Aaron Neville (1991)

"Everybody's Somebody's Fool" (MGM 12899)
Connie Francis (1960)

"The Fool" (Dot 15481)
Sanford Clark (1956)

"Funny How Time Slips Away" (Cadence 1441)
Johnny Tillotson (1963)

"Goody Goody" (Gee 1039)
Frankie Lymon and The Teenagers (1957)

"Heartaches" (Epic 9179)
Somethin' Smith and The Redheads (1956)

"Heartaches By The Number" (Columbia 41476)
Guy Mitchell (1959)

"Heartbreak (It's Hurtin' Me)" (King 5356)
Little Willie John (1960)

"Hurt" (Liberty 55343)
Timi Yuro (1961)

"I Can't Stop Loving You" (ABC-Paramount 10330)
Ray Charles (1962)

"I Can't Turn You Loose" (Volt 130)
Otis Redding (1965)

"I Fall To Pieces" (Decca 31205)
Patsy Cline (1961)

"I Heard It Through The Grapevine" (Tamla 54176)
Marvin Gaye (1968)

"(I Know) I'm Losing You" (Gordy 7057)
The Temptations (1966)

"I Pity The Fool" (Duke 332)
Bobby Bland (1961)

"I Was Such A Fool (To Fall In Love With You)" (End 1062)
The Flamingos (1960)

"I'll Never Fall In Love Again" (Parrot 40018)
Tom Jones (1967)

"I'm A Fool To Care" (Smash 1702)
Joe Barry (1961)

"If You Don't Come Back" (Atlantic 2201)
The Drifters (1963)

"Lonely Teardrops" (Brunswick 55105)
Jackie Wilson (1958)

"My Heart Cries For You" (Columbia 78-39067)
Guy Mitchell (1950)

"Poor Little Fool" (Imperial 5528)
Ricky Nelson (1958)

"She Cried" (United Artists 415)
Jay and The Americans (1962)

"Smoke From A Distant Fire" (Warner Brothers 8370)
The Sanford/Townsend Band (1977)

"Stardust" (Reprise 20, 059)
Frank Sinatra (1962)

"The Sun Ain't Gonna Shine (Anymore)" (Smash 2032)
The Walker Brothers (1966)

"Suspicious Minds" (RCA Victor 47-9764)
Elvis Presley (1969)

"These Foolish Things Remind Me Of You" (Federal 12129)
The Dominoes (1953)

"Tryin' To Live My Life Without You" (Capitol 5042)
Bob Seger (1981)

"What Becomes Of The Brokenhearted" (Soul 35022)
Jimmy Ruffin (1966)

"Who Will The Next Fool Be" (Sun 1110)
Charlie Rich (1970)

"Wisdom Of A Fool" (Capitol 3597)
The Five Keys (1956)

"You've Lost That Lovin' Feeling" (Philles 124)
The Righteous Brothers (1964)

Expressing Positive Feelings About A New Object Of Affection

Idealism may be cloaked in hyperbole. While the emotional roller coaster of being deeply in love and then encountering either infidelity or outright rejection should prompt a reflective mood toward initiating new romantic relationships, such an objective approach to love is likely to be temporary. Somehow, wounded lovers tend to rebound into the dating game far too quickly. Undeniably, human beings crave companionship and affection. Seeking a new soul mate is a complicated process that often involves several stages of consideration. Among these are fantasizing about a perfect match, assessing elements of physical attractiveness, feeling and exhibiting behaviors that amount to falling in love, and, finally, engaging in sexual activities. Granted, this is a gross oversimplification of the romantic cycle. Yet popular recordings frequently engage in such consolidated behavioral formats. This abbreviated sketch offers a reasonable overview of the tales of courtship and romance that dominate song lyrics. These situations also provide additional opportunities for songwriters and singers to exercise hyperbole. Usually, listeners validate the rapid, exhilarating, and over-stated mini-dramas that illustrate strong, positive feelings about a new object of affection. Songs often function as audio vignettes and melodic melodramas that anticipate or parallel the idealized worlds of romance experienced by the listening audience (Bridges and Denisoff; Carey; Edwards; Furia and Lasser; Hayakawa; Horton; Moore; Scheurer, "The Beatles"; Scheurer, "Thou Witty").

Dreaming can manifest either the creation of an ideal loved one or the fixation on a particularly interesting man or woman. Johnnie Ray sang "All I Do Is Dream Of You" with the same zeal expressed by The Everly Brothers in "All I Have To Do Is Dream". Both recordings harken to a desired but still distant lover. More conscious reveries are depicted in "Daydream" by The Lovin" Spoonful and "Daydream Believer" by The Monkees. Still, The Pickens Sisters are much more specific in "Did You Ever See A Dream Walking?". The amount of attention focused on dream-related longing within song lyrics is remarkable. Illustrations include: "Dream" by Dinah Washington, "Dream Baby (How Long Must I Dream)" by Roy Orbison, "Dream Lover" by Bobby Darin, "Dream A Little Dream Of Me" by Mama Cass, "Just A Dream" by Jimmy Clanton, "My Prayer" by The Platters, "A Wonderful Dream" by The Majors, and "You Make My Dreams" by Daryl Hall and John Oates. Wishful thinking rather than dreaming stokes the hyperbolic imagination of Smokey Robinson as he laments "I've Made Love To You A Thousand Times" even though it was only in his mind.

Physical attraction sometimes stimulates dreams, but it is also essential to initiating face-to-face romantic interactions. Art Mooney was captured by a "Baby Face", while

Roy Orbison ogled "Oh, Pretty Woman". In both cases, the visage of beauty drew eye contact and sparked mutual interest. This visual magnetism is celebrated in "Can't Take My Eyes Off You" and "My Eyes Adored You" by Frankie Valli, "Did You Ever See A Dream Walking" by Fats Domino, "Look At That, Look At That" by The Fabulous Thunderbirds, and "Young Blood" by The Coasters. Hyperbolic descriptions of loved ones often reach unearthly proportions in lyrics. Both male and female companions assume heavenly characteristics in "Angel Baby" by Rosie and The Originals, "Angel Eyes" by The Jeff Healy Band, "Earth Angel (Will You Be Mine)" by The Penguins, "My Special Angel" by The Vogues, "Next Door To An Angel" by Neil Sedaka, and "You're The Sweetest Girl This Side Of Heaven" by Guy Lombardo. Of course, not all attractive creatures are angelic in either temperament or behavior. It's clear that ZZ Top's "Sharp Dressed Man" is trolling for sex rather than seeking a life-time romantic relationship. And Little Richard reminds everyone that "The Girl Can't Help It" if her prime physique is tempting more men than she can mention. Commercial recordings are populated with salutes to high-stepping, hip-shaking women who are incredibly attractive -- but who are also unwilling to settle for monogamy, domesticity, or even adoration by a single boyfriend. Once again, hyperbole is utilized in lyrics to depict frisky, feisty, fickle, and fortune-hunting females. Exceptional ladies justify extravagant descriptions in recordings like "Brick House" by The Commodores, "Foxey Lady" by Jimi Hendrix, "Reet Petite (The Finest Girl You Ever Want To Meet)" by Jackie Wilson, "She's A Bad Mama Jama (She's Built, She's Stacked)" by Carl Carlton, "She's Got It" by Little Richard, "She's Lookin' Good" by Wilson Pickett, "So Tough" by The Kuf-Linx, "39-21-46" by The Showmen, and "You Sexy Thing" by Hot Chocolate.

Neither dream-like compatibility nor extreme physical beauty can guarantee a stable, lasting romantic relationship, though. Falling madly in love opens the door for uncontrollable urges, irrational expectations, and other foolish behaviors. Complete adoration produces hyperbolic mood swings from absolute infatuation, loyalty, and selflessness to obsession, jealously, and selfishness. The sense of mindless approval and praise for a loved one is embodied in many songs, including "The Way You Do The Things You Do" by The Temptations. It also generates an unhealthy surrender of self as illustrated in "Bend Me, Shape Me" by The American Breed and "I'm Your Puppet" by James and Bobby Purify. Being mesmerized by a lover, like Albert King in "The Very Thought Of You" or The Platters in "(You've Got) The Magic Touch", is a form of blindness to reality. It is similarly unhealthy and self-deluding to seek to control the behavior of others through witchcraft, voodoo, or chemistry. Yet recordings frequently suggest such functional alternatives. Such artificial modes of relationship creation or retrieval are outlined in "I Put A Spell On You" by Screamin' Jay Hawkins and "Love Potion Number Nine" by The Coasters.

Mental instability can be an undesired result of romantic stress. Such psychological trauma obviously manifests itself in physical problems as well. Among the common complaints voiced by overly intense lovers are shortness of breath, anxiety, hot flashes, and cold chills. In popular recordings these ailments can seem life-threatening. Just listen to the lyrics of "Breathless" and "Great Balls Of Fire" by Jerry Lee Lewis, "Cold Sweat" by James Brown, "Dizzy Miss Lizzy" by Larry Williams, and "Fever" by Little

Willie John. More generalized psychiatric concerns are articulated by Patsy Cline in "Crazy" and "I Fall To Pieces", by Ivory Joe Hunter in "I Almost Lost My Mind", and by Al Jolson in "You've Simply Got Me Cuckoo". The most frequently used term to depict the unpredictable behavior of an over-stimulated lover is...fool. In "Some Enchanted Evening", Ezio Pinza reminds listeners that fools attempt to supply reasons for their demented deeds, while wise men accept love as a natural cause of foolishness. Brook Benton repeats the adage that "Fools Rush In" where angels fear to tread. ZZ Top capsules the motivation of physical attraction in "A Fool for Your Stockings" and Undisputed Truth confesses "I'm A Fool For You". The hyperbole of foolish fantasies and unexamined commitments can be found in love song after love song.

"All I Do Is Dream Of You" (Columbia 40046)
Johnnie Ray (1953)

"All I Have To Do Is Dream" (Cadence 1348)
The Everly Brothers (1958)

"Angel Baby" (Highland 1011)
Rose and The Originals (1960)

"Angel Eyes" (Arista 9808)
The Jeff Healy Band (1989)

"Baby Face" (MGM 10156)
Art Mooney (1948)

"Bend Me, Shape Me" (Acta 811)
The American Breed (1967)

"Breathless" (Sun 288)
Jerry Lee Lewis (1958)

"Brick House" (Motown 1425)
The Commodores (1977)

"Can't Take My Eyes Off You" (Philips 40446)
Frankie Valli (1967)

"Cold Sweat" (King 6110)
James Brown (1967)

"Crazy" (Decca 31317)
Patsy Cline (1961)

"Daydream" (Kama Sutra 208)
The Lovin' Spoonful (1966)

"Daydream Believer" (Colgems 1012)
The Monkees (1967)

"Did you Ever See A Dream Walking?" (Victor 24468)
The Pickens Sisters (1934)

"Did You Ever See A Dream Walking" (Imperial 5875)
Fats Domino (1962)

"Dizzy, Miss Lizzy" (Specialty 626)
Larry Williams (1958)

"Dream" (Mercury 71958)
Dinah Washington (1962)

"Dream A Little Dream Of Me" (Dunhill 4145)
Mama Cass (1968)

"Dream Baby (How Long Must I Dream)" (Monument 456)
Roy Orbison (1962)

"Dream Lover" (Atco 6140)
Bobby Darin (1959)

"Earth Angel (Will You Be Mine)" (DooTone 348)
The Penguins (1954)

"Fever" (King 4935)
Little Willie John (1956)

"A Fool For Your Stockings" (Warner Brothers 3361)
ZZ Top (1979)

"Fools Rush In" (Mercury 71722)
Brook Benton (1960)

"Foxey Lady" (Reprise 0641)
Jimi Hendrix (1967)

"The Girl Can't Help It" (Specialty 591)
Little Richard (1957)

"Great Balls Of Fire" (Sun 281)
Jerry Lee Lewis (1957)

"I Almost Lost My Mind" (MGM K10578)
Ivory Joe Hunter (1950)

"I Fall To Pieces" (Decca 31205)
Patsy Cline (1961)

"I Put A Spell On You" (Okeh 7072)
Screamin' Jay Hawkins (1956)

"I'm A Fool For You" (Gordy 7139)
Undisputed Truth (1974)

"I'm Your Puppet" (Bell 648)
James and Bobby Purify (1966)

"I've Made Love To You A Thousand Times" (Tamla 1655)
Smokey Robinson (1983)

"In Dreams" (Monument 806)
Roy Orbison (1963)

"Just A Dream" (Ace 546)
Jimmy Clanton (1958)

"Look At That, Look At That" (CBS Associated 05838)
The Fabulous Thunderbirds (1986)

"Love Potion Number Nine" (King 6385)
The Coasters (1971)

"My Eyes Adored You" (Private Stock 45003)
Frankie Valli (1974)

"My Prayer" (Mercury 70893)
The Platters (1956)

"My Special Angel" (Reprise 0766)
The Vogues (1968)

"Next Door To An Angel" (RCA Victor 8086)
Neil Sedaka (1962)

"Oh, Pretty Woman" (Monument 851)
Roy Orbison (1964)

"Reet Petite (The Finest Girl You Ever Want To Meet)" (Brunswick 55024)
Jackie Wilson (1957)

"Sharp Dressed Man" (Warner Brothers 29576)
ZZ Top (1983)

"She's A Bad Mama Jama (She's Built, She's Stacked)" (20th Century 2488)
Carl Carlton (1981)

"She's Got It" (Specialty 584)
Little Richard (1956)

"She's Lookin' Good" (Atlantic 2504)
Wilson Pickett (1968)

"So Tough" (Challenge 1013)
The Kuf-Linx (1958)

"Some Enchanted Evening" (Columbia 4559)
Ezio Pinza (1949)

"39-21-46" (Minit 32007)
The Showmen (1967)

"The Very Thought Of You" (Tomato 10009)
Albert King (1979)

"The Way You Do The Things You Do" (Gordy 7028)
The Temptations (1964)

"A Wonderful Dream" (Imperial 5855)
The Majors (1962)

"You Makes My Dreams" (RCA 12217)
Daryl Hall and John Oates (1981)

"You Sexy Thing" (Big Tree 16047)
Hot Chocolate (1975)

"You're The Sweetest Girl This Side Of Heaven" (Columbia 2188)
Guy Lombardo and His Orchestra (1930)

"(You've Got) The Magic Touch" (Mercury 70819)
The Platters (1956)

"You've Simply Got Me Cuckoo" (Columbia 3984)
Al Jolson (1923)

"Young Blood" (Atco 6087)
The Coasters (1957)

Afterthoughts

Hyperbole is verbal adrenaline. It is designed to jump-start thoughts and actions, to provoke interest in specific persons or events, or to trigger extreme feelings of love or hate, fear or laughter. The frequent use of hyperbole in song lyrics is related to the brevity of time that the recorded format provides for communication. Composers and performers craft their audio vignettes to attract immediate attention. Granted, a catchy melody is also important to seizing a listener's ear. But lyricists and singers know that distinctive words and phrases create drama, build persuasive monologues, prompt reveries, or make bold assertions that may resonate in a listener's thoughts long after the music ceases. Merely telling tales is what books and newspapers do. Popular songs must stimulate feelings. To accomplish this, lyrics often focus on experiences that have universal meaning and emotional power (DeNora; Frith, "Song" and "Meaning"; Frith, "Sound Effects"; Goodall; Grossberg; Jourdain; Kawin; Lewis, "Meaning's In The Music"; Middleton; Moore; Neal; Walley; Weinstein; Wolfe and Haefner).

Hyperbole is a particularly effective lyrical device when the listening audience is young, naive, inexperienced, or gullible. When singers brag and boast about their skills in terms that defy reality, only the untutored actually believe their rants. Similarly, when performers harken to midnight settings where monsters dwell and creatures crawl, only small children cower in fear. And when the musical contributions of specific artists are attributed to heavenly inspiration, only fanatics will say, "Amen". Hyperbole demands an agreed-upon suspension of reality. It is an expected, welcomed, almost joyful instance of incredibility in an otherwise sane, sanitized, standardized existence. For this reason hyperbole thrives in love songs. The object of affection, ranging from an unknown but shapely woman strolling along a busy boulevard to a gorgeous bride about to walk down the aisle, is depicted as lyrical perfection. She's heavenly. To be with her is to be in Paradise.

Such hyperbolic descriptions in lyrics have become the ideal images of courtship, marriage, and eternal bliss for many young Americans. The other extreme of romantic relationships is also extravagantly depicted in songs. The excruciating pain of separation from a loved one, the attendant suffering and tears, and the ultimate recriminations are all painted in the most vibrant hyperbolic shades. Adoration and devotion shift quickly to rejection and revulsion in recordings. Romantic involvements are seldom stable. Extremes of breaking up and making up, steady dating and random cheating, marriage and divorce are the chief elements of lyrical drama. Human partnerships are cycles that vacillate between heaven and hell. There is little time on discs for calm, routine, easy personal interactions. The 120 seconds allotted to a single song is usually crammed with profound extremes. From the peaks of passion as communicated in "All Of Me", "Because Of You", "It Had To Be You", and "Too Marvelous For Words" to the depths of despair as told in "Cryin', Prayin', Hopin' Waitin'", "Crying Time", "Heartbreak Hotel", and "I'll Never Fall In Love Again", hyperbole is dominant. The recording industry, lyricists, vocalists, and listeners are co-conspirators in sustaining this system of extravagant audio illusion.

"All Of Me" (Columbia 10834)
Willie Nelson (1978)

"Because Of You" (Columbia 39362)
Tony Bennett (1951)

"Cryin', Prayin', Waitin', Hopin'" (RCA Victor 6154)
Hank Snow (1955)

"Crying Time" (ABC-Paramount 10739)
Ray Charles (1966)

"Heartbreak Hotel" (RCA Victor 47-6420)
Elvis Presley (1956)

"I'll Never Fall In Love Again" (Scepter 12273)
Dionne Warwick (1969)

"It Had To Be You" (Bluebird 30-0825)
Earl Hines (1944)

"Too Marvelous For Words" (Decca 1185)
Bing Crosby, with Jimmy Dorsey and His Orchestra (1937)

Works Cited

Bridges, John, and R. Serge Denisoff. "Changing Courtship Patterns In Popular Song: Horton And Carey Revisited." POPULAR MUSIC AND SOCIETY, 10:3 (Fall 1986): 29-45.

Carey, James T. "Changing Courtship Patterns In The Popular Song." AMERICAN JOURNAL OF SOCIOLOGY, 74 (May 1969): 720-731.

Cooper, B. Lee. "Personal Relationships, Love, And Sexuality," in A RESOURCE GUIDE TO THEMES IN CONTEMPORARY AMERICAN SONG LYRICS, 1950-1985 (Westport, Connecticut: Greenwood Press, 1986): 131-181.

Cooper, B. Lee. "The Sky Is Crying: Tales Told In Tearful Tunes." POPULAR MUSIC AND SOCIETY, 27:1 (Winter 2004): 107-115.

Cooper, B. Lee. "Wise Men Never Try: A Discography Of Fool Songs, 1945-1995." POPULAR MUSIC AND SOCIETY, 21:2 (Summer 1997): 115-131.

Davis, Hank. "Not-So-Subtle Sexual Content In Early Pop Music." GOLDMINE, No. 666 (February 3, 2006): 12.

DeNora, Tia. "Music And Self-Identity," in THE POPULAR MUSIC READER, edited by Andy Bennett, Barry Shank, and Jason Toynbee (New York:Routledge, 2006): 141-147.

Edwards, Emily D. "Does Love Really Stink? The 'Mean World' Of Love And Sex In Popular Music Of The 1980s," in ADOLESCENTS AND THEIR MUSIC: IF IT'S TOO LOUD, YOU'RE TOO OLD, edited by Jonathan Epstein (New York: Garland Publishing, 1994): 225-249.

Farber, Barry A. ROCK 'N' ROLL WISDOM: WHAT PSYCHOLOGICALLY ASTUTE LYRICS TEACH ABOUT LIFE AND LOVE. Westport,Connecticut: Praeger, 2007.

Frith, Simon. "Songs As Texts" and "The Meaning Of Music," in PERFORMING RITES: ON THE VALUE OF POPULAR MUSIC (CAMBRIDGE,MASSACHUSETTS: Harvard University Press, 1996): 158-182, 249-268.

Frith, Simon. SOUND EFFECTS: YOUTH, LEISURE, ANDTHE POLITICS OF ROCK 'N' ROLL. New York: Pantheon Books, 1981.

Furia, Philip. THE POETS OF TIN PAN ALLEY: A HISTORY OF AMERICA'S GREAT LYRICISTS. New York: Oxford University Press, 1990.

Furia, Philip, and Michael Lasser.AMERICA'S SONGS: THE STORIES BEHIND THE SONGS OF BROADWAY, HOLLYWOOD, AND TIN PAN ALLEY. New York: Routledge, 2006.

Gabree, John. "Cheatin': Tell Us About It, Singer Man." COUNTRY MUSIC, 2 (December 1973): 42-45.

Goodall, Jr., H.L. LIVING IN THE ROCK 'N' ROLL MYSTERY: READING CONTEXT, SELF AND OTHERS AS CLUES. Carbondale, Illinois:Southern Illinois University Press, 1991.

Green, Jeff (comp.). THE GREEN BOOK OF SONGS BY SUBJECT: THE THEMATIC GUIDE TO POPULAR MUSIC (4th edition, updated andexpanded). Nashville, Tennessee: Professional Desk Services, 1995.

Grossberg, Lawrence. "The Politics Of Youth Culture: Some Observations On Rock And Roll In American Culture." SOCIAL TEXT, 8 (Winter 1983-84): 104-126.

Hayakawa, S. I. "Popular Songs Vs. The Facts Of Life. "ETC: A REVIEW OF GENERAL SEMATICS, 12 (Winter 1955): 83-95.

Horton, Donald. "The Dialogue Of Courtship In Popular Song," in ON RECORD: ROCK, POP, AND THE WRITTEN WORD (edited bySimon Frith and Andrew Goodwin (New York: Pantheon Books, 1990): 14-26.

Hoskyns, Barney. SAY IT ONE MORE TIME FORTHE BROKEN-HEARTED: THE COUNTRY SIDE OF SOUTHERN SOUL. London: Bloomsbury Books, 1998.

Johnson, Christopher D. HYPERBOLES: THE RHETORIC OF EXCESS IN BAROQUE LITERATURE AND THOUGHT. Cambridge, Massachusetts: Harvard University Press, 2010.

Jourdain, Robert. MUSIC, THE BRAIN, AND ECSTASY: HOW MUSIC CAPTURES OUR IMAGINATION. New York: Quill/HarperCollins,2002 (c1997).

Kawin, Bruce F. TELLING IT AGAIN AND AGAIN: REPETITION IN LITERATURE AND FILM. Ithaca, New York: Cornell University Press, 1972.

Lewis, George H. "The Meaning's In The Music And The Music's In Me: Popular Music As Symbolic Communication." THEORY, CULTURE, AND SOCIETY, 1:3 (1983): 133-141.

Macken, Bob, Peter Fornatale, and Bill Ayres (comps.). "Twenty Emotions And Themes Of Love," in THE ROCK MUSIC SOURCE BOOK (Garden City, New York: Anchor Press/Doubleday, 1980): 484-558.

McLaurin, Melton A., and Richard A. Peterson (eds.). YOU WROTE MY LIFE: LYRICAL THEMES IN COUNTRY MUSIC. Philadelphia, Pennsylvania: Gordon and Breach, 1992.

Middleton, Richard. VOICING THE POPULAR: ON THE SUBJECTS OF POPULAR MUSIC. New York: Routledge, 2006.

Moore, John. "The Hieroglyphics Of Love: The Torch Singers And Interpretation." POPULAR MUSIC, 8:1 (January 1989): 31-58.

Neal, Mark Anthony. WHAT THE MUSIC SAID: BLACK POPULAR MUSIC AND BLACK PUBLIC CULTURE. New York: Routledge, 1999.

Pessen, Edward. "Tin Pan Alley's Many Ways Of Love, 1920-1945." POPULAR MUSIC AND SOCIETY, 14 (Winter 1990): 39-47.

Rogers, Jimmie N. "Audience Attitudes As Indicated By Cheatin' Messages In Popular Country Songs." STUDIES IN POPULAR CULTURE, 3 (1980): 2-10.

Rogers, Jimmie N. THE COUNTRY MUSIC MESSAGE: REVISITED. Fayetteville, Arkansas: University of Arkansas Press, 1989.

Scheurer, Timothy E. "The Beatles, The Brill Building, And The Persistence Of Tin Pan Alley In The Age Of Rock." POPULAR MUSIC AND SOCIETY, 20:4 (Winter 1996): 89-102.

Scheurer, Timothy E. "'Thou Witty': The Evolution And Triumph Of Style In Lyric Writing, 1890-1950," in AMERICAN POPULAR MUSIC – VOLUME ONE: THE 19TH CENTURY AND TIN PAN ALLEY, Edited by Timothy E. Scheurer (Bowling Green, Ohio: Bowling Green State University Popular Press, 1989): 104-119.

Schlueter, Carol J. FILLING UP THE MEASURE: THE POLEMICAL HYPERBOLE IN FIRST THESSALONIANS 2:14-16. Sheffield, England: JSOT Press, 1994.

Stein, Robert H. DIFFICULT SAYINGS IN THE GOSPELS: JESUS' USE OF OVERSTATEMENT AND HYPERBOLE. Grand Rapids, Michigan: Baker Book House, 1985.

Tawa, Nicholas E. "The Ways Of Love In The Mid-Nineteenth Century American Song," in AMERICAN POPULAR MUSIC – VOLUME ONE: THE 19TH CENTURY AND TIN PAN ALLEY, edited by Timothy E. Scheurer (Bowling Green, Ohio: Bowling Green State University Popular Press, 1989): 47-62.

Walley, David. TEENAGE NERVOUS BREAKDOWN: MUSIC AND POLITICS IN THE POST-ELVIS AGE (Second Edition). New York: Routledge, 2006 (c1998).

Webb, Stephen H. BLESSED EXCESS: RELIGION AND THE HYPERBOLIC IMAGINATION. Albany, New York: State University of New York, 1993.

Weinstein, Deena. "Rock: Youth And Its Music," in ADOLESCENTS AND THEIR MUSIC: IF IT'S TOO LOUD, YOU'RE TOO OLD, edited by Jonathan S. Epstein (New York: Garland Publishing, 1994): 3-23.

Weisman, Eric Robert. "Wine, Women, And Song: Frank Sinatra And The Rhetoric Of Whoopee." PENNSYLVANIA SPEECH COMMUNICATION ANNUAL, 32 (1976): 67-79.

Whitburn, Joel (Comp). POP MEMORIES, 1890-1954. Menomonee Falls, Wisconsin: Record Research, 1986.

Whitburn, Joel (Comp). TOP POP SINGLES, 1955-2012. Menomonee Falls, Wisconsin: Record Research, 2013.

Whitburn, Joel (Comp). TOP R&B/HIP-HOP SINGLES, 1942-2004. Menomonee Falls, Wisconsin: Record Research. 2004.

Wolfe, Arnold S. and Margaret Haefner. "Taste Cultures, Culture Classes, Affective Alliances, And Popular Music Reception: Theory, Methodology, And Application To A Beatles Song." POPULAR MUSIC AND SOCIETY, 20:4 (Winter 1996): 127-155.

(This commentary was originally published as B. Lee Cooper. "The Hyperbolic Hit Parade: A Discographic Study of The Extravagant Lyrical Assertions in Romantic Recordings," POPULAR MUSIC AND SOCIETY, 38:5 (December 2015): 611-624.)

SPIRITUAL IDEAS AND RELIGIOUS IMAGERY

Contemporary American recordings rarely reference religious figures, doctrines, or practices beyond the confines of Old and New Testament orthodoxy. While embracing Christianity as a set of humane principles and Jesus Christ as a supernatural being and a social philosopher, most pop songs ignore the spiritual tenets that differentiate Roman Catholics from United Methodists from Free Will Baptists. Examples of non-denominational anthems include "All God's Children Got Soul", "Amen", "Are You Ready?", "The Bible Tells Me So", "Brother Love's Traveling Salvation Show", "Crying in The Chapel", "Deck of Cards", He's Get The Whole World (In His Hands)", "Oh Happy Day", "Put Your Hand In the Hand", "Spirit in The Sky", "Turn! Turn! Turn!", and "A Wonderful Time Up There". In contrast to these popular spiritual perspectives, a few recordings do emphasize more traditional Christian beliefs and practices. For example, prayer is acknowledged in both "The Lord's Prayer" and "Our Father (Which Art in Heaven)". Inspirational songs and gospel tunes are also reprised in recordings such as "Amazing Grace", "Go Tell It on The Mountain", "I'll Fly Away", "Just A Closer Walk With Thee", "Oh, Rock My Soul", "(There'll Be) Peace in The Valley (For Me)", "Touch The Hem of His Garment", and "Will the Circle Be Unbroken". Similarly, the birth of Christ is faithfully recalled in "Adeste Fideles (Oh, Come All Ye Faithful)", "Ave Maria", "Little Drummer Boy/ Peace on Earth", "Oh Holy Night", and "Silent Night, Holy Night". Beyond the familiar Bethlehem perspective, though, images of Christ in contemporary lyrics are remarkably diverse. The Lamb of God is directly addressed in "Dear Mr. Jesus", "Dropkick Me, Jesus (Through the Goalposts of Life)", "Jesus Gave Me Water", "Jesus Is a Soul Man", "Jesus Is Just Alright", "Jesus Was a Capricorn", "Put Christ Back into Christmas", and "Superstar - Jesus Christ Superstar". Finally, numerous other recordings illustrate personal spirituality and love for humanity while only peripherally commenting on organized religion. Among these recordings are "Bridge Over Troubled Water", "Do They Know It's Christmas?", "Give Peace A Chance", "He Ain't Heavy, He's My Brother", "Imagine", "Let It Be", "Love Train", "Put A Little Love in Your Heart", and "You've Got A Friend".

Discographic Illustrations

"Adeste Fideles (Oh, Come All Ye Faithful)" (Decca 23777)
Bing Crosby (1960)

"All God's Children Got Soul" (Elektra 45671)
Dorothy Morrison (1969)

"Amazing Grace" (Elektra 45709)
Judy Collins (1970)

"Amen" (ABC-Paramount 10602)
The Impressions (1964)

"Are You Ready?" (Columbia 45158)
Pacific Gas and Electric (1970)

"Ave Maria" (RCA Victor 45-0071)
Perry Como (1949)

"The Bible Tells Me So" (Coral 61467)
Don Cornell (1955)

"Bridge Over Troubled Water" (Columbia 45079)
Simon and Garfunkel (1970)

"Brother Love's Traveling Salvation Show" (Uni 55109)
Neil Diamond (1969)

"Christian's Automobile" (Peacock 1780)
The Dixie Hummingbirds (1957)

"Crying In The Chapel" (Jubilee 45-5122)
The Orioles (1953)

"Day By Day" (Bell 45210)
Godspell's Original Cast (1972)

"Dear Mr. Jesus" (PowerVision 8603)
Power Source (1987)

"Deck Of Cards" (Dot 15968)
Wink Martindale (1959)

"Do They Know It's Christmas?" (Columbia 04749)
Band Aid (1984)

"Dropkick Me, Jesus (Through the Goalposts of Life)" (RCA 10790)
Bobby Bare (1976)

"Dust In the Wind" (Kirshner 4274)
Kansas (1978)

"Eleanor Rigby" (Capitol 5715)
The Beatles (1966)

"Ezekiel Saw De Wheel" (Columbia A-3370)
The Fisk Jubilee Singers (1921)

"Friendship Train" (Soul 35068)
Gladys Knight and The Pips (1969)

"Give Peace A Chance" (Apple 1809)
John Lennon (1969)

"Go Tell It on The Mountain" (Columbia 4-42633)
Mahalia Jackson (1962)

"God Bless America" (MGM 12841)
Connie Francis (1959)

"God, Love, And Rock and Roll" (Westbound 170)
Teegarden and Van Winkle (1970)

"God Knows" (Warner Brothers 8554)
Debby Boone (1978)

"Golden Gate Gospel Train" (Bluebird 7126)
The Golden Gate Jubilee Quartet (1937)

"The Gospel Train Is Coming" (Vocalion 1082)
Edward J. Clayborn (1927)

"Gotta Serve Somebody" (Columbia 11072)
Bob Dylan (1979)

"He" (Verve 10406)
The Righteous Brothers (1966)

"He Ain't Heavy, He's My Brother" (Epic 10532)
The Hollies (1969)

"He's Got the Whole World (In His Hands)" (Capitol 3891)
Laurie London (1958)

"How I Got Over" (Gotham 674)
Clara Ward and The Ward Singers (1950)

"I Believe" (London 9672)
The Bachelors (1964)

"I Don't Know How to Love Him" (Capitol 3027)
Helen Reddy (1971)

"I Heard the Voice of Jesus" (Warner Brothers 7397)
Turley Richards (1970)

"I Knew Jesus (Before He Was A Star)" (Capitol 3548)
Glen Campbell (1973)

"I Know What God Is" (RCA Victor 7670)
Perry Como (1960)

"I'll Fly Away" (Okeh 6890)
The (CBS) Trumpeteers (1952)

"If You See My Savior" (Vocalion 1710)
Thomas A. Dorsey (1939)

"Imagine" (Apple 1840)
John Lennon (1971)

"Jesus Gave Me Water" (Specialty 802)
The Soul Stirrers (1951)

"Jesus Is A Soul Man" (Warner Brothers 7322)
Lawrence Reynolds (1969)

"Jesus Is Just Alright" (Warner Brothers 7661)
Doobie Brothers (1972)

"Jesus Met the Woman at the Well" (Decca 48178)
The Famous Blue Jay Singers of Birmingham Alabama (1950)

"Jesus Take a Hold" (Capitol 2838)
Merle Haggard (1970)

"Jesus Was a Capricorn" (Monument 8558)
Kris Kristofferson (1973)

"Just A Closer Walk with Thee" (Roulette 4234)
Jimmie Rodgers (1960)

"Lady Madonna" (Capitol 2138)
The Beatles (1968)

"Let It Be" (Apple 2654)
Beatles (1970)

"Let's Talk About Jesus" (Peacock 1584)
Bells of Joy (1952)

"Little Drummer Boy/ Peace on Earth" (RCA PH-13400)
David Bowie and Bing Crosby (1982)

"Lord I Can't Just Keep from Crying" (Columbia 14425-D)
Blind Willie Johnson (1935)

"The Lord's Prayer" (Jubilee 5045)
The Orioles (1950)

"Lord's Prayer" (A&M 1491)
Sister Janet Mead (1974)

"Love Train" (Philadelphia International 3524)
The O'Jays (1973)

"Mary Don't You Weep" (Vee-Jay 5003)
The Swan Silvertones (1959)

"Me And Jesus" (Mercury 73278)
Tom T. Hall (1972)

"Michael (Row the Boat Ashore)" (United Artists 258)
The Highwaymen (1961)

"Mighty Clouds uf Joy" (Scepter 12320)
B.J. Thomas (1971)

"Move On Up A Little" (Apollo 164)
Mahalia Jackson (1947)

"My Sweet Lord" (Apple 2995)
George Harrison (1970)

"Oh Happy Day" (Pavillion 20001)
The Edwin Hawkins Singers (1969)

"Oh Holy Night" (Jubilee 5045)
The Orioles (1950)

"Oh, Rock My Soul" (Warner Brothers 5442)
Peter, Paul, and Mary (1964)

"The Old Ship Zion" (Apollo 223)
The Roberta Martin Singers (1950)

"Operator" (Atlantic 3292)
The Manhattan Transfer (1975)

"Our Father (Which Art in Heaven)" (Peacock 1550)
The Five Blind Boys (1950)

"People Get Ready" (ABC-Paramount 10622)
The Impressions (1965)

"People Get Ready" (Epic 05416)
Jeff Beck and Rod Stewart (1985)

"Put A Little Love in Your Heart" (Imperial 66385)
Jackie DeShannon (1969)

"Put Your Hand in The Hand" (Kama Sutra 519)
Ocean (1971)

"Put Christ Back Into Christmas" (Decca 28940)
Red Foley (1953)

"Reverend Mr. Black" (Capitol 4951)
The Kingston Trio (1963)

"The Shrine of St. Cecilia" (Capitol 3696)
Faron Young (1957)

"Signs" (Lionel 3213)
The Five Man Electrical Band (1971)

"Silent Night (Christian Hymn)" (Decca 48119)
Sister Rosetta Tharpe (1949)

"Silent Night, Holy Night" (Apollo 750)
Mahalia Jackson (1962)

"Some Children See Him" (Rhino CD R2-70714)
The Inner Voices (1990)

"Spirit in The Sky" (Reprise 0885)
Norman Greenbaum (1970)

"Superstar - Jesus Christ Superstar" (Decca 32603)
Murray Head, with The Trinadad Singers (1971)

"Swing Down Chariot" (Columbia 37834)
The Golden Gate Quartet (1947)

"Tell It on The Mountain" (Warner Brothers 5418)
Peter, Paul, and Mary (1964)

"(There Was A) Tall Oak Tree" (Era 3012)
Dorsey Burnette (1960)

"(There'll Be) Peace in The Valley (For Me)" (RCA EPA-4054)
Elvis Presley (1957)

"Touch Me Lord Jesus" (Gotham 605)
The Angelic Gospel Singers (1949)

"Touch the Hem of His Garment" (Specialty 896)
The Soul Stirrers (1956)

"Turn! Turn! Turn!" (Columbia 43424)
The Byrds (1965)

"Who Will Answer?" (RCA Victor 47-9400)
Ed Ames (1967)

"Will the Circle Be Unbroken" (Epic BN 26196)
The Staple Singers (1966)

"A Wonderful Time Up There" (Dot 15690)
Pat Boone (1958)

"Woodstock" (Atlantic 2723)
Crosby, Stills, Nash and Young (1970)

"You Gave Me A Mountain" (ABC 11174)
Frankie Laine (1969)

"You'll Never Walk Alone" (RCA Victor 47-9600)
Elvis Presley (1968)

"You've Got a Friend" (Warner Brothers 7498)
James Taylor (1971)

Print References

Gavin Baddeley. LUCIFER RISING: SIN, DEVIL WORSHIP, AND ROCK 'N' ROLL. London: Plexus Books, 1999.

Paul Baker. CONTEMPORARY CHRISTIAN MUSIC. Westchester, Illinois: Crossway Books, 1985.

James H. Cone. THE SPIRITUALS AND THE BLUES: AN INTERPRETATION. New York: Seabury Press, 1972.

B. Lee Cooper. "Religion," in A RESOURCE GUIDE TO THEMES IN CONTEMPORARY AMERICAN SONG LYRICS, 1950-1985 (Westport, Connecticut: Greenwood Press, 1986): 223-233.

B. Lee Cooper. "Rock Music and Religious Education: A Proposed Synthesis." RELIGIOUS EDUCATION, 70 (May-June 1975): 289-299.

R. Serge Denisoff. "The Religious Roots of the American Song of Persuasion." WESTERN FOLKLORE, 29, No. 3 (1970): 175-184.

Michael J. Gilmour. CALL ME THE SEEKER: LISTENING TO RELIGION IN POPULAR MUSIC. New York: Continuum, 2005.

David Graham. HE WALKS WITH ME. New York: Simon and Schuster, 1977.

Edward F. Heenan and H. Rosanne Falkenstein. "Religious Rock: What Is It Saying?" POPULAR MUSIC AND SOCIETY, 2 (Summer 1973): 321-326.

Tony Hilfer. "'Wreck on the Highway': Rhetoric and Religion in a Country Song." JEMF QUARTERLY, 21 (Fall-Winter 1985): 116-119.

Jay R. Howard. "Contemporary Christian Music: Where Rock Meets Religion." JOURNAL OF POPULAR CULTURE, 26 (Summer 1992): 123-130.

Alton B. Pollard III. "Religion, Rock, and Eroticism." JOURNAL OF BLACK SACRED MUSIC, 1 (Spring 1987): 47-52.

Jimmie N. Rogers and Stephen A. Smith. "Country Music and Organized Religion," in ALL THAT GLITTERS: COUNTRY MUSIC IN AMERICA, edited by George H. Lewis (Bowling Green, Ohio; Bowling Green State University Popular Press, 1993): 270-284.

William D. Romanowski. "Roll Over Beethoven, Tell Martin Luther the News: American Evangelicals and Rock Music." JOURNAL OF AMERICAN CULTURE, 15 (Fall 1992): 78-88.

Davin Seay, with Mary Neely. STAIRWAY TO HEAVEN: THE SPIRITUAL ROOTS OF ROCK 'N' ROLL - FROM THE KING AND LITTLE RICHARD TO PRINCE AND AMY GRANT. New York: Ballantine Books/Epiphany Press, 1986.

Robert L. Stone. "Make a Joyful Noise: A Brief History of the House of God Church and the Sacred Steel Musical Tradition." LIVING BLUES, No. 176 (January-February 2005): 14-21.

Stephen R. Tucker. "Pentecostalism and Popular Culture in the South: A Study of Four Musicians." JOURNAL OF POPULAR CULTURE, 16 (Winter 1982): 68-80.

Steve Turner. HUNGRY FOR HEAVEN: SEARCH FOR MEANING IN ROCK AND RELIGION. London: Hodder and Stoughton, 1995.

(This commentary was originally published as B. Lee Cooper. "Religious Images," in PROMINENT THEMES IN POPULAR SONGS, edited by B. Lee Cooper and Frank W. Hoffmann (Charleston, South Carolina: Paw Paw Press, 2015): 285-293.)

Little Richard

WEDDING BELLS

VALENTINE'S DAY: THE SOUND OF WEDDING BELLS - 33 TUNES TO WED BY
Various Artists
CD, Bear Family Records BCD 17654, 2022

Why do couples wed? Reasons abound. The most frequent answer is because they love each other and wish to spend the rest of their lives together. But other motives also exist. Sometimes couples marry to please their parents. Sometimes they desire legal confirmation or religious affirmation of their shared future. Responses to "Why did you get married?" can range from the romantically sublime to the financially ridiculous. Just pause and contemplate several weird matrimonial stimulations. Consider an elderly businessman divorcing his middle-aged mate and marrying a younger, more beautiful trophy wife. Or think about the angry father of a pregnant teenage girl forcing a shotgun wedding upon an unlucky young man. Or speculate about an enterprising lower level male executive marrying the boss's daughter as a means of insuring career advancement. Or, in a parallel circumstance, a golddigger female secretary marrying her boss to assure her own financial future. Likewise, imagine a widower and a divorcee seeking to rebound from crushing grief and loneliness by rushing into a second marriage. Is there song material in any of these situations?

Living happily ever seems like a fairy tale ending that seldom describes life after marriage. Nevertheless, the majority of popular recordings approach matrimony from this mythic ideal. Dating and romantic affection invariably lead to engagement and marriage in most songs. In 1955 Frank Sinatra and Dinah Shore each released a recording of "Love And Marriage." This was the vocalized epitome of normative social progression. It's still the quintessential tune concerning marital inevitability. No matter the age or the season, not matter the rhyme or the reason - when it comes to emotional attachment and binding matrimony, you can't have one without the other.

VALENTINE'S DAY: THE SOUND OF WEDDING BELLS is a marvelous, thoughtful assembly of 33 unconventional songs that explore varying plans and plots, dreams and schemes concerning tying the knot. Granted, there are a few idealistic ditties that managed to creep into this audio tent of mismatched couples and misunderstood marital intentions. But the majority of tunes anthologized by Bear Family compiler Marc Mittelacher are chocked full of matrimonial doubt, self-interest, insincerity, and dark humor. The spectrum of wedding-related perspectives begins with joyful, predictable, traditional ceremonies. These warm feelings are communicated via lyrics from "Love And Marriage" (1961) and "When A Boy From The Mountains (Weds A Girl From The Valley)" (1936). They are also echoed in the instrumentations of "Caribbean Honeymoon" (1960), "Honeymoon Hotel" (1934), "Love Bells" (1940), and "White Wedding" (1956). Beyond these recordings, though, matrimonial planning gets more vague, more complicated, and more qualified. High schoolers and other young adults express their hopes and dreams in "Ding Dong Rock A Billy Wedding" (1957), "Gonna Marry That Gal" (1955), "Honeymoonin'" (1959), "Teenage Wedding" (1960), and

"Wedding Bells (Just For You And Me)" (1961). Wonderful times together and pledges of enduring love abound among these youthful dreamers. Marital obligations and financiaal responsibilities are seldom considered.

More thoughtful, carefully negotiated female perspectives about marriage are offered by Sunny Gale, Brenda Lee, Ginny Arnell, and Eva Boswell in their recordings of "Church Bells May Ring" (1960), "Let's Jump The Broomstick" (1959), "Married To You" (1962), and "Ready, Willing, and Able" (1955). But more skeptical male perspectives are voiced by Bill Darnel, The Belvederes, The Brooks Brothers, and The Tarriers in "The Hook" (1954), "Let's Get Married" (1956), "Married" (1961), and "Pretty Boy" (1957). These tunes predict that flirting, fun times, and strong physical attraction won't necessarily lead to the alter.

Even more complex personal relationships and socio-economic circumstances are explored throughout VALTENINE'S DAY: THE SOUND OF WEDDING BELLS. Rikki Henderson can't quite comprehend that "Peggy Sue Got Married" (1959) and Gene Vincent decries the reality that "Wedding Bells (Are Breaking Up That Old Gang Of Mine)" (1956). The Knockouts ponder the significant female marital choice between "Rich Boy / Boy Boy" (1960). It gets even more dicey, though. O.C. Holt laments seeing the girl of his dreams getting married in a "Pink Wedding Gown" (1959). Ann Cole warns the former lover of her groom-to-be "Don't Stop The Wedding" (1962), while June Valli admits that she has accepted the proposal of a man who is second in her heart in "The Wedding" (1958). A surprise ending is featured in "Jeannie's Wedding" (1961), when the bride ditches the groom at the altar in favor of an old boy friend - the song's singer Otis Blackwell. Finally, Betty Hutton and Tennessee Ernie Ford declare that "The Honeymoon's Over" (1954) after cheating and quarreling begin to replace loving and snuggling.

Unanticipated events and unexpected emotions dominate the pre-matrimonial commentaries presented in VALENTINE'S DAY: THE SOUND OF WEDDING BELLS. The obscure recordings are frivolous, yet funny. However, there are several key audio omissions that beg for inclusion. From a whimsical viewpoint, the Bear Family compiler should have tapped comical tunes like "Aba Daba Honemoon" (1950) by Kitty Kallen and Dick Haymes, "The Big Bopper's Wedding" (1958) by The Big Bopper, "I'm Henry VIII, I Am" (1965) by Herman's Hermits, "If You Want To Be Happy" (1963) by Jimmy Soul, "Keep Your Hands To Yourself" (1986) by The Georgia Satellites, "One Mint Julep" (1952) by The Clovers, and "Wedding Boogie" by The Johnny Otis Congregation. Other obvious contenders for any compilation confronting peculiar wedding circumstances are "Daisy Bell" (1893) by Dan Quinn, "Hey Paula" (1962) by Paul and Paula, "It's Gonna Work Out Fine" (1961) by Ike & Tina Turner, "If I Were A Carpenter" (1968) by The Four Tops, and "Wedding Bell Blues" (1969) by The 5th Dimension.

Bear Family's VALENTINE'S DAY: THE SOUND OF WEDDING BELLS faces direct commercial competition from only two other marriage-tune anthologies. Rhino Records released a two-disc, 28-song collection titled ROCKIN' & ROLLIN' WEDDING SONGS in 1992 and Fantastic Voyage Records/Future Noise Music issued a single-disc, 24-

tune compilation in 2011. What sets this Bear Family disc apart, though, is the reliance upon previously unissued hillbilly/folk/orchestral recordings that explore the more petty and preposterous problems of matrimony. What this collection lacks in respect to musical quality (such as pop hits by familiar artists), it compensates for in eccentricity of lyrics and dark humor related to marital perspectives.

Herman's Hermits

"WHITE CHRISTMAS"...AND "UNCHAINED MELODY"

IRVING BERLIN'S WHITE CHRISTMAS: 28 WILDLY ECLECTIC VERSIONS OF THE MOST FAMOUS CHRSTMAS SONG OF ALL
Various Artists
CD, Jasmine Records JASMCD 2729, 2021

THE UNCHAINED MELODY: 29 KILLER VERSIONS
Various Artists
CD, Jasmine Records JASMCD 2719, 2021

I HUNGER FOR YOUR TOUCH - UNCHAINED MELODY: 31 VERSIONS OF THE WORLD-FAMOUS LOVE SONG
Various Artists
CD, Bear Family Records BCD 17128, 2014

The vast majority of recorded songs dwell in obscurity. This sonic limbo status was never intended. On the contrary, record companies seek to produce hits, hits, and more hits. Recorded music is invariably composed with high hopes. It is thoughtfully arranged to yield popular success and carefully orchestrated to generate energy. Recordings are vocalized with gusto and sincerity. Nevertheless, most audio releases fail to receive public recognition and never attain financial success. Fewer still receive praise from rock journalists and music critics. And even fewer manage to sustain numerical designations on America's "Top 100" pop music charts as displayed in either BILLBOARD or CASH BOX. Commercial success within the American recording industry is a Darwinian-like battle for survival. Extinction always threatens. Audio adaptation vies with formulaic compromise to secure a sweet spot in the public buying forum. Record label promotion of new songs is highly competitive. So is the fierce struggle among composers to have demos of their lyrics/melodies pitched to established recording stars. Each new release is then introduced to audiences by radio and TV disc jockeys, by artists at their concerts, and by record companies within new albums. When a hit song finally emerges, the corporate celebration explodes. Money flows into record company coffers. Artists get paid. Composers reap royalties. But quickly the process of searching for a follow-up hit recording commences. This endless cycle churns on and on.

Once a recorded song secures commercial hit status, it becomes a favorable target for re-issue. It is a pre-approved popular artifact. Admittedly, there are only a few hundred songs that have been re-recorded, re-charted, and classified as pop favorites during multiple decades. These tunes qualify as standards. Examples include the patriotic anthem "The Star-Spangled Banner." This song was a pop hit for Gilmore's Band (1892), Margaret Woodrow Wilson (1915), Jimi Hendrix (1969), and Whitney Houston (1991, 2001). Similarly, the sacred Christmas hymn "Silent Night" was converted into pop music gold by The Haydn Quartet (1905), Bing Crosby (1936, 1938, 1942, 1947, 1957, and 1960), Mahalia Jackson (1962), and Pentatonix (2014). Other songs that have demonstrated this same multi-decade chart popularity in the U.S. are: "Blue

Moon," "Blue Skies," "Body and Soul," "Bridge Over Troubled Water," "Jingle Bells," "Let It Be," "My Blue Heaven," "Over The Rainbow," "Peg O' My Heart," "Rudolph, The Red-Nosed Reindeer," "Since I Don't Have You," "St. Louis Blues," and "Star Dust." There are two additional classics that merit acknowledgement - "White Christmas" and "Unchained Melody," Discographers employed by European re-issue giants Jasmine Records and Bear Family Records have recently assembled well-deserved tributes to the Bing Crosby tune and to the song that became a signature performance for Bobby Hatfield of The Righteous Brothers.

Jasmine liner notes scribe Roger Dopson addresses the majesty and longevity of IRVING BERLIN'S WHITE CHRISTMAS. This 28-track collection of "White Christmas" renditions sparkles with diversity. It begins with the 1942 Bing Crosby version and ends with a 1957 cut by Elvis Presley. The compiler explores R&B releases by The Ravens (1948) and Clyde McPhatter, Bill Pinkney, and The Drifters (1954). He also features performances by pop music legends Frank Sinatra (1944) and Ella Fitzgerald (1960). He highlights several instrumental versions, including releases by Mantovani (1952) and Chet Atkins (1961). He touches on gospel and inspirational approaches by Sister Rosetta Tharpe (1949) and Mahalia Jackson (1955). Dopson also examines a quirky jazz reading of the holiday melody by Big Maybelle (1958), a doo-wop arrangement by The Statues (1960), a homespun country piece by Walter Brennan (1962), and international versions of "White Christmas" from the Indonesian duo The Blue Diamonds (1960), the U. K.'s Emile Ford & The Checkmates (1960), Jamaica's Simms & Robinson (1960), and Belgium's Vic Borrell & His Orchestra. There are only two flaws in this outstanding compilation. First, the presentation of the recordings on the CD should have followed the same chronological pattern detailed in the liner notes. A random arrangement seems pointless. Second, it would have been even more impressive if Dopson had added a few post-1962 versions of "White Christmas." Such a supplement might have included BILLBOARD-charted renditions by Andy Williams (1963), Michael Bolton (1992), and Michael Buble & Bing Crosby (2012).

THE UNCHAINED MELODY and I HUNGER FOR YOUR TOUCH -- UNCHAINED MELODY provide two incredibly in-depth historical perspectives on the creation, vocal evolution, and music chart triumphs of a distinctive American tune. The 2021 Jasmine anthology assembled by Roger Dopson features 29 different versions of "Unchained Melody" that were released between 1955 and 1962. The 2014 Bear Family collection organized by Hank Davis expands the time frame of releases well beyond the early 1960s, but sadly fails to provide consistent information about the dates of production or of chart success. The Davis compilation acknowledges the flimsy film roots of the song and emphasizes The Righteous Brothers' 1965 revival of "Unchained Melody" as a cultural touchstone moment. That is, 21st century listeners of mixed generations, genders, and ethnicities have come to respect the Bobby Hatfield vocal version of the song as the epitome of all renditions. Understandably, there is a huge amount of duplication within these two honorific songlists.

THE UNCHAINED MELODY traces an uneven seven-year sonic trail. It features the birth pangs of "Unchained Melody" as an Alex North-Hy Zaret film score, an unsuccessful Academy Award nominee, and a pop music chart wonder. The audio renditions for this period feature Todd Duncan's understated movie version from the film "Unchained," Les Baxter's No. 1 instrumental hit, and various 1955 vocal successes by Al Hibbler, Roy Hamilton, and others. The Jasmine compiler builds his case for the song's sustained greatness by citing the repetitions of releases. For vocals, Dopson lists Sam Cooke (1960), Ricky Nelson (1958), and The Lettermen (1962). For instrumentals, the compiler cites Mantovani (1957), Liberace (1955), Floyd Cramer (1961), Chet Atkins (1957) and Duane Eddy (1962). This is Dopson's case for the song's greatness.

There are several other distinctive performances featured in THE UNCHAINED MELODY. The Fleetwoods offer a scintillating acappella treatment of "Unchained Melody" from 1959. And Gene Vincent establishes the rock-star-as-balladeer template in 1957. Dopson opens the mixed genre interpretation gateway even further with country artists Marty Robbins (1961) and Conway Twitty (1962) as well as pop stars Pat Boone (1960) and June Valli (1955). Even R&B stalwart Bobby Day (1959) took a crack at "Unchained Melody." Despite all this sonic firepower, though, this collection seems hopelessly antique without the inclusion of tenor Bobby Hatfield's over-the-top Phil Spector-produced version.

I HUNGER FOR YOUR TOUCH -- UNCHAINED MELODY genuflects to the 1955 film "Unchained" by featuring Todd Duncan's screen rendition along with Harry Belafonte's 1956 Academy Award nomination performance of the North-Zaret tune. But it is obvious that the film soundtrack driving this 2014 compilation is the 1991 blockbuster "Ghost," starring Patrick Swayze and Demi Moore. Thus The Righteous Brothers are heralded for regenerating interest in "Unchained Melody" on two separate occasions. Of course, nothing can match the renewing force of a beautiful love story being filtered through an emotion-dripping vocal performance. Therefore, Hank Davis utilizes "Ghost"-related artwork on his CD cover and among his liner notes to market this Bear Family compilation.

Beyond the hype for the 1965 Righteous Brothers' tune and the 1991 "Ghost" connection, though, the performances exhibited throughout this CD are outstanding. They include undated versions of "Unchained Melody" by Giselle MacKenzie, Willie Nelson, Charlie Rich, Elvis Presley, Vito & The Salutations, Waylon Jennings, Eddy Arnold, David Allan Coe, Hank Snow & Chet Atkins, Diana Ross & The Supremes, Ray Coniff, and Phil Phillips. Now that's audio diversity. It's also indelible proof of a song's universal appeal to performers and to audiences alike. It's too bad that Hank Davis elected to omit key discographic details from the otherwise excellent I HUNGER FOR YOUR TOUCH - UNCHAINED MELODY.

Songs with multiple decades of commercial success merit the description as standards. Similarly, near universal public recognition of the words and melodies of classic tunes continue to make wedding receptions and karaoke lounge singing fun. Of course, compact disc salutes to single songs are rare. But "Ghost Riders In The Sky," "Kansas City," and "Rudolph, The Red-Nosed Reindeer" have received such acknowledgements. Both "White Christmas" and "Unchained Melody" are undoubtedly important and lasting audio achievements within American popular culture. Arguably, Bing Crosby and Bobby Hatfield have provided the most memorable versions of these two tunes. Lucky us.

RECORDING GIANTS AND PERFORMING HEROES

Chuck Berry

CHUCK BERRY

Chuck Berry, the poet laureate of rock 'n' roll, has been the foremost spokesman on the nature and impact of automobiles in 20th century popular culture. No other songwriter has approached his lyrical ingenuity for utilizing four-wheeled imagery to depict the realms of freedom and mobility, romantic relations and money, and authority and class. Berry emerged as a popular recording artist in 1955. "Maybellene", his initial release on Chess Records, soared to No. 5 on the BILLBOARD "Pop" charts. His hit production flourished over the next decade. Signature tunes included: "Roll Over Beethoven" (1956), "Rock & Roll Music" (1957), "Sweet Little Sixteen" (195 in 8), "Johnny B. Goode" (1958), "Little Queenie" (1959), "Let It Rock" (1960), and "No Particular Place To Go" (1964). Berry's legend grew during the late '60s and early '70s as performers like The Beatles and The Rolling Stones covered his material and lauded his influence. Berry even crashed the "Pop" charts again in 1972 with live and raunchy renditions of "My Ding-A-Ling" and "Reelin' & Rockin'". During the next two decades Berry was inducted into the Rock and Roll Hall of Fame, issued his autobiography, became the topic of many books and articles, and starred in the film "Hail, Hail Rock and Roll". He became a legend in his own lifetime.

Chuck Berry was a total performer. He composed the majority of songs he recorded; he was a relaxed and enthusiastic stage performer; he was an articulate vocalist and a scintillating guitarist; and his duckwalk dance step was known worldwide. The major themes in Berry's songs were quite personal, at least to his fans. Specifically, his song-poems detailed observations and insightful commentaries about young people living in urban-industrial mid-century America. The topics of Berry's recordings captured this perspective. He noted the lack of relevance in public educational experiences ("School Day" and "Anthony Boy"); he depicted the heavy reliance on popular music as a means of communication and celebration ("Rock & Roll Music" and "Round and Round"); he encapsulated the confusing process of adolescent maturation ("Sweet Little Rock and Roller", "Almost Grown", and "Sweet Little Sixteen"); he fabricated and breathed vitality into a series of 20th century Horatio Algers ("Johnny B. Goode" and "Bye, Bye Johnny"); he condemned the fickleness of the female heart ("Nadine (Is It You?)" and "Little Queenie"); and he described the simplistic sense of patriotism among American teens ("Back In The U.S.A.").

The topical consistency of Chuck Berry's self-penned tunes were only one sign of his lyrical genius. He was a language-creating marvel as well. In addition to employing standard slang terminology in his car songs, with "machine" meaning automobile and "cruisin'" meaning driving, Berry initiated fascinating verbal images to symbolize the characters or scenes that he described. For instance, Johnny B. Goode didn't just lounge near a train track and play his guitar. Instead, he "...strums to the rhythm that the drivers make...". And the young man chasing the naughty Nadine doesn't just call out her name. He is described as "...campaign shoutin' like a Southern diplomat...". And students at a dance didn't just enjoy listening to the records. They are "...feelin' the music from head to toe...".

Throughout his songwriting and recording career, automobile imagery dominated Chuck Berry's lyrical context. He chronicled the sociological impact of this particular technology thoroughly and accurately. Undeniably, this balladeer of teenage existence, this canny oral historian, understood the central role of the car culture on dating and mating, on drinking and movie-going, and on escaping from parents and school principals as well. In 1970 journalist Michael Lydon wrote, "Serious and comic as only a genius can be; arrogant, beautiful, and demonically energetic, Chuck Berry has indelibly marked our times." What is seldom acknowledged, though, is how skillfully and cogently this master lyricist adapted the automobile to his own poetic ends. In the meantime, one cannot ignore the fact that even in the 21st century car usage remains a topic of national attention and sharply divided opinions. Shifting gas prices, increased levels of pollution, and the cost of new engine technologies are common newspaper subjects. Just as Berry explored the sociology and psychology of teenage motorcar use, contemporary songsmiths are dealing with the complex issues of traffic congestion, environmental pollution, energy availability, and other concerns related to society's love-hate relationship with automobiles.

The following pages trace Chuck Berry's use of motorized vehicle imagery within his recordings. The centrality of cars and drivers vary tune to tune. But the visions of life through the windshield and rearview mirror are never less than stunning. Berry remains the undisputed master of motorvatin' music. He understands carhops and juke boxes; he applauds hot rod chases and women who adore fast cars; and he is sympathetic to young men in raggedy Fords who long to drive Cadillacs, Lincolns, and Thunderbirds.

"Maybellene" - Fast cars and fickle females have sustained Chuck Berry's lyrics for five decades. "Maybellene" was the first. This 1955 tale illustrated two persistent themes in Chuck Berry's songs. First, the dude with the biggest, most elegant car will invariably capture the attention of any girl ("Maybellene, why can't you be true?"); and second, the pursuit of a wayward woman is never successful ("You've started back doin' the things you used to do"). The driver of the Cadillac Coup de Ville remains unidentified, although one suspects that his financial resources far exceed those of the singing hero driving the V-8 Ford. Fate, in the form of a sudden cloudburst, enables the over-heated Ford to catch the 110-mile-per-hour speeding Cadillac at the top of the hill. Then what happens? Chuck Berry doesn't depict a battle between the two drivers over the fair damsel. Instead, he returns to the original refrain - "Mabellene, why can't you be true?" Somehow, one senses that the man with the V-8 Ford will be chasing his girl again in the near future.

"Nadine (Is That You?)" - If dating a girl like Maybellene was a problem, having a fiancée like Nadine would be unbearable. Chuck Berry utilizes traffic congestion - crowded buses, loaded taxis, and endless lines of honking cars - to set the scene for this romantic chase. Nadine, who is reportedly always "…. up to something new," is spotted doubling back from a corner and moving toward a coffee-colored Cadillac. As the hero calls out to gain her attention, she abandons the Caddie and gets into "…. a Yellow Cab headin' up-town." The song provides no resolution since the pursuer is left at the mercy of his own cab driver and must be content "leanin' out the taxi window, tryin' to make her hear." Obviously, private transportation is superior to public vehicles - and courtship via buses, on foot, or in cabs is depicted by Chuck Berry as a losing battle.

"Come On" - This tune, both comic and tragic, finds a disabled automobile to be only one of a growing list of problems for a young man. "Everything is wrong," he declares, "since me and my baby parted." It may be difficult to establish a causal relationship between lost love and failing technology, but Chuck Berry achieves it. The hero's car won't start. To further complicate matters, he loses his job and can't even afford to hire a mechanic. Dolefully noting his immobilized vehicle, the hero expresses the frustrated wish that "…somebody's gonna come along and run into it and wreck it." One surmises that a token amount of insurance money might be gained from such an accident - although certainly not enough to resolve all of the problems detailed in this down-and-out song.

"No Money Down" - A new Cadillac symbolizes power, sex, social mobility, notoriety, freedom, and…the pot of gold at the end of the rainbow for the owner of a "broken down ragged Ford." The salesman in this tune is initially silent, but stands beneath a tempting "No Money Down" sign. When the prospective car buyer rolls into the lot, however, the dealer offers to put him in a car "that'll eat up the road." The salesman soon learns that he is facing a young man who knows exactly what he wants. The list of accessories requested for the yellow, four-door Cadillac Coup de Ville staggers the mind - wire-chromed wheels and a Continental spare, power steering and power brakes, air conditioning and automatic heat, "a full Murphy bed in my back seat," short-wave radio, television, telephone ("You know I gotta talk to my baby when I'm ridin' alone."), four carburators and two straight exhaust pipes, railroad airhorns, and a military spotlight. One doubts that this car deal can be consumated. Nevertheless, the values of the would-be owner are clearly articulated. A peppy, ostentatious buggy to replace a tired, drab Ford - and the whole world will be fine.

"No Particular Place To Go" - Thus tune demonstrates Chuck Berry at his comic best. Initially, it appears to be a typical tale of automotive seduction. The boy is "cruising and playing the radio" with a sweet young thing seated close beside him. He steals a kiss, she whispers softly in his ear, and they continue "…cuddling more and driving slow, with no particular place to go." The romantic mood is shaken, however, when the car is unexpectedly transformed from a lovers' chariot into a four-wheeled chastity belt. Just as the couple is ready to take a stroll in the moonlight, the young woman discovers that her safety harness will not release. The final verse is classic Berry: "Riding along in my calaboose, still trying to get her belt unloose. All the way home I held a grudge, for the safety belt that wouldn't budge." Here is the motorcar as entrapment, a classic example of technologically enforced morality.

"Too Much Monkey Business" - This song brings to mind Jim Croce's "Workin' In the Carwash Blues." The hero is really down on his luck. Too many bills and too much hard work. If it's not the antics of a woman trying to steal his freedom by forcing him to settle down, it's the mechanical thievery of a telephone stealing his dime, or the exile of Uncle Sam robbing him of physical autonomy and years of freedom through military service in Yokohama. The two automobile-related commentaries in this song are brief. The first is a derogatory reference to the inferiority and sterility of military vehicles - "Army car! Arrgh...." The second is a negative attitude expressed about post-military employment at a local filling station - "Too many tasks, wipe the windows, check the tires, check the oil - dollar gas?!!!" There is not joyous speculation about owning the gas station, or driving a shiny Coup de Ville. Only frustration by being forced to endure...too much monkey business.

"Move It" - This upbeat tune contains two illustrations of Chuck Berry's most creative automobile imagery. The cars mentioned here are utilized as symbols of sexual liberation and unthinking authority. In the first case, the singer yearns to possess a shapely disco queen who ".... drives a mustang" and "let's her hair hang." The second case is more complex, though. The driver of a '55 Ford finds that his engine has mysteriously died on the freeway. Traffic begins to pile up behind him, despite the fact that he has rolled the disabled car toward the curb and raised the hood to indicate mechanical distress. When Officer Lamar arrives, his only recommendation to resolve the automobile problem is terse, "Move it!" The omission of a statement of sympathy, an offer of direct aid, or even a call for assistance is indicative of police mentality in high traffic areas. "You cannot stop it here! Get it out of here!" is the authoritarian patrolman's heartless refrain. The stalled automobile symbolizes not only unexpected trouble, but also an opportunity for someone else on the highway to play the role of Good Samaritan. Unfortunately, other motorists are simply "...tryin' to drive around." Only the policeman responds, unsatisfactorily.

"Almost Grown" - Coming-of-age, that anthropological combination of physical maturation and economic independence, is a common theme in Chuck Berry's songs. The automobile is frequently a focal point for youthful expenditures, purchases of personalizing accessories (as in "No Money Down"), the never-ending quest for gasoline ("I'm burnin' aviation fuel - no matter what the costs."), and pleasure-riding in the countryside. From the perspective of the young man in this tune, the acquisition of a car is a symbol of social stability. He's a reformed soul who's "...doing all right in school," hasn't broken any rules,"...ain't never been in dutch" [with the police?], doesn't "...browse around too much," and doesn't "run around with no mob." In short, he's respectable. But youthful uncertainty permeates the lyric. The "little car" he plans to buy will reportedly halt all his browsing and provide entry into the adult world.

"Carol" - "Come into my machine, so we can cruise on out," says Carol's would-be date. He wants to take her to a "Swingin' Little Joint" that's located "not too far back off the highway, not so long a ride." The romantic approach is straight forward. No frills. The automobile is simply a source of horizontal mobility. But the slang term "My Machine" utilized to describe the young man's vehicle hints that the engine may not be a stock variety and that the car's body may have been artistically personalized. Nonetheless, Carol is an object of pursuit - not unlike the fickle

Maybellene and the fleeting Nadine - and both the automobile and the dancehall figure prominently in the would-be lover's chase.

"If I Were" - This highly speculative love song offers an automobile metaphor in which a desirable female is cast as a Mercedes Benz and the day-dreaming boy is a (Cadillac) Fleetwood Brougham. The idealized relationship is simple and straightforward: "...everytime I see you rollin' on the highway, I think I'd have to follow you home." There the Fleetwood longs to lodge in the Benz' double garage, bumper to bumper. Instead of just settling down and living happily ever after, the Cadillac yearns for a fast-paced life where there's "nobody home but the Benz and the Brougham, ready, rarin' to roll out together." This is truly a four-wheeled fairy tale.

"Back In The U.S.A." - This paen to America, or more precisely, to the urban centers of the United States ("New York, Los Angeles, oh, how I yearned for you. Detroit, Chicago, Chattanooga, Baton Rouge. Let alone just to be at my home back in ol' St. Lou.") is punctuated by two automobile-related yearnings. The returning world traveler, who exudes love for his homeland, indicates that high on his list of things "missed" are freeways and drive-ins. It should be obvious that traffic congestion and greasy hamburgers are not considered social problems by this urban patriot; instead, lines of cars zooming along multilane highways and dozens of automobiles sandwiched together beneath the watchful eyes of drive-in restaurant operators and their carhop employees are signs of social progress, economic stability, and personal joy.

"You Never Can Tell" - The message of this song – directed toward skeptical middle class parents - is clear. Don't make snap judgments concerning the likely failure of teenage marriages. The automobile once again functions in several sociological ways. First, it illustrates economic stability and independence from the older generation; second, it establishes the individualistic style of the young couple under observation ("They bought a souped-up jitney, 'twas a cherry red fifty-three"); and finally, it becomes a source of personal pleasure and geographical mobility ("They drove it down to New Orleans to celebrate their anniversary"). The skepticism of the "old folks" apparently is not totally overcome by this single instance of marital bliss, though as the refrain indicates - "It goes to show you never can tell."

(This commentary was originally published as B. Lee Cooper, "Nothin' Outrun My V-8 Ford: Chuck Berry And The American Motorcar, 1955-1979," JOHN EDWARDS MEMORIAL FOUNDATION QUARTERLY, 16 (Spring 1980), pp. 18-23. It also appeared as B. Lee Cooper. "Cruisin' And Playin' The Radio: Exploring Images of The American Automobile Through Popular Music," INTERNATIONAL JOURNAL OF INSTRUCTIONAL MEDIA, 7 (1979-1980): 327-334.)

Solomon Burke

SOLOMON BURKE

KING OF ROCK 'N' SOUL
Solomon Burke
William Hogeland, compiler
CD, Factory of Sounds FOS 2205184, 2019

THE DEFINITIVE SOUL COLLECTION
Solomon Burke
John Tottenham, compiler
2 CDs, Rhino R2-77666, 2006

Solomon Burke was destined for vocal majesty. At his birth in 1940 his grandmother dedicated him to lead The House of God For All People. This worship site later became known as Solomon's Temple. By age 7 the precocious child was giving sermons; by age 9 he was the lead singer in the gospel choir; and by age 12 he was labeled "The Wonder Boy Preacher", with his own Sunday radio program. But musical life beyond church walls also beckoned the multi-talented Solomon Burke. Strongly influenced by the commercial success of Roy Hamilton's inspirational hit "You'll Never Walk Alone", Burke signed a recording contract with Apollo Records in 1954. Not surprisingly, his dual commitment to spiritual tunes and popular songs continued over the next five decades. Burke's primary commercial success came with Atlantic Records between 1960 and 1969. Producers Jerry Wexler and Bert Berns provided particularly valuable suggestions concerning song selections during Burke's halcyon soul music years. After 1970 Burke experienced only limited pop recognition on a variety of labels including Bell, Savoy, MGM, Chess, and Fat Possum. But he persisted as a preacher, a singer, and a touring spectacle of worldwide acclaim.

Taken together, KING OF ROCK 'N' SOUL and THE DEFINITION OF SOUL COLLECTION trace the arc of Solomon Burke's studio recording career from his obscure mid-50s releases on the Apollo label to his final BILLBOARD-charted hit in 1975 for Chess Records. The KING OF ROCK 'N' SOUL collection presents many rare, self-penned tunes and several uncharted b-side numbers. Unfortunately, the liner notes are brief and the non-chronological order of the playlist is confusing. Highlights from this 31-song assemblage are Burke's earliest releases ("I'm In Love", "No Man Walks Alone", and "To Thee"), two numbers issued under the recording pseudonym Little Vincent ("This Little Ring" and "It's All Right"), the quirky flip-side of Burke's initial Atlantic hit ("Be-Bop Grandma"), and the fascinating cover versions of several mid-century R&B and country songs ("A Tear Fell", "I Almost Lost My Mind", "I Really Don't Want to Know", and "Gotta Travel On"). By contrast, THE DEFINITIVE SOUL COLLECTION features informative, thorough liner notes, a meticulously organized discography, and full chart information about each anthologized song. The 30 recordings assembled by John Tottenham begin with "Just Out of Reach (Off My Two Open Arms", "Cry To Me", and "Down in The Valley" and end with "Get Out of My Life Woman", "Proud Mary", and "You and Your Baby Blues". This exemplary collection also features two of Burke's very best releases ("Everybody Needs Somebody to Love" and "Got to Get You Off Of My Mind"), plus several other fan favorites ("The Price" and "Tonight's The Night").

Solomon Burke was an extremely important, distinctive soul music star. First, as a very young performer he amalgamated the personas of Stevie Wonder, Sam Cooke, and Al Green. Burke was a child prodigy who achieved musical stardom as both a singer and a composer; he was unflinching in his commitments to both church hymns and commercial tunes; and he was an unlikely sex symbol and verbally suggestive performer during his audience-appealing theater acts. Second, he was as prescient as Ray Charles in recognizing the commercial potential of adopting classic country songs and infusing them with emotive gospel fervor. Throughout his career Burke borrowed freely from the songbooks of Eddy Arnold, Bobby Bare, Patsy Cline, Billy Grammer, and Jim Reeves. Of course, that several other black vocalists followed Brother Ray and King Solomon down this country-covering pathway. Note the country re-issue hits by Brook Benton, Bobby "Blue" Bland, Fats Domino, Joe Hinton, Aaron Neville, Esther Phillips, Candi Staton, and Bettye Swann.

Finally, it must be acknowledged that Solomon Burke was a bodacious, flirtatious, crowd-pleasing, soul-stirring stage phenomenon. Although he couldn't match the startling dance moves of James Brown or The Temptations or the sensual charisma of Jackie Wilson or Marvin Gaye, Burke manifested the call-and-response banter of an emotional evangelist who sought to praise romantic interludes as blessed release from mundane earthly existence. Fortunately, a few of his "live" performances have been preserved. They manifest soulful, sexually suggestive monologues that both precede and follow sonic gems from Burke's extensive vocal playbook. Among the best of these stage sets are: LIVE AT THE HOUSE OF BLUES (Black Top Records, 1994), SOUL ALIVE! (Rounder Records, 2002), and THE LAST GREAT CONCERT – SWITZERLAND 2008 (Rock Beat Records, 2012). Undeniably, Solomon Burke was a force of nature, both from the pulpit and from the bandstand.

Solomon Burke charted 31 R&B tunes and 32 pop hits between 1961 and 1978. His powerful legacy was acknowledged at his 2001 induction into The Rock and Roll Hall of Fame. The studio recording achievements of Burke are well-displayed in THE DEFINITIVE SOUL COLLECTION - and his gospel, pop, R&B, and country roots are unearthed in KING OF ROCK 'N' SOUL. But both anthologies overlook the dynamism of Solomon Burke's live musical extravaganzas. Black audiences at the Apollo Theater in Harlem, at the Regal Theater in Chicago, at the Howard Theater in Washington, D.C., and in the Royal Theater in Baltimore viewed the uninhibited performing skills of a vocal colossus. Aretha Franklin and Wilson Pickett, who shared the Atlantic studios with Burke, undoubtedly enjoyed the stories of "The Bishop of Soul" as a chitlin' circuit warrior prowling Southern musical venues. It is always an important task to assemble collections of significant studio recordings that have achieved BILLBOARD prominence. But to tell the full tale of a complicated, energetic, self-assured performing dynamo like Solomon Burke, a broader sonic brush is required. One must capture the excitement of a throng of fans being titillated, coaxed, cajoled, scolded, and thoroughly entertained by an artist pulling the emotional strings of sin and sex, salvation and seduction, and love in its myriad meanings. Solomon Burke was never humble. He was born to preach, to sing, and to satisfy audiences. During his seventy years on earth, he fulfilled that calling. Recordings of his hit songs and "live" stage performances extend his magical musical ministry to future generations.

(This commentary was originally published as B. Lee Cooper. "Review of KING OF ROCK 'N' SOUL by Solomon Burke and THE DEFINITIVE SOUL COLLECTION by Solomon Burke," POPULAR MUSIC AND SOCIETY, 43:3 (July 2020): 359-360.)

Ray Charles

RAY CHARLES

TRUE GENIUS
Ray Charles
6 CDs, Tangerine Records TRC 2107, 2021

Crafting an anthology of recordings as a tribute to the life-time excellence of a master singer is a challenging task. But denying audio representation to the initial portion of that singer's professional career seems like a huge historical error. For example, it's possible, though not advisable, to tell the Frank Sinatra story from a post-1952 Capitol Records / Reprise Records perspective without acknowledging the influence of his prior associations with Tommy Dorsey, Harry James, and Columbia Records. Similarly, it's possible, though not advisable, to tell the Elvis Presley story from a post-1955 RCA Victor Records perspective without acknowledging the influence of Sam Phillips and Sun Records. Likewise, it's possible, though not advisable, to tell the Aretha Franklin story from a post-1966 Atlantic Records/Arista Records perspective without acknowledging the influence of 1950s gospel singers, John Hammond, and Columbia Records. It's even possible, though certainly not advisable, to tell the The Rolling Stones story from a post-1970 Rolling Stone Records perspective without acknowledging the immense influence of 1950s American blues and rock 'n' roll singers, Brian Jones, and London Records. Actually, none of these abbreviated approaches to audio anthology history construction seem reasonable - or accurate.

The artistic legacy and recorded achievements of Ray Charles are extensive, distinctive, and well-documented. His audio influence impacted both black and white audiences from the 1950s into the early 21st century. Ray Charles intersperced gospel harmonies and boogie woogie rhythms; he borrowed jazzy pop stylings from Nat King Cole and cool bluesy phrasing from Charles Brown; and he added jazz rifts, female vocal ensembles, and piano magic to traditional country ballads - turning many of them into BILLBOARD-charted pop hits. Ray Charles released a few blues tunes on Swing Time Records in 1951 and 1952. Then he joined Ahmet Ertegun, Jerry Wexler, Tom Dowd, and the dynamic studio session players at Atlantic Records in New York City. Over the following seven years Ray Charles expanded his horizons as a singer, keyboardist, composer, arranger, and producer. He shook thunder and lightning from the sonic heavens with hit recordings like "I've Got a Woman," "A Fool for You," "Drown In My Own Tears," "Hallelujah I Love Her So," and "What'd I Say." For some unexplainable reason, the 6-disc TRUE GENIUS anthology ignores all of these early Atlantic cuts. Granted, the post-1960 Ray Charles recordings were worthy of critical praise, exerted tremendous influence over future artists, and helped define a life-time of musical superiority. But why would John Burk, Valerie Erwin, and Cheryl Pawelski issue a 90-song tribute to the Genius of Soul - and omit the sonic roots of his professional career?

Working with audio releases from labels like ABC-Paramount, Columbia, CrossOver, Impulse, and Tangerine, the compilers of TRUE GENIUS were undeniably blessed with numerous high quality recordings. They took advantage of Ray Charles' genre-jumping innovations, stylistic experimentations, and performances with other vocal and instrumental stars. In all, 90 tracks are provided. The most rare cuts are the final nine songs from a "live" concert venue in Stockholm, Sweden in 1972. Tunes on this disc vary from "Alexander's Ragtime Band" to "I Can't Stop Loving You." There is also considerable attention paid to Ray Charles' work on patriotic and civil rights music. Segments illustrating these themes include "America the Beautiful," "Compared to What," "There'll Be No Peace Without All Men As One," and "Living for The City." Predictably, the very best of Ray Con My Mind," "Hit the Road Jack," "Unchain My Heart," "You Are My Sunshine," "Busted," and "Cryin' Time." Instrumental hits like "One Mint Julep" are also acknowledged.

The TRUE GENIUS compilers seem particularly fascinated by Ray Charles as a collaborative performer. A large portion of the multi-disc anthology is committed to his performances with Betty Carter ("Baby, It's Cold Outside"), Cleo Laine ("Summertime"), Hank Williams, Jr. ("Two Old Cats Like Us"), Willie Nelson ("Seven Spanish Angels"), Billy Joel ("Baby Grand"), Lou Rawls and Milt Jackson ("Save The Bones for Henry Jones"), and Norah Jones ("Here We Go Again"). Truthfully, very few of these playful concoctions are either memorable or valuable in portraying the majesty of Ray Charles as a musical innovator. Elsewhere, TRUE GENIUS hits home with the funny mischief depicted in "Hardhearted Hannah," "I've Got News For You," "Sticks and Stones," "Let's Go Get Stoned," and "Makin' Whoopie." The Tangerine compilers are also diligent in displaying Ray Charles' penchant for commandeering hits from others. Examples of these transformative ventures include several works by The Beatles - "Eleanor Rigby," "Let It Be," "Something," and "Yesterday." Yes, TRUE GENIUS even samples Ray's marvelous motion picture soundtrack material, including "The Cincinnati Kid" and "In the Heat of The Night."

Despite overlooking his groundbreaking Atlantic years, TRUE GENIUS offers an interesting and insightful perspective on Ray Charles as an American musical icon from 1960 until his death in 2004 at age 73. Assembling a whopping 90 tracks, this 2021 Tangerine Records salute is a worthwhile acquisition for those seeking an introduction to Ray Charles. However, the incredible gaps in the TRUE GENIUS anthology demand that true fans consider acquiring other collections to fill in their understanding and appreciation for the artist. Where to start? First, one should secure THE GENIUS IN PERSON (Jasmine, 2011), a 2-disc gem that highlights Ray Charles' classic appearances at the 1959 Newport Jazz Festival and the following year at Herndon Stadium in Atlanta. Next, one should consider purchasing either the 3-disc RAY CHARLES - THE BIRTH OF SOUL (Atlantic, 1991) or the monster 8-disc PURE GENIUS - THE COMPLETE ATLANTIC RECORDINGS, 1952-1959 (Atlantic/Rhino, 2005). Third, for those more interested in the ABC-Paramount years, the 5-disc SINGULAR GENIUS - THE COMPLETE ABC SINGLES (Concord Music, 2011) is an excellent choice. So is THE COMPLETE COUNTRY AND WESTERN RECORDINGS, 1959-1986 (Rhino, 1998), a 5-disc collection that displays all of Ray Charles' sparkling country music repertoire. Finally, for individuals seeking the very best, most informed and most informative overview of Ray Charles' career, the 5-disc compilation GENIUS

AND SOUL - THE 50TH ANNIVERSARY COLLECTION (Rhino, 1997) fills the bill. This magnificent tribute was assembled by James Austin, David Ritz, and Billy Vera. It captures every important nuance of the nimble, inventive, explosive, and influential Brother Ray.

Sam Cooke

SAM COOKE

CUPID: THE VERY BEST OF SAM COOKE, 1961-1962
Sam Cooke
Roger Dopson, compiler
CD, Jasmine JASCD 991, 2018

WIN YOUR LOVE FOR ME: THE COMPLETE SINGLES, 1956-1962
Sam Cooke
Gary Blailock, compiler
2 CDs, Hoo Doo 600894, 2017

THE SONGWRITER
Sam Cooke and Various Artists
Glenn Gretlund, compiler
2 CDs, Not Now Music NOT2CD567, 2015

BRING IT ON HOME: BLACK AMERICA SINGS SAM COOKE
Various Artists
Tony Rounce, compiler
CD, Ace CDCHD 1420, 2014

SAM COOKE'S SAR RECORDS STORY, 1959-1965
Various Artists
Alisa Coleman and Peter Guralnick, compilers
2 CDs, Abkco 3122-2, 2004

Sam Cooke was born on January 22, 1931. He died from a gunshot wound on December 11, 1964. Music dominated his brief life. As a youngster he performed before several Baptist congregations as a member of the mixed-gender Singing Children quintet; as a teenager he founded and fronted The Highway Q.C.'s, a Chicago-based all-male gospel group; and during his early 20s he became the lead singer for the nationally-recognized Soul Stirrers. Expanding his vocal repertoire and enlarging his listening audience during 1957, Sam Cooke emerged as a top-selling pop and R&B artist on the Specialty and Keen record labels. This commercial singing success, coupled with Cooke's songwriting prowess, prompted RCA Victor Records to sign him to a long-term contract in 1960. As part of these negotiations, RCA also agreed to distribute releases from the Sar label that Cooke had founded in 1959. Thus, Sam Cooke spent the final five years of his professional life perfecting his skills as a performer, composer, arranger, producer, talent scout, and recording industry executive. His artistic influence across the realms of gospel, pop, rock 'n' roll, R&B, and soul music echoes into the 21st century. Accolades for his remarkable musical contributions and performing legacy are understandably numerous, including Rock and Roll Hall of Fame (1986), Songwriters Hall of Fame (1987), Chairman's Award from the

Apollo Theatre Foundation (1993), Pioneer Award from the Rhythm & Blues Foundation (1999), and NARAS Grammy Lifetime Achievement Award (1999).

The five CD releases cited above - CUPID (2018), WIN YOUR LOVE FOR ME (2017), THE SONGWRITER (2015), BRING IT ON HOME (2014), and SAM COOKE'S SAR RECORDS STORY (2004) - capsule this artist's impact on American popular music. CUPID features 30 recordings released during a particularly productive 24-month period in the early sixties. Cooke displays versatility and virtuosity as he experiments with older tunes - "Chains of Love", "Driftin' Blues", "Nobody Knows You When You're Down and Out", and "Send Me some Lovin'" - and crafts brand new numbers - "Bring It on Home to Me", "Soothe Me", "Nothing Can Change This Love", and the title song. WIN YOUR LOVE FOR ME is a massive two-disc, 60-song compilation of Cooke classics. The hits span from "Lovable", "I'll Come Running Back to You", and "You Send Me" to "Chain Gang", "Having A Party", and "Twistin' the Night Away". THE SONGWRITER offers a two-CD treat of 20 hits sung by Sam Cooke and 20 more Cooke compositions performed by other artists. The composer himself offers "Wonderful World", "Only Sixteen", "Somebody Have Mercy", and "(Don't Fight It) Feel It". Then Johnnie Taylor sings "Rome (Wasn't Built in A Day)", The Soul Stirrers perform "Wade in The Water", The Simms Twins do "Soothe Me", and The Flamingos contribute "Nobody Loves Me Like You".

Continuing the line of tribute discs, BRING IT ON HOME is a 24-song salute to Sam Cooke's influence among major black vocalists of the '60s and '70s. This assembly of tunes features "(Ain't That) Good News" by The Supremes, "Shake" by Otis Redding, "That's Heaven to Me" by The Soul Stirrers, "Win Your Love" by Lou Rawls, and "A Change Is Gonna Come" by Brenton Wood. Finally, SAM COOKE'S SAR RECORDS STORY offers audio snapshots of the composer, producer, and arranger leading a variety of black artists through their recording sessions. Sam Cooke is a rigorous stylistic taskmaster. During the sessions he barks out instructions and provides encouraging hints. This two-disc, 56-song compilation of Sar Records productions includes "I'm A Pilgrim" by The Soul Stirrers, "When A Boy Falls in Love" by Mel Carter, "Meet Me at The Twistin' Place" by Johnnie Morisette, and "It's All Over Now" by The Valentinos.

Beyond this hefty helping of recent releases, though, there are additional Sam Cooke collections that also warrant attention. These compilations either highlight Cooke's earliest recordings or offer broad, enlightening cross-sections from his numerous '50s and '60s albums. For example, SAM COOKE WITH THE SOUL STIRRERS (Specialty, 2002) is a 3-CD, 84-track box set that emphasizes the artist's gospel roots between 1951 and 1957. Similarly, THE KEEN RECORDS STORY is a 3-CD anthology providing 46 songs by Cooke from his pre-RCA Victor period. Illustrations of other excellent Cooke hit song compilations include THE SINGLES COLLECTION (Not Now Music, 2013), featuring 55 songs; PORTRAIT OF A LEGEND, 1951-1964 (ABKCO, 2003), with 30 tunes; GREATEST HITS (RCA, 1998), with 22 recordings; and THE MAN AND HIS MUSIC (RCA, 1986), featuring 28 numbers. It's particularly heartening to find so many uncharted Cooke gems like "Touch the Hem of His

Garment", "That's Heaven to Me", and "Jesus Gave Me Water" anthologized in these collections.

Music historian Peter Guralnick heralded Sam Cooke's remarkable musical career in DREAM BOOGIE (Little, Brown, and Company, 2005). But few other writers have been able to capture the dynamism of Cooke's rare and diverse talents. Why is that so? Complex aesthetic figures often defy standard journalistic analysis. Sam Cooke exhibited the same gospel-into-pop fervor that propelled Ray Charles; he pursued the same ongoing aesthetic experimentation that has been manifested by Bob Dylan; he demonstrated the performing energy and sexual charisma of Jackie Wilson; he manufactured hit-after-hit like Chuck Berry; and he was a master of dealing with mixed fan bases, as was Bobby Darin. Cooke's personal trove of hit recordings is exceeded only by his residual impact on future singing stars like Aretha Franklin, Otis Redding, Lou Rawls, Marvin Gaye, and other soulful giants. Cooke proved that black music was inherently American music. He also demonstrated that black music was simultaneously personal and universal, spiritual and sexual, sweet and sorrowful. Sam Cooke was the essence of American music and American culture during the meaningful transition from segregation to integration. These five informative releases glorify an artist who advanced the quality of his country's musical heritage. His audio legacy is a... more wonderful audio world.

(This commentary was originally published as B. Lee Cooper. "Review of CUPID by Sam Cooke, WIN YOUR LOVE FOR ME by Sam Cooke, THE SONGWRITER by Sam Cooke and Various Artists, BRING IT ON HOME by Sam Cooke, and SAM COOKE'S SAR RECORDS STORY by Sam Cooke and Various Artists," ROCK MUSIC STUDIES, 6:1 (February 2019): 72-73.)

Aretha Franklin

ARETHA FRANKLIN

ARETHA
Aretha Franklin
Rhino Entertainment R2-643463, 2020

Shrewd music historians like Peter Guralnick, Jack Hamilton, and Erin Torkelson Weber caution readers about the difficulty of comprehending the audio genius of recording artists via written words. The oft-repeated and delightfully humorous indictment that writing about music is like dancing about architecture is accurate. Journalistic interpretations of personal musical quality tend to change with each new album released. Opinions also vary over time. As a musical career unwinds over years and even decades, perspectives of fellow artists, music critics, fans, and even family members vacillate. The rollercoaster reports of weekly BILLBOARD "Pop" chart rankings rise and fall over a career, casting a particular performer as imaginative, inspirational, and influential in good times and repetitive, formulaic, or old-fashioned in bad times. Few recording artists are able to manifest creativity and vibrance throughout their entire careers. Examples of such sustained greatness among male performers include Louis Armstrong, Johnny Cash, Ray Charles, and Frank Sinatra. The primary female illustration, of course, is Aretha Franklin.

ARETHA is a 4-CD compilation featuring 81 songs that span the remarkable professional career of The Queen of Soul. Diligent Rhino compilers David Nathan and Patrick Milligan present a variety of audio snippets that offer a distinctive overview of the vocal pyrotechnics, piano-playing virtuosity, song selection skills, and fascinating personal observations of Aretha Franklin. This is not a just "Greatest Hits" anthology. However, monster releases like "Respect," "I Never Loved A Man (The Way I Love You)," and "Since You've Been Gone" are included. This is not just a memory lane stroll through Aretha's halcyon Atlantic Records years, either. Nathan and Milligan coax insights from early Columbia Records material as well as from many post-Atlantic productions. ARETHA is a thoroughly planned, fully documented, broad-stroke sonic portrait of a phenomenally flexible artist. It covers six decades of excellence.

Aretha Franklin vocalizes her own soulful biography, with insightful editing help from the two Rhino compilers. She presents powerful studio performances that were released as singles ("Freeway of Love"). She delivers ebullient live performances ("Dr. Feelgood"). She offers playful yet meaningful duets with male artists ("Spirit in The Dark" with Ray Charles and "I Knew You Were Waiting (For Me)" with George Michael). She also probes gospel tunes with a female superstar ("Oh Happy Day" with Mavis Staples). There are even several previously unheard cuts that expand appreciation for Aretha's experimental nature. She performs an alternative take of a chart-topping hit ("Chain of Fools") along with a demo version of a pop standard ("Try A Little Tenderness"). Rarities abound. Frankly, that's a large part of the sonic magic that's sprinkled throughout ARETHA.

This magnificent Rhino collection features two very different introductory commentaries. The first is penned by Detroit journalist and women's rights activitist Rochelle Riley. As a self-identified fangirl and a life-time admirer of Aretha Franklin, this uncritical observer casts the artist as a divine musical messenger who crafted memorable anthems of freedom and dignity. Riley views Aretha's total songbook as a rich compendium of gospel truth ("Amazing Grace"), a guidebook for black civil rights ("A Change Is Gonna Come"), and a continuing dialogue of mutual respect among male and female romantic partners ("Do Right Woman - Do Right Man"). Riley is dogmatic in her determination to define Aretha as a black female freedom fighter and a role model for independent thought and action. Yes, the ideas of The Rev. Martin Luther King, Jr., Harry Belafonte, Sam Cooke, and dozens of other Afro-American activists are folded into the vocalized assertions of Lady Soul.

The second introductory essay is a 16-page history of Aretha Franklin's professional singing career. It is crafted by soul music afficionado David Nathan. This perceptive scholar and co-compiler of ARETHA notes that there was unanimous agreement among late '50s record executives like John Hammond, Clive Davis, Jerry Wexler, and Amhet Ertegun that the young Aretha was an original, voracious new talent. Nathan depicts the many collaborative interactions among Aretha and Wexler, Quincy Jones, Curtis Mayfield, and other musicians that helped to generate her remarkable treasury of hits. He also reminds readers that Aretha's personal life was frequently volatile and unstable - and that her Detroit roots always held strong, even when her soulful singing success had yielded world-wide fame. Nathan is clearly as awed by Aretha as Rochelle Riley. But he justifies his admiration factually through a chronological review of Aretha's early gospel touring, Columbia studio recordings, Atlantic Records international acclaim, and her post-1980 legacy status. Obviously, it's hard to overlook rewards like a 1987 Rock and Roll Hall of Fame induction, a 1991 Grammy Legend Award, a 1994 Grammy Lifetime Achievement Award, and the 1994 Kennedy Center Honors recognition. Nahan also mentions Aretha singing the national anthem in 2009 at Barack Obama's Presidential Inauguration and reprising her hit "(You Make Me Feel Like) A Natural Woman" in 2015 when the Kennedy Center honored singer-songwriter Carole King.

Predictably, there is no shortage of Aretha Franklin material on compact discs. Re-issued recordings range from the 1964 Columbia release UNFORGETTABLE: A TRIBUTE TO DINAH WASHINGTON (Legacy, 1995) to Atlantic's 1971 album ARETHA: LIVE AT THE FILLMORE (Rhino, 2006) to the huge five-disc assemblage ARETHA FRANKLIN - ORIGINAL ALBUM SERIES (Rhino, 2009). The Columbia/Legacy imprint also issued ARETHA FRANKLIN - JAZZ TO SOUL in 1992. Many, many single-CD collections featuring Aretha's "greatest hits" are also available. The premiere collection of her numerous Atlantic recordings is the 4-CD set titled QUEEN OF SOUL (Rhino, 1992). In 2007 Rhino Records issued a fascinating double-disc collection titled ARETHA FRANKLIN: RARE AND UNRELEASED RECORDINGS FROM THE GOLDEN REIGN OF THE QUEEN OF SOUL. Previously uncirculated demos and unissued outtakes were on full display throughout this 35-song review. One suspects that the 2020 ARETHA anthology was inspired in part by this earlier exploration of rarities. But compilers Nathan and Milligan wisely selected both hit tunes and rarities over a multi-decade time span to portray the artist's performing development, piano styling, proclivity for genre-hopping, and creative vocal stylings. In ARETHA, the songstress emerges as a thoughtful, flexible, innovative, and risk-taking professional, with a broad appreciation for the recordings of her contemporaries as well as a deep loyalty to the traditional American songbook. Nimble phrasing, interesting instrumentation, and emotional intensity make Aretha's cover recording efforts sparkle.

Her commercial recording statistics are staggering. Aretha Franklin ruled the BILLBOARD album charts with 48 studio, concert, and greatest hits releases between 1962 and 2013. She also placed 101 single recordings on the "R&B" charts between 1960 and 2014 - and 88 songs on the "Pop" charts between 1961 and 1998. That's remarkable! ARETHA is a superb audio vehicle for displaying the musical gifts that enabled The Queen of Soul to reign supreme. It illustrates the development and enhancement of the raw talent that she displayed as a child in her father's New Bethel Baptist Church in downtown Detroit. Although she was born in Memphis and catapulted to recording superstardom in New York City, Aretha remained personally rooted in the Motor City. It is ironic, of course, that Rev. C.L. Franklin directed his gifted daughter toward the well-established Columbia Records operation in New York City rather than encouraging her to join the smaller local recording franchise being managed by Berry Gordy, Jr. It would have been amazing if Motown Records had added Aretha Franklin to that outstanding stable of '60s black singers that included Mary Wells, Diana Ross and The Supremes, Tammi Terrell, and Martha Reeves and The Vandellas, along with Smokey Robinson and The Miracles, The Four Tops, Marvin Gaye, The Temptations, and Stevie Wonder.

Jerry Lee Lewis

JERRY LEE LEWIS

JERRY LEE LEWIS: SPECIAL EDITION
Rik Flynn, editor
London: Vintage Rock/Anthem Publishing, 2019

Biographical profiles of popular musicians are often fabricated and invariably flexible. They exist not as an accurate, permanent historical record, but as malleable promotional material. Pop bios are strangely assembled beasts. Initially, agents and publicists strive to attract new fans by releasing tantalizing tidbits about newly discovered artists. Then record company advertisers strive to cultivate excitement over upcoming releases and cast new artists as either innovative or traditional, rebellious or reflective, upbeat or low-key. Fan magazine writers add startling or unexpected side stories to earlier biographical sketches of pop musicians. And fanzines also use concert photos and quotations from other performers to create more interesting images of new artists. Finally, music critics and rock journalists issue their own opinions concerning the quality of new recordings, the context of an artist's lyrical material, and stylistic comparisons with both older and contemporary performers. This deluge of information forms the literary persona of a new artist.

If a popular musician's career extends beyond one or two charted hits, though, it is likely that more lengthy, in-depth biographical probing will commence. The initial persona will be enhanced and expanded - and possibly even fact-checked. A pop biography may appear. Though picture-filled and sketchy, this lifetime overview usually emphasizes teenage performing activities, fledgling songwriting attempts, and lists of early musical influences. Photos of parents, high school friends, enthusiastic concert goers, and the artist in action are mandatory, too. When a musician's success secures nationwide attention and chart-topping repetition, major music journalists and popular culture historians begin to develop more authoritative biographies. Often labeled either "authorized" or "unauthorized", these book-length probes constitute investigations that sing praises and reveal flaws, correct early myths and assemble evidence about future recording plans. The complex lives of performing stars are no longer reduced to a few friendly quotes or to elegant picture sequences. Instead, childhood motivations, years of musical tutelage, initial professional rejections and failures, prior recording contracts, failed and successful romantic relationships, alcohol and drug use, conflicts and cooperation with session players, and the myriad of career-related ups and downs are documented with footnotes.

Subjects of such severe biographical scrutiny include Louis Armstrong, Frank Sinatra, Elvis Presley, Bob Dylan, Pete Townshend, Bruce Springsteen, Madonna, Keith Richards, Beyoncé, and many other prominent musicians. Occasionally, a resourceful editor even assembles a decade-by-decade compilation of literary perspectives covering the entirety of an artist's musical career. A fine example of this chronological survey approach is Richard Kostelanetz's B.B. KING READER: SIX DECADES OF COMENTARY (Hal Leonard, 2005). An even more fascinating longitudinal biography approach, though, is the historical analysis of the twisting and turning interpretations over the past 50 years concerning the creative forces, conflicting interests, and competing values among The Fab Four. This 2016 study, titled THE BEATLES AND THE HISTORIANS (McFarland), was penned by Erin Torkelson Weber. She dissected the mishmash of facts and fables that inhabit nearly all early biographies of Liverpool's most famous quartet. Wherever fandom and scholarship intersect, the truth about an artist's life can be elusive.

Over the past three years London's Anthem Press has issued several biographical profiles of American rock 'n' roll performers. The handsome, well-illustrated, magazine-size publications have featured Chuck Berry, Buddy Holly, Little Richard, and Elvis Presley. Compiled by Rik Flynn and assembled by the editorial staff of VINTAGE ROCK magazine, these 130-page career overviews are tributes to the lives and careers of 20th century U.S. musicians whose classic recordings still resonate within the U.K. This review concentrates on the most recent volume in this on-going Anthem Press series - JERRY LEE LEWIS: SPECIAL EDITION. This 2019 study follows the formulaic design established in the earlier volumes. It is reasonable to speculate that one can judge the value of the entire series by assessing the content of the most recent release. Of course, one anticipates that compiler Flynn and his VINTAGE ROCK staff are already prepping future issues on James Brown, Ray Charles, Fats Domino, and Carl Perkins.

JERRY LEE LEWIS: SPECIAL EDITION is a colorful 130-page magazine containing 20 carefully crafted essays that cover the life, recordings, and performing career of Ferriday, Louisiana's most volatile native son. Experienced music writers like Bill Dahl, Randy Fox, Douglas McPherson, and Jack Watkins provide knowledgeable commentaries about The Killer's antics and achievements over the past seven decades. Specific topics covered include: Jerry Lee's rise and fall as a rock 'n' roll piano player and vocal star at Sun Records in Memphis; reflections on The Killer's studio work and stage performances from knowledgeable insiders like guitarist Roland Janes, drummer J.M. "Jimmy" Van Eaton, bassist J.W. Brown, fiddler Kenny Lovelace, and session director Jerry Kennedy; perspectives on Jerry Lee's contributions to country music, including his first appearance at the Grand Ole Opry; and reactions to his farewell concert at The London Palladium on September 6, 2015. In addition, recent Jerry Lee biographer Bill Bragg discusses his private interview sessions with the elderly rocker, David Burke traces the off-screen conflicts between The Killer and Dennis Quaid during the filming of the 1989 autobiographical movie "Great Balls of Fire", and Julie Burns highlights the sibling admiration between Jerry Lee and his sister, Linda Gail Lewis. The final essay in the volume features photographs of personal memorabilia -- pipes, knives, and recording awards - displayed at Jerry Lee's retirement abode, the Lewis Ranch in Nesbit, Mississippi.

While the aforementioned biographical perspectives are intriguing, editor Rik Flynn has much more to offer in respect to discographic and bibliographic information about Jerry Lee. First, the myriad of photographs and LP cover reproductions are remarkable. They range from the 1956 Sun Studios snapshot of the young Jerry Lee brashly joining Johnny Cash, Carl Perkins, and Elvis Presley as the "Million Dollar Quartet" to a very recent black-and-white portrait of a grey-haired old Jerry Lee wearing pajamas and slippers, supported by a fancy cane. Second, Randy Fox offers retrospective reviews on two key Jerry Lee Lewis albums. One is the raucous "LIVE" AT THE STAR-CLUB, HAMBURG (1964), where a defiant rocker reasserted his claim to being the wildest performer in the world. The other is a remembrance of a less successful studio attempt to re-ignite Jerry Lee's fading pop career. Unfortunately, SOUTHERN ROOTS: BACK HOME IN MEMPHIS (1973) turned out to be an artistic and commercial failure. Third, editor Flynn extends the analysis of Jerry Lee's recording work by assessing his vast vinyl output and lauding the superb vinyl compilations issued by England's Charly Records and Germany's Bear Family Records. Moving on to smaller discs, Flynn then offers an 8-page, 40-disc salute to Jerry Lee's most popular, influential 45 r.p.m. releases. This homage expands from "Whole Lot Of Shakin' Going On", "Lewis Boogie", and "Great Balls of Fire" to "Middle Age Crazy", "Me and Bobby McGee", and "Thirty-Nine and Holding". Finally, in a section labeled "Killer Reading", Douglas McPherson annotates eight books that are essential to understanding the talented, perverted, haunted, energetic, enigmatic, driven, self-destructive, and unpredictable Jerry Lee Lewis.

JERRY LEE LEWIS: SPECIAL EDITION is either a slick, well-illustrated fanzine masquerading as a scholarly study, or a thorough, thoughtful historical biography disguised as a colorful piece of fandom fun. Truthfully, it is all of these things. The impressive array of recordings examined, the vast reservoir of photos displayed, the attention to book-length biographies, and the provocative interviews with Jerry Lee's session players and family members make this 2019 volume worthwhile reading for fans and popular music scholars alike. While none of the essays approach the eloquence of Nick Tosches or Colin Escott in depicting Jerry Lee's complex and troubled psyche, the writers gathered by Rik Flynn do justice to the immense talent and grand personal missteps that characterize the topsy-turvy career of The Killer. This collection of commentaries accurately describes Jerry Lee's idiosyncratic song selections, his arrogant and self-centered demeanor, and his charismatic, crowd-pleasing performing style. Wily popular culture commentator Mark Duffett has cautioned his fellow scholars to be more appreciative of the contributions of music fans in helping to understand the popularity of particular recording stars. To comprehend the majesty of Jerry Lee Lewis throughout his lengthy career, it is obligatory to abandon rationality and reserve, to downplay objectivity and nuance. In this biographical circumstance, fandom and fanzines can offer invaluable judgments about artistic eccentricity and outlandish behavior. Editor Rik Flynn takes us on a swinging safari into the deep jungles of Ferriday, Memphis, and Nashville to view the most untamed creature ever to prowl and howl and pound on a piano. Enjoy the outlandish excursion.

References

Rick Bragg. JERRY LEE LEWIS: HIS OWN STORY. New York: HarperCollins, 2014.

Mark Duffett (ed.). FAN IDENTITIES AND PRACICES IN CONTEXT: DEDICATED TO MUSIC. Oxford: Routledge, 2016.

Mark Duffett (ed.). POPULAR MUSIC FANDOM: IDENTITIES, ROLES, AND PRACTICES. Oxford: Routledge, 2014.

Colin Escott. JERRY LEE LEWIS: THE KILLER, 1963-1977 (Three Volumes). Hamburg, Germany: A Bear Family Publication, 1987.

Richard Kostelanetz (ed.). THE B.B. KING READER: SIX DECADES OF COMMENTARY. Milwaukee, Wisconsin: Hal Leonard Corporation, 2005

Erin Torkelson Weber. THE BEATLES AND THE HISTORIANS: AN ANALYSIS OF WRITINGS ABOUT THE FAB FOUR. Jefferson, North Carolina: McFarland and Company, 2016.

Nick Tosches. HELLFIRE: THE JERRY LEE LEWIS STORY. New York: Dell Publishing, 1982.

(This commentary was originally published as B. Lee Cooper. "Review of JERRY LEE LEWIS: SPECIAL EDITION by Rik Flynn," ROCK MUSIC STUDIES, 6:3 (October 2019): 271-273.)

JERRY LEE LEWIS AND ELVIS PRESLEY

JERRY LEE LEWIS: HIS OWN STORY
Rick Bragg
New York: HarperCollins Publishers, 2014
ISBN: 978-0-06-207822-3
498 pp.   Hb $27.99

ELVIS PRESLEY: A SOUTHERN LIFE
Joel Williamson
New York: Oxford University Press, 2015
ISBN: 978-0-19-986317-4
369pp.   Hb $34.95

Jerry Lee Lewis and Elvis Presley were undeniably Southern boys. But they were poor boys with hardscrabble backgrounds, little formal education, and limited social skills. Their shared experiences included strong maternal ties, strict Pentecostal beliefs, deep fascination with black music, unfettered attraction to young women, and self-starting musical talent. Physically relocated from Ferriday, Louisiana and Tupelo, Mississippi to Memphis, Tennessee, Jerry Lee and Elvis were initially tutored in music by Sam Phillips and his stable of rowdy rockabillies at Sun Records. Fame greeted both young men quickly. Elvis emerged in 1954 as the swiveling, hip-shaking Hillbilly Cat and, after signing contracts with RCA Victor Records and manager Colonel Tom Parker, began his life-time reign as The King Of Rock 'N' Roll in 1957. Jerry Lee, the pumping piano man and Ferriday fireball, stormed onto the world stage singing "Whole Lot OfShakin' Going On" in 1957. Although his meteoric rise to rock legend status ended in self-destruction within two years, Jerry Lee persisted as a performer of country, blues, pop, and rock recordings for the next six decades. From their shared 1935 birth dates until their simultaneous 1986 inductions into the Rock And Roll Hall Of Fame, Elvis and Jerry Lee were mythic figures and tragic examples of musical stardom gone awry.

Why did Jerry Lee Lewis and Elvis Presley flounder? How did their Southern backgrounds contribute to their problems? Fans and scholars have crafted various responses to these questions. Perhaps Jerry Lee and Elvis were haunted by religious guilt over their commitments to the Devil's music and to their manic indulgences in sexual promiscuity. Maybe they viewed their failed marriages to virginal child-brides (Myra Brown and Priscilla Beaulieu) as personal responsibilities. They undeniably considered themselves to be above the law and beyond redemption - and played fast and loose with alcohol, drugs, guns, motorcycles, fast cars, and willing women. And they found little satisfaction in the wealth they accumulated from recordings, concerts, and motion pictures.

Neither fame nor fortune could erase their inherent doubts and guilt; neither stardom nor fan adulation could provide security or comfort. Both Jerry Lee and Elvis seemed to be trapped in devilish musical deals that put hellhounds on their trails, even as their recordings drew larger audiences and increased their professional profiles. As their careers progressed, both Jerry Lee and Elvis developed a legacy of insecurity, loneliness, and isolation. Of course, Elvis died on August 16, 1977, from a poisonous polypharmacy that stopped his heart. But Jerry Lee continues to stagger forward and recently greeted fans at the 2015 Rock And Roll Hall Of Fame induction ceremonies. Since Elvis' death, Jerry Lee reportedly overcame his whiskey and drug addictions. But he still suffers from shingles, bouts of pneumonia, and arthritis. It is fascinating to read the observations of Rick Bragg and Joel Williamson as they attempt to sort through the facts and fictions surrounding the extraordinary Southern lives of these two out-of-control musical giants.

University of Alabama English professor Rick Bragg read widely about his subject, then interviewed Jerry Lee Lewis for several weeks to ascertain The Killer's perspective on his long, complicated life. The authorized biography that resulted from this exercise is chronologically-structured, fact-filled, and well-written. Sadly, Bragg functions as an apologist for the self-centered greed and self-destructive behaviors that define Jerry's Lee's life. The story is interesting, but often unbalanced. The bizarre Lewis Family relationships among Elmo Lewis, Lee Calhoun, Mickey Gilley, and Jimmy Swaggart are hilarious; and Jerry Lee's fond memories of Steve Allen, Jack Clement, Kenny Lovelace, Moon Mullican, and Del Wood are understandable. But all of this is couched in the seemingly endless cycle of random sexual encounters, marriages, infidelities, and divorces. Then there are deaths and more deaths. Among the most devastating to Jerry Lee were the losses of his older brother (Elmo Kidd Lewis, Jr. in 1938), his baby son (Steve Allen Lewis in 1962), his mother (Mamie Herron Lewis in 1971), and his oldest son (Jerry Lee Lewis, Jr. in 1973). But many other wives and relatives also departed as Jerry Lee pounded the piano and toured across America. The most informative sections of Bragg's reporting concern Jerry Lee's pre-Sun Records tutelage as a pianist and his penchant for accumulating a diverse repertoire of songs. Lacking songwriting skills, Jerry Lee gleefully plundered the songbooks of fellow rockers Chuck Berry, Ray Charles, Little Richard, and Carl Perkins. Bragg reveals little new material about his subject, while crafting a more mellow interpretation of the flawed rocker. Upon reflection, one wonders why anyone would seek to cast a ferocious musical man-eater like Jerry Lee as a relatively tame, domesticated pussy cat.

Even more puzzling, though, is the strange Elvis Presley biography assembled by University of North Carolina at Chapel Hill humanities professor Joel Williamson. This study lacks research depth and musical insight. It reads like a howling diatribe against drug abuse, womanizing, and the evils of popular culture. Williamson posits that Elvis' original stage sexuality created a life-time cadre of insatiable female fans. These young women, initially captivated in 1954, 1955, and 1956, loyally followed their musical heartthrob through staged television performances, the absence of overseas military service, onto the motion picture screen with B-rated films, into a short-lived 1968 TV comeback show, and then on to the Las Vegas concert circuit. For Williamson, the immediate intimacy of female adoration for Elvis stunted his future performing creativity. It also enabled Colonel Parker, his slavish Memphis mafia followers, and others to offer false security against the loss of audience appeal. This interpretation of Elvis, flooded with sexual encounters and drug abuse, seems much more psychoanalytical and moralistic than cultural and historical. At various points throughout the biography, Williamson drifts aimlessly through his own Southern social class theories into sexual liberation ideas. Sadly, he never reaches a reasonable or convincing conclusion about the musical motivation behind the Presley persona.

Jerry Lee Lewis and Elvis Presley were redneck rockabillies. They unleashed energetic, emotion-laden recordings on an unsuspecting American audience and gained immediate recognition as wild men. Teenagers, males and females alike, were "Breathless" in their praise of "Heartbreak Hotel". It was a sign of youth and rebellion, pleasure and financial freedom to purchase "Great Balls Of Fire" and "Hound Dog". While Elvis may have seemed caged in Graceland in the '60s, Jerry Lee roamed wild and free across America asking "What'd I Say" in juke joints and at county fairs. Both men remained boys of the South. They personified rock 'n' roll at its best and worst. While they were inventive, loud, attractive, rhythmic, and commanding on stage, they were also infantile, emotionally brittle, insecure, under-educated, limited in commercial vision, and sexually motivated. Neither Rick Bragg nor Joel Williamson possesses the requisite fan ardor or the necessary musical enthusiasm and knowledge to chronicle the lives of these two giants. Bragg comes across as a diligent, thoughtful scribe, but an uncritical transmitter of tales. Williamson is a Southern culture elitist and condescending anti-popular culture commentator who misunderstands and misrepresents both the rockabilly revolution and The Hillbilly Cat. Contemporary readers will be better served to re-visit the classic studies by Colin Escott, Peter Guralnick, and Nick Tosches if they wish to experience the explosive nature of the two firebrands that launched the rock revolution from Memphis.

(This commentary was originally published as B. Lee Cooper. "Review of JERRY LEE LEWIS: HIS OWN STORY by Rick Bragg and ELVIS PRESLEY: A SOUTHERN LIFE by Joel Williamson," ROCK MUSIC STUDIES, 4:2 (May 2017): 157-159.)

Jerry Lee Lewis on guitar and Elvis Presley on piano

LITTLE RICHARD

DIRECTLY FROM MY HEART: THE BEST OF THE SPECIALTY AND VEE-JAY YEARS
Little Richard
Chris Clough (comp.)
3 CDs, Specialty/Concord Music Group SPC 76988-02, 2015

Little Richard lit the fuse in 1956. Rock 'n' roll exploded across America to the frenetic sounds of "Tutti Frutti", "Long Tall Sally", "Ready Teddy", and "Lucille". Released on the Los Angeles-based Specialty Records label, Little Richard's rhythmic anthems demonstrated gospel fervor, boogie-woogie piano pounding, vocal pyrotechnics, and suggestive (if sometimes silly) lyrics. His music captured the imagination of white teenagers. Undeniably, the manic musical messenger from Macon, Georgia was a unique popular culture figure. He was clearly unlike any of his recording contemporaries. He wasn't a leather-jacketed menace like Gene Vincent or a televised choir boy like Ricky Nelson; he wasn't a rhythmic machine like Bo Diddley or a gifted lyricist like Chuck Berry; and he wasn't a handsome rockabilly like Elvis Presley or a country-swing convert like Bill Haley. Little Richard was an irrepressible force of nature (similar to Jerry Lee Lewis) who had honed his performing style and musical talent in black churches, carnivals, night clubs, and gay bars. Sporting make-up and mascara, grooming his hair into a stunning pompadour, and flirting with both women and men,

Little Richard discovered like-minded friends in New Orleans. More importantly, he readily absorbed the stage personas of Crescent City favorites Roy Brown, Esquerita, and Billy Wright. Although he failed to achieve success with the RCA Victor or Peacock labels during the early 1950s, he struck recording gold on Specialty at the end of the decade. Between 1956 and 1959 Little Richard charted 16 pop hits, including "Slippin' And Slidin' (Peepin' And Hidin')", "Rip It Up", "The Girl Can't Help It", "Keep A Knockin'", "Good Golly Miss Molly", and "Kansas City". But at the height of his performing prominence, Little Richard abandoned his musical career for evangelical ministry. Fortunately for youthful rock music enthusiasts in the United States and in the United Kingdom, his quixotic return to religion was short-lived. Over the next five decades Little Richard spent brief, unspectacular interludes performing for several labels, including Manticore, MCA, Mercury, Modern, Okeh (a subsidiary of Columbia), and Vee-Jay. While he produced tunes ranging from "Bama Lama Bama Loo" to "Great Gosh A'Mighty" for these new labels, his post-'50s recordings always seemed mild in comparison to his fiery Specialty releases.

Concord Music Group compiler Chris Clough, along with liner notes author Billy Vera, has assembled a three-disc, 64-song salute to Little Richard's 1956-1965 recording period. DIRECTLY FROM MY HEART features 43 Specialty releases and 21 Vee-Jay recordings. The former songs are brilliant, bodacious, and electric, while the latter tunes are mostly uninspired covers of "Goodnight Irene", "Money Honey", "Lawdy Miss Claudy", "Blueberry Hill", "Only You", and "Short Fat Fanny". The Specialty releases exude creativity, imagination, and verve. The Vee-Jay recordings present an artist contributing boundless energy on inferior material. It's clear that Clough and Vera would have been better stewards of Little Richard's legacy if they had abbreviated their compilation by one disc.

Countless anthologies of Little Richard's recordings have been issued over the past 25 years. None offer complete overviews of his remarkable career. For example, HE'S GOT IT (Blue Label, 2007) highlights 10 RCA Victor and Peacock tunes - from "Get Rich Quick" to "Little Richard's Boogie" - along with 10 Specialty numbers - from "I'm Just A Lonely Guy" to "All Around The World". This collection covers only seven years. A much larger compilation titled LITTLE RICHARD RIPS IT UP (Golden Stars, 2009) offers 42 songs from 1951 to 1959, but nothing beyond that end date. Similarly, LITTLE RICHARD ROCKS (Bear Family, 2011), THE VERY BEST OF...LITTLE RICHARD (Specialty, 2008), THE GEORGIA PEACH (Specialty, 1991), and THE ESSENTIAL LITTLE RICHARD (Specialty, 1989) offer an endless array of Specialty releases, but only occasional hints that the performer ever recorded in the '60s, '70s, or later for other labels. To balance these omissions one must be diligent in searching for specialized collections such as THE EXPLOSIVE LITTLE RICHARD (Edsel, 2007) and LITTLE RICHARD: THE KING OF ROCK AND ROLL (Reprise, 2004).

These anthologies explore British and American releases from the 1960s, while totally ignoring earlier material. From yet another perspective, it is fascinating to note that Little Richard's post-Specialty singing career is dotted with collaborative ventures. He recorded with Canned Heat ("Rockin' With The King", 1972), Bachman-Turner Overdrive ("Take It Like A Man", 1976), The Beach Boys ("Happy Ending", 1987), Bon Jovi ("You Really Got Me Now", 1990), Living Colour ("Elvis Is Dead", 1990), Elton John ("The Power", 1993), and Solomon Burke ("Everybody's Got A Game", 1996). Beyond observations about individual greatest hits and star-level collaborations, it is especially interesting to trace the influence of Little Richard upon other successful artists. Over the past 65 years, his impact has been noteworthy. Elvis Presley, Bill Haley, Pat Boone, Jerry Lee Lewis, and The Everly Brothers were among the '50s recording giants who borrowed Little Richard tunes. Later, John Lennon, Creedence Clearwater Revival, The Kinks, Heart, MC5, and Bruce Springsteen also raided Little Richard's vault of rock numbers as well.

DIRECTLY FROM MY HEART is a typical accumulation of Little Richard's marvelous Specialty hits, cobbled together with a lackluster group of Vee-Jay releases. Richard Wayne Penniman deserves better. This founding father of rock 'n' roll merits a box set that surveys his entire recording career. The future compiler of this multi-disc tribute should carefully sift through the rich audio wheat and be sure to discard all of the recorded chaff. The final anthology should be chronologically broad and artistically diverse. It should feature examples of Little Richard singing gospel tunes and illustrations of his vibrant concert performances. It should also join the magnificent Specialty releases with rarities like the 1962 single "I'm In Love Again" by Little Richard and The World Famous Upsetters. There are already enough Specialty-only compilations on the market. It's time for a truly thoughtful, thorough retrospective on the musical mayhem and regal rocking of...the man who would be Rock 'N' Roll's King.

(This commentary was originally published as B. Lee Cooper. "Review of DIRECTLY FROM MY HEART: THE BEST OF THE SPECIALTY AND VEE-JAY YEARS by Little Richard," ROCK MUSIC STUDIES, 4:1 (February 2017): 80-81.)

Keb' Mo'

KEB' MO'

GOOD TO BE...
Keb' Mo'
CD, Rounder Records CD 1166101542, 2022

For the first four decades of his life, Kevin Roosevelt Moore was an evolving, experimental, uninspiring musical critter. Professional fame and fortune eluded him. Nevertheless, he obviously absorbed a variety of sonic stylings and gained valuable performing experience. After adopting the Keb' Mo' persona during the early 1990s, he focused diligently upon powerful Delta blues guitar licks and heartfelt personal songwriting. This new approach really worked. For the next thirty years he thrived professionally by mixing autobiographical revelations with his cultural heritage, deeply personal feelings and strong political observations, and rich blues rhythms with sensitive, sincere lyrics. The range of his topical commentaries is staggering. For instance, he lauds extended family holiday celebrations in "Jingle Bell Jamboree" (2000). He decries female fickleness in "Perpetual Blues Machine" (1996). He manifests a working man's logic about money management in "Soon as I Get Paid" (1998). He honors the blues tradition in "Henry" (1998). He longs for the freedom of youthful irresponsibility in "The Old Me Better" (2014)). And he stresses the adult joy of psychic escape and independence in "She Just Wants To Dance" (2016).

The successful, productive, and richly rewarded Keb' Mo' is an important 21st century bluesman. His recorded commentaries are lucid and liberating, sometimes expressing frustration or disappointment, but always rebounding to the potential of life's abundant opportunities. Like his Delta blues heroes, Keb' Mo' explores the human condition through a lyrical frame of personal relationships and social networks. Sometimes he's Sigmund Freud wearing a green fedora. Sometimes he's a combination of Big Bill Broonzy/Johnny Mercer/Paul Simon with a big, wide grin and an insightful set of bluesy lyrics. Sometimes he's Ralph Ellison spinning the tales of invisible people while strumming a National Steel guitar. But in the end, Keb' Mo' is Everyman - just trying of make sense of his long and winding seven-decade journey.

Happily married to Robbie Brooks Moore and comfortably residing in suburban Nashville, the Compton-born Keb' Mo' is admired by fellow musicians and blues fans alike. His trophy case displays a W.C. Handy Award along with five well-deserved Grammy acknowledgments. The lanky, African-American singer-songwriter has nothing left to prove. In fact, GOOD TO BE..., his latest CD venture for Rounder Records, feels more like a sonic statesman's farewell address than a stepping stone toward something new and different. The Guitar Man is still at his peak. He's not sick. He's not tired. He's not bored. He's not jaded. But he's now 71 years old. It's reasonable to reflect - and to share a few ideas for a final time.

What does GOOD TO BE... hold in store for a 21st century listener? The title tune presents an autobiographical retrospective. "Good To Be (Home Again)" commemorates the singer's recent return visit to Compton, his boyhood stomping ground. Reveries abound about local barber shops and good times in L.A.'s black urban culture. But youthful memories are joined by adult reflections on the joy of a life well-lived. Next, Keb' Mo' revisits his long-time fascination with complex, confusing, but very satisfying romantic involvements. He lauds the supportive, healing majesty provided by the love of a good woman in "So Easy." "Sunny and Warm." "Good Strong Woman," and "Like Love." The marvel of becoming a better man via a healthy, honest relationship with a sensitive, supportive woman is detailed in "So Good to Me." And the peculiar ecstasy of exchanging thoughts of love silently is depicted in "Quiet Moments." Such radiant feelings are standard fare for this thoughtful chronicler of romance.

The remaining tunes on this self-revelatory CD provide provocative examples of heart-breaking, soul-searching, and politically-charged observations from a canny senior citizen. This is no ordinary bluesman. This is no African-American copycat trading on traditional Mississippi jargon or old-fashioned country blues imagery. GOOD TO BE... is the work of a mature, enlightened, deceptively profound yet still uncertain Everyman moving closer and closer to life's end. Whimsical at times. Serious at times. But always direct, cunning, and insightful. In "'62 Chevy," for example, Keb' Mo' begs for forgiveness concerning an unidentified misstep that has interrupted a blossoming relationship. Then in "All Dressed Up" he expresses regret for ignoring his mother's sound advice about an ill-advised romantic affiliation. And in "The Medicine Man" Keb' Mo' probes the quest for much-needed political and social reformation. He cites problems ranging from the dreaded COVID-19 pandemic and Stop-The-Steal electoral politics to racial inequality and damaging climate change. Borrowing the words from a familiar Bill Withers song, Keb' Mo' also stresses the need for mutual caring and personal assistance. Moving beyond "Lean on Me," Keb' Mo' name-checks the Rev. Martin Luther King, Jr. as the model for both the energy and the goodwill necesssary to promote meaningful social change. Finally, the elder bluesman declares his positive expectations for radical improvements in "Louder." Keb' Mo' projects increasingly vocalized rebellion among youthful protesters, greater political power exerted by coming generations, and the hope for constructive results around the world. Global transformation seeems to be at hand.

GOOD TO BE.. is a career capstone recording. It echoes the critical style and hopeful spirit of artists like Robert Johnson, Big Bill Broonzy, Sonny Boy Nelson, and Taj Mahal. Storytellers all. It demonstrates the universality of Keb' Mo' as a guitarist and singer-songwriter, but also as an enthusiastic musical collaborator with diverse artists like Vince Gill, Darius Rucker, Kristen Chenoweth, Christone "Kingfish" Ingram, and The Old Crow Medicine Show. It offers thoughtful and thought-provoking insights into life, love, and day-to-day survival. It also beckons modern listeners to appreciate the music of other 21st century blues artists like Joe Bonamassa, Gary Clark, Warren Haynes, and Derek Trucks. And finally, it solidifies the legacy of Keb' Mo' as a successful Delta blues preacher, composer, multi-instrumentalist, humanitarian, and soothsayer.

ROY ORBISON

THE ROY ORBISON CONNECTION: 34 ROOTS AND COVERS OF ROY ORBISON
Various Artists
CD, Bear Family Records BCD 17607, 2021

Rock 'n' roll kingmaker Sam Phillips couldn't get it done. He was unable to generate recording stardom for the multi-talented Roy Orbison. Granted, the singer/songwriter/guitarist from Vernon, Texas lacked the good looks and stage charisma of Elvis Presley. Orbison wasn't as instrumentally dynamic or as self-assured as Jerry Lee Lewis, either. And he didn't possess the uncomplicated lyrical skills and crowd-pleasing country style of Johnny Cash. It didn't take long for Orbison himself to recognize that his affiliation with Sun Records was not propelling his career forward. He abandoned the Memphis music scene in 1957. Then he watched The Everly Brothers score a major hit with his honorific salute "Claudette." In 1958 Roy Orbison moved to Nashville and signed a recording contract with RCA Victor. Even under the skillful guidance of Chet Atkins, no Orbison hit recordings surfaced. Finally, Roy's Nashville singing career was jump-started when he joined Fred Foster's Monument Records during 1960. What happened? Roy began collaborating on songwriting and string-drenched production arrangements with fellow artist Joe Melson. Great new songs and the rich recording quality of Monument studios allowed the majesty of Roy's octave-spanning, ethereal vocals to sparkle. Over the next four years, the BILLBOARD Pop charts featured a remarkable number of Orbison hits.

Roy Orbison crafted his recordings as if they were three-minute dramas. He projected emotional intensity that rivaled the performances of European operatic soloists. "Crying" and "Running Scared" illustrate this style. Orbison also created lyrics, melodies, and rhythms within his tunes designed to expose a sense of sustained romantic longing. "Dream Baby (How Long Must I Dream)" and "In Dreams" manifest this approach. Beyond personal reflection in ballads, though, Roy could brag and strut with the best American rockers. "Candy Man" and "Mean Woman Blues" are songs of assertion and confidence. Nevertheless, personal pain and doubt were almost always present in Orbison releases. Think of "Only the Lonely (Know How I Feel)." "Love Hurts," and "Oh, Pretty Woman." Patterns of vocal angst, orchestral power, and nagging uncertainty were the audio trademarks of Monument's newest superstar. Roy Orbison scored 38 BILLBOARD Pop hits between 1956 and 1989. He was inducted into the Rock and Roll Hall of Fame in 1987, toured with The Traveling Wilburys (Bob Dylan, George Harrison, Jeff Lynne, and Tom Petty) during 1988, and was posthumously granted a Grammy Lifetime Achievement Award in 1998. Both Sam Phillips and Chet Atkins probably puzzled over their inabilities to successfully launch the career of the former lead singer of The Teen Kings.

Bear Family compilers Bill Dahl, Nico Feuerbach, and Marc Mittelacher present an intriguing treasury of 34 recordings in THE ROY ORBISON CONNECTION. Each of the anthologized songs was either composed by or performed by Roy Orbison. But all of the tracks in this Bear Family collection were released by other artists. Some are well-known singers like The Everly Brothers ("Claudette" and "Love Hurts"), Jerry Lee Lewis ("Down the Line" and "Mean Woman Blues"), and Willie Nelson ("Pretty Paper"). Others are much less familiar performers like Ronnie Cord ("Only the Lonely"), Dalida ("Je T'aime (It's Over)"), and Vernon Taylor ("Sweet and Easy to Love"). The compilers seem to be particularly interested in the numerous Orbison covers released on the Embassy label. Examples of Embassy singers who specialized in such re-issues include Les Carle ("In Dreams"), Don Duke ("Only the Lonely"), Rikki Henderson ("Dream Baby (How Long Must I Dream)"), and Paul Rich ("Running Scared").

There are also several examples of Roy Orbison song sampling among performers from musical genres ranging from pop and rockabilly to country and rock 'n' roll. These include Gene Pitney ("Today's Teardrops"), Janis Martin ("Ooby Dooby"), Narvel Felts ("Go, Go, Go"), and Bobby Fuller ("Rock House"). Totally unexpected audio entries featured in THE ROY ORBISION CONNECTION include a black quintet named The Velvets. They successfully tackle "Lana." And bandleader Ray Ellis presents an extraordinary instrumental version of "Crying." Variety rules among Roy Orbison cover clones.

How effective are these cover artists in duplicating the tone, phrasing, harmonics, and rhythm patterns of The Monument Master? That is, do these re-recordings bring the vitality of the original Orbison releases to mind - or are they simply pale duplications of inspired artistry? Personally, I found the collection to be vibrant and interesting. Sound-alike efforts by Don Duke, Mike Redway, and Paul Rich are reasonable, no strained. The stylistic variations introduced by Dalida, The Everly Brothers, Jerry Lee Lewis, Del Shannon, and The Velvets are fascinating. Only the performances by Les Carle, Sid King, Vernon Taylor, Kris Jensen, and The Schneider Sisters seem wooden and subpar. Of course, there are too many recycled versions of "Go, Go, Go," "Only the Lonely," and "Ooby Dooby" within this 34-song collection. What the Bear Family compilers should have done is to permit Roy Orbison to speak for himself throughout this disc. Frankly, the magnificent range of his voice puts all copycats to shame. His reading of lyrics is flawless. And the orchestration and production arrangements on the original Monument releases perfectly emphasize the drama of each song. THE ROY ORBISON COLLECTION compilers mistakenly assume that all 21st century listeners are broadly acquainted with the entire Orbison songbook. Sadly, they aren't. So this collection should have featured several original Sun/Monument releases as the sonic roots of each cover rendition.

Like Clyde McPhatter, Elvis Presley, Jackie Wilson, and a few other influential rock era vocalists, Roy Orbison possessed the aural power and harmonic range to shake rafters and break glass. His brilliant songwriting and lyrical storytelling made his audio tales throb with pathos. Ironically, his best love songs were masterpieces of self-doubt and misery. Yet Orbison could also rock with the best. As stated above, this 34-song collection needs to be pared in half - and then supplemented with 17 original Roy Orbison hits. Notwithstanding the major revision requested in the 2021 Bear Family release, 21st century song lovers ought to examine the following CD resources: THE

ANTHOLOGY (Not Now Music, 2013), ROY ORBISON (Monument/Legacy, 2011), ROY ROCKS (Bear Family, 2006), and THE COMPLETE SUN SESSIONS (Varese Sarabande, 2001). Upon hearing Roy Orbison plead, preach, and prophesize in person, a contemporary music fan will appreciate why so many '50s and '60s artists sought to copy his songs.

Roy Orbison

JIMMY REED

ROCKS
Jimmy Reed
CD, Bear Family Records BCD 17572, 2021

MR. LUCK: THE COMPLETE VEE-JAY SINGLES
Jimmy Reed
3 CDs, Craft Recordings/Concord Music Group CR 00006, 2017

MR. LUCK: A TRIBUTE TO JIMMY REED -- LIVE AT THE ROYAL ALBERT HALL
The Ronnie Wood Band
CD, BMG 53868242, 2021

Jimmy Reed was an entertainer. He amused himself and made new childhood chums by strumming a guitar and playing the harmonica. As a young married man and a bluecollar worker, he performed on weekends in local bars and juke joints. But Jimmy Reed was never a child prodigy, a trained musician, a gifted instrumentalist, or a show-stopping vocalist. He just loved center stage -- and small black audiences applauded his self-trained efforts. His loyal wife supported this entertaining zeal. Then a Chicago-based record company began to release Reed's personalized songs. Jukeboxes across the U.S. magnified public interest in the distinctive blues tunes of Jimmy Reed. He continued to please black audiences with his down home sound, but also acquired numerous young white fans with his rhythmic recordings. This commercial integration increased the size of his small concert venues, too. The simple but emotive playing style, the uncomplicated lyrics of love and loss, and the homey vocalizations by Jimmy Reed changed the popular music world.

Who was Jimmy Reed? For some, he was a bedeviled soul, plagued by chronic alcoholism and late onset epilepsy. He died in 1976 after a seizure. His blues songs were cathartic and his stage performances helped him overcome an innate sense of loneliness. The tenth child of a black sharecropping family from Jim Crow/Depression era Mississippi, Reed lacked formal education and spent his early working years in cotton fields, meat packing plants, and steel mills. He drifted from the Delta to Chicago to Gary, Indiana, where he finally secured his first recording contract. He had listened eagerly to elder bluesmen like Charley Patton, Sonny Boy Williamson, and Rice Miller. He had occasionally performed with his childhood buddy Eddie Taylor. Finally, he logged undistinguished service in the U.S. Navy during World War II, married his teenage sweetheart Mary Lee Davis in 1945, and honed his limited skills on guitar and harmonica at Club Jamorbee. He re-united with Taylor in 1952, signed a recording contract with Vee-Jay Records in 1953, and launched an unexpectedly successful music career.

Who was Jimmy Reed? He began his unlikely professional recording career as a young vocalist in a gospel quartet associated with the Pilgrim Rest Missionary Church of

Shaw, Mississippi. He also developed rudimentary skills on the harmonica and the guitar while listening to touring country blues singers. Jimmy Reed eventually fled the Delta via the Illinois Central Railroad. He purchased a one-way ticket to Chicago. Initially, he worked as a YMCA janitor and later as a coal hiker for the Hefter Coal Company. In his spare time, he practiced his guitar licks, harmonica melodies, and lyric rhyming skills. Mama Reed. his helpful wife and trusted confidant, assisted him in composing song poems and simple melodies. It was Vivian Carter, part-owner of the newly incorporated Vee-Jay Records company, who "discovered" the gentle, compassionate, and amazingly marketable Jimmy Reed in 1953. Teamed with Eddie Taylor on rhythm guitar and Earl Phillips on drums, Reed released a decade of chart worthy, blues-oriented shuffle recordings. Mama Reed's lyrical stories had found the perfect rhythmic interpreter.

Bear Family compiler and liner notes scribe Roland Heinrich Rumtreiber has created a 29-song tribute to the "Jimmy Reed Sound." ROCKS is an exceptional salute vehicle - and Rumtreiber is a superb music historian and audio analyst. But he muddies the ethnomusicological waters by defining Reed as a many-different-things-to-many-different-people recording chameleon rather than a signature blues stylist. For instance, the compiler argues that Reed became more commercially popular among whites than Leadbelly, B.B. King, or Bobby "Blue" Bland. He also states that Reed's recordings served as a bridge for numerous artists with garage band, ska, skiffle, and even rockabilly backgrounds. From Link Wray and Jimmy Vaughan to Mick Jagger and Eric Burden, Rumtreiber hears Reed influences echoing and expanding. Nevertheless, the compiler defines Reed's vocal and instrumental skills as severely limited. Rumtreiber casts Eddie Taylor as an under-appreciated guru and forgotten Svengali behind most of Jimmy Reed's hit records. According to the compiler, Taylor tutored, cajoled, assisted, and molded the distinctive "Jimmy Reed Sound." To further illustrate this point, Rumtreiber ends the ROCKS collection with four solo releases by Taylor - "Bad Boy," "E.T. Blues," "Big Town Playboy," and "Train Fare."

Seeking to provide even greater historical clarity concerning the "Jimmy Reed Sound," Rumtreiber expands on Eddie Taylor's musical roots. This exercise involves references to blues resources including Robert Johnson, Leroy Carr, and Scrapper Blackwell. Beyond Taylor, though, the compiler also lauds the lyric influences exerted by Mama Reed and the supplementary studio session assistance provided by John Brim, Albert King, Henry Gray, Lefty Bates, Willie Dixon, and Lonnie Brooks. It's a wonder that Jimmy Reed could tie his own shoes without assistance, according to Rumtreiber. Even the post-1950s "Jimmy Reed Highway" of adoring audio acolytes - including The Blues Brothers, Dale Hawkins, Lazy Lester, Omar Dykes, Charlie Rich, Neil Young, and many others -- seem more indebted to the shuffle rhythms and quaint blues tunes rather than to the main artist. Somehow, Jimmy Reed gets discounted, under-appreciated, and under-rated in an anthology that sparkles with his signature songs - "Ain't That Loving You Baby," "Big Boss Man," "Bright Lights Big City," "High and Lonesome," and many more.

MR. LUCK: THE COMPLETE VEE-JAY SINGLES is an 88-cut compilation featuring Jimmy Reed's most important songs from his most important label. This collection presents a recording-by-recording annotated history of Reed's tunes, session-playing cronies, and successes or failures within the R&B/pop music marketplace between 1953 and 1964. Grammy-winning songwriter and harmonica specialist Scott Billington produced and drafted the detailed liner notes for this thoughtful. insightful, loving tribute to Jimmy Reed. All of the expected hits are represented. So are many surprisingly interesting non-hit recordings. The session-by-session commentaries by Billington make this anthology glitter with facts and ideas about the nature and meaning of Reed's music. Clearly, he was an artist with a magic touch. And his recordings were appreciated during his brief life-time as well as into the next century.

MR. LUCK: A TRIBUTE TO JIMMY REED is a rollicking 18-song concert performance that was originally taped in 2013 at London's Royal Albert Hall. The disc offers impassioned vocals by Ronnie Wood, Mick Hucknall, and Bobby Womack and exquisite guitar renderings by Wood and Mick Taylor. This splendid salute to Reed's music is spellbinding. The CD cover explains the genesis of this salutary effort. "It's all about those visceral chords that send a shiver down your spine. It's the shift from the lowdown pain of the blues to the power of rock 'n' roll." The entire disc sizzles. There are pulse-pounding interpretations of the title track, "Good Lover," and "You Don't Have to Go." There are heart-felt repetitions of "Honest I Do," "Big Boss Man," and "High and Lonesome." And there is a singularly touching eulogy to Jimmy Reed's complex career in the biographical tune "Ghost Of The Man," This remarkable retrospective release is a confession of faith concerning the long-time influence of Mama Reed's husband.

Who was Jimmy Reed? He wasn't a guitar virtuoso like Aaron "T-Bone" Walker or B.B. King. He wasn't a dynamic stage performer like James Brown or Jackie Wilson, either. He wasn't a harmonica wizard like Little Walter. He wasn't a poly-rhythmic dynamo like Bo Diddley. He wasn't a sexually suggestive macho man like Howlin' Wolf or Muddy Waters. And he certainly wasn't a brown-eyed handsome man - or a fast-talkin', duck walkin' rocker - like Chuck Berry. No one knew exactly what to think of Jimmy Reed's fundamental talents. The premiere blues recording entrepreneur of Chicago - Leonard Chess - rejected him as a potential representative for Chess/Checker Records. But on the local Vee-Jay label Jimmy Reed demonstrated the ability to attract middle-aged African-American record buyers along with white teenage music fans. The latter group often seemed transfixed with the bump-and-grind sexuality that was latent within the hypnotic rhythms of Reed's best tunes.

Who was Jimmy Reed? Critics who misunderstood and misinterpreted Reed's casual precision as a bluesman often condemned his work as formulaic and mundane. But Reed and his talented musical compatriots elevated orgasmic sonic suggestions into high audio art. Yes, the little girls understood. So did the lustful little boys. It was never about excelling at electronic modulation or speed tripping across guitar frets. Reed relied upon a steady rolling shuffle. It was simultaneously muddy and clean, unpretentious and reliable. Jimmy Reed attracted many fans in the U.S.A. and abroad. He accumulated several professional musicians as loving followers as well. Beyond

America's shores, Eric Clapton, The Rolling Stones, Jeck Beck, The Yardbirds, and The Animals were haunted and intrigued by Reed's lopping rhythmic style. In Louisianna, Elmore James, Slim Harpo, and others exhibited blues innovations directly linked to Reed's performing format. In Texas, young Jimmy Vaughan and The Fabulous Thunderbirds lionized Reed's musical approach. And in Memphis, Elvis Presley couldn't get Reed's rhythm patterns out of his head.

These three 21st century compilations of Jimmy Reed's material invite a new generation of listeners to be mesmerized by lilting rhythms that invariably suggest seduction and satisfaction. The discs also reveal a unique group of African-American love ballads. Personal vulnerability and romantic frustration are obvious within Reed's moaning vocal demeanor. His tunes invite silent passions to bubble and unspoken feelings to leap toward action. Jimmy Reed repeatedly returns to the eternal lover's question - "Baby, What You Want Me to Do?"

MARTY ROBBINS

TWENTIETH CENTURY DRIFTER: THE LIFE OF MARTY ROBBINS
Diane Diekman
Urbana: University of Illinois Press, 2012

THE ESSENTIAL MARTY ROBBINS, 1951-1982 (Columbia Legacy C2K 48537)
Marty Robbins
Liner Notes by Rich Kienzle. New York: Sony Music/Columbia Records, 1991

Capturing artistic vitality in print is challenging. The 20th Century maxim that writing about music is like dancing about architecture still rings true today. Nevertheless, music journalists and rock critics continue to flail away on their computers attempting to describe red-hot concert performances and brilliant studio albums. Their reviews invariably fall short. The electricity inherent in musical pursuits is always best communicated through audio media rather than in print. Hearing performers, whether Nat King Cole, Elvis Presley, The Beatles, Madonna, Eminem, or Beyonce, produces a much deeper impression than reading even the most perceptive written commentaries about their musicianship. Yet music historians continue to draft biographies. Through sentences, paragraphs, and chapters, they strive to transcribe the lyrical lightning and the sonic thunder manifested by distinctive artists. Great rock biographies do exist, of course. Charles White has skillfully chronicled the provocative lifestyle and performing mania of Little Richard; Rick Coleman has carefully traced the piano-pounding magic and historical influence of Fats Domino; and Nick Tosches has unmasked the personal insanity and professional obsessions of Jerry Lee Lewis. In an extraordinary autobiographical effort, Keith Richards has revealed his own musical motivations and reveled in his lengthy tenure with The Rolling Stones. But without personally experiencing hit recordings such as "Tutti Frutti", "Blueberry Hill", "Whole Lot of Shakin' Going On", and "(I Can't Get No) Satisfaction", one doubts that any of these superb manuscripts would enable a reader to comprehend the musical genius of these four premiere performers.

A CD tribute anthology or a box set of historic hits offers the ideal blend of written personal profile information and key audio tracks that can accurately reflect a musician's biography. In such cumulative ventures, a music historian usually addresses readers through liner notes. These commentaries briefly capsule the life-time pursuits of the featured singer. Interspersed among stories about musical influences, record company affiliations, inspirations for particular songs, and lists of awards and honors, the compiler always assesses the definitive audio performances featured within the set. In 1991, for instance,

Sony Music issued THE ESSENTIAL MARTY ROBBINS, 1951-1982 as part of its extensive Columbia County Classics Collection. This two-disc, 48-song compilation provided thoughtful liner notes by Rich Kienzle. Carefully melding highlights of Marty Robbins' life and recordings, Kienzle transcended print medium by inviting his readers to commune with Marty Robbins on his own lyrical and rhythmic terms. Supported by songs like "Tennessee Toddy", "Singing The Blues", "Knee Deep In The Blues", "Mister Teardrop", "Smokin' Cigarettes and Drinkin' Coffee Blues", "Tonight Carmen", "Feleena (From El Paso)", "Some Memories Just Won't Die", and "El Paso City", the historical facts of the print commentary were confirmed through vocal harmony, lyrical logic, and rhythmic rejuvenation. Kienzle's observations also enabled the songs themselves to gain greater meaning, too. They were no longer isolated pleasures or random sonic events. Now they were bound together by a historical interpretation that offered a vision linking biography, motivation, talent, artistry, and achievement. Thus, the coherence between printed text and audio performance could be critically assessed by each reader/listener. Thus, the final judgment concerning musical greatness, always personal in nature, is both guided and enriched.

Traditional biography persists, of course. Despite the existence of a nearly perfect print/audio perspective on Marty Robbins from Columbia Records, the University of Illinois Press has issued a new book-length study. Diane Diekman has assembled a thoroughly documented, factually accurate biography of this American music legend. This 280-page study addresses Robbins' early family experiences, his adoration of singing cowboy Gene Autry and country/pop vocalist Eddy Arnold, his long-time recording and performing affiliations with New York's Columbia Records and Nashville's Grand Ole Opry, his noteworthy composing efforts and persistent album generating activities, his zealous but relatively unsuccessful NASCAR circuit flirtations, and his death in 1982 due to lung and kidney failure after a fourth heart attack. This biographical text is lucid and entertaining.

However, as details concerning cross-country bus rides to concerts, sporadic encounters with fans and supportive instrumentalists, and shifting business arrangements populate page after page, the magic of Mary Robbins' distinctive musical contributions is regrettably upstaged. For example, his marvelous versatility in song selection and his stylish flexibility in vocalizing are seldom acknowledged. Robbins was a uniquely gifted performer. Genre-hopping diversity was his trademark. He covered country classics ("Kaw-Liga" and "Cool Water"), experimented with rockabilly raves ("That's All Right" and "Maybelline"), performed teen-oriented pop tunes ("A White Sport Coat (And A Pink Carnation)"), composed memorable gunfighter ballads ("El Paso" and "Big Iron"), dabbled in steel guitar rhythms ("The Hawaiian Wedding Song" and "Beyond The Reef"), and released a variety of other hit songs ("Don't Worry", "Devil Woman", "Ruby Ann", and "My Woman, My Woman, My Wife"). While casually mentioned by Diekman, the expansive nature of this artist's repertoire is never fully plumbed. Similarly, the author makes no meaningful attempts to contrast Robbins' three-decade musical trajectory with any of his country music contemporaries, whether Johnny Cash, Elvis Presley, the Every Brothers, Roy Orbison, Merle Haggard, Jerry Lee Lewis, or Charlie Rich. Although Diekman does mention the titles of most of Robbins' hit songs within her text, she fails to offer a formal discography to illustrate the subject's songwriting prowess and his distinctive approach to re-recording classic tunes. TWENTIETH CENTURY DRIFTER is the literary equivalent of offering an array sheet music without providing a piano - or of listing the song titles on a jukebox without spending the quarters necessary to play those recordings. There is no musical life to be found in this workman-like biography. This is especially sad since Marty Robbins, the subject of this book, was incapable of defining his priorities or expressing his values in any way other than through composing, playing, singing, and recording.

The success of THE ESSENTIAL MARTY ROBBINS, 1951-1982 and the failure of the TWENTIETH CENTURY DRIFTER are not merely functions of personal taste. These two commercial productions -- one a CD box set and the other a literary profile - manifest very different approaches to the same biographical subject. Documenting the lives of kings and queens or statesmen and corporate leaders can be achieved through print alone. However, this is not the case in respect to 20th Century musicians. Without blending their carefully crafted audio productions with information from their diaries, autobiographies, and secondary written sources, no exploration of lives that have been dedicated to music can ever be accurate or complete. This is why Rich Kienzle's approach to Marty Robbins succeeds and Diane Diekman's doesn't.

Works Cited

Rick Coleman. BLUE MONDAY: FATS DOMINO AND THE LOST DAWN OF ROCK 'N' ROLL. Cambridge, Massachusetts: Da Capo Press, 2006.

Keith Richards, with James Fox. LIFE. Boston: Little, Brown and Company, 2010.

Nick Tosches. HELLFIRE: THE JERRY LEE LEWIS STORY. New York: Dell Publishing, 1982.

Charles White. THE LIFE AND TIMES OF LITTLE RICHARD: THE QUASAR OF ROCK. New York: Harmony Books, 1984.

(This commentary was originally published as B. Lee Cooper. "Marty Robbins," in DISCS OF DISTINCTION: ESSAYS ON REMARKABLE RECORDINGS BY EXCEPTIONAL ARTISTS, edited by B. Lee Cooper and Frank W. Hoffmann (Charleston, South Carolina: Paw Paw Press, 2015): 135-137.)

Marty Robbins

NINA SIMONE

NINA SIMONE: THE DEFINITIVE COLLECTION, 1958-1962
Nina Simone
Paul Watts, compiler
4 CDs, Acrobat ACQCD 7124, 2018

FOREVER YOUNG, GIFTED, AND BLACK: SONGS OF FREEDOM AND SPIRIT
Nina Simone
Richard Seidel, compiler
CD, RCA/Legacy 82876-74413-2, 2006

NINA SIMONE SINGS THE BLUES
Nina Simone
Richard Seidel, compiler
CD, RCA/Legacy 82876-73334-2, 2006

BITTERSWEET: THE VERY BEST OF NINA SIMONE
Nina Simone
Paul Williams, compiler
CD, 7N/BMG/House of Hits 66748-77010-2, 2000

Born in 1933, Eunice Kathleen Waymon was young, gifted, and black in Tryon, North Carolina throughout the 1940s. She was raised in a typically segregated community, participated actively in her parents' African Episcopal Methodist Church, and studied classical piano under the guidance of British tutor Muriel Mazzonovich. Eunice's childhood musical stimulation came from Bach, Beethoven, Brahms, Chopin, and Schubert. After graduating with honors from a private high school in Asheville and prepping at the Julliard School in New York, Eunice was inexplicably denied admission to Philadelphia's prestigious Curtis Institute of Music. Where does a female African-American musical prodigy turn when a classical music career option is snatched away? Upon the advice of her most recent music tutor, Eunice accepted a job playing jazz piano at the Midtown Bar & Grille in Atlantic City in 1954. The club owner suggested that she sing as well as play for his customers. Performing the "devil's music" for hire and singing in her husky contralto, Eunice decided to adopt a new stage persona. She became Nina Simone. Within four years she released an album on Cincinnati's Bethlehem Records. Her professional singing, songwriting, and piano playing career was launched.

As a songstress, Nina Simone's style defies singular descriptors. Her childhood roots were rich in gospel music and spiritual songs. Her teenage years and post-high school learning was devoted to classical piano technique and rigorous concerto performances. Pop radio and sound recordings were her only links to contemporary audio culture. As a young commercial artist she eagerly explored the realms of blues and jazz, pop and soul, and even world music. Her eclectic repertoire ranged from "Children Go Where I

Send You", "Little Liza Jane", and "Trouble In Mind" to "I Loves You, Porgy", "It Don't Mean A Thing If It Ain't Got That Swing", and "House Of The Rising Sun". This diversity of interests prompted mixed and misleading labels like folk interpreter, jazz diva, and even High Priestess of Soul. The latter title stemmed from two associations. First, Nina developed strong cultural affiliations with Lorraine Hansbery, Leroi Jones, James Baldwin, Miriam Makeba, and Langston Hughes. Second, she produced marvelous social commentaries such as "Backlash Blues", "I Wish I Knew How It Would Feel To Be Free", "Mississippi Goddam", and "The Times They Are A-Changin'".

Nina sang truth to power throughout her career. She barked on behalf of various black civil rights causes; she battled for female equality; and she befriended those involved in gay rights activities. But her music always defined her as a unique creature, involved with many causes but artistically above the fray. She also produced several incredibly sensual love songs, including "Do I Move You?" and "In The Dark". She crafted a number of important social statements like "Why (The King Of Love Is Dead)" and "To Be Young, Gifted, and Black". And she was playful, cynical, sexy, and fun on tunes like "Nobody Knows You When You're Down And Out" and "I Want A Little Sugar In My Bowl". During the later years of her life, she was diagnosed with bi-polar disorder. Then she became a frequently-quoted, anti-American expatriate living in the south of France. At age 70, she died of breast cancer in 2003.

Nina Simone: The Definitive Collection, 1958-1962 is an extensive four-disc, 76-song introduction to the artist's fascinating songlist. This excellent assemblage of early recordings samples eight albums released on the Bethlehem and Colpix labels. It also includes several Colpix single releases that achieved national hit status. Nina Simone's distinctive arrangements are especially noteworthy on her "live" performance recordings from The Town Hall, The Village Gate, and The Newport Jazz Festival. But her studio material is important as well. Although sometimes over-orchestrated, the numerous Duke Ellington tunes on this compilation are inspired and inspiring. Nina seems particularly attuned to "Mood Indigo", "Do Nothin' Till You Hear From Me", "Hey Buddy Bolden", and "Solitare". Her versions of "Black Is The Color Of My True Love's Hair", "Summertime" (both as an instrumental piece and as a vocal rendition), and "Fine And Mellow" are superb. And her emotional presentations of "Work Song", "Forbidden Fruit", "Brown Baby", and Nina's Blues" are thoughtful and provocative.

Forever Young, Gifted, And Black, Nina Simone Sings The Blues, and Bittersweet: The Very Best Of Nina Simone complete the arc of Simone's recording career on the Phillips and RCA Victor labels. Nearly all of her Billboard "R&B" and "Pop" hits are enrolled on one or more of these single-disc anthologies. Each of the compilations pursues a different perspective. Forever Young, Gifted, And Black offers the protest-oriented, social justice proclamations within Simone's personal songbook. These tunes include "Revolution" (not the Lennon-McCartney song), "Ain't Got No - I Got Life", and the prophetic title tune. This CD should have been dedicated to ideas and memories of Malcolm X and Martin Luther King, Jr. Nina Simone Sings The Blues presents a far more intimate, introspective, and romantic side of the artist. Aural illustrations include "Since I Fell For You", "Blues For Mama", and "My Man's Gone Now". Finally,

Bittersweet features a broad overview of Nina's most popular numbers. Assembled here are pop classics like "My Baby Just Cares For Me" and "Don't Smoke In Bed", novelties like "I Put A Spell On You", and familiar Simone hits like "I Loves You, Porgy", "To Love Somebody", "Trouble in Mind", and "I Want A Little Sugar In My Bowl".

What is the historical context of this female artist's fame? Nina Simone never attained the national superstar status of Diana Ross, Aretha Franklin, or Donna Summer. She never reached the regional soul diva standing of either Irma Thomas or Ann Peebles. Nina wasn't a stage-stealing dancer like Tina Turner, a brilliant pop composer like Carole King, a folkie heroine like Odetta, or a jazz idol like Billie Holiday. But in some ways, she was a rare gem unto herself, defying comparison by raging for individual recognition. The classically-trained musician turned club artist and recording performer established a strong base of audience support in the Northeast, particularly between Greenwich Village and Harlem. Her multiple albums, both live and studio performances, allowed nationwide exposure to her songs of faith, love, protest, and personal pain.

Since her genius was best exhibited in stage venues, Nina's concert audiences understood her moods and style changes far better than her record-buying followers. Her instantly recognizable voice and her inspired piano playing were a large part of her force-of-nature persona. Her unwillingness to be taken for granted - as a black woman, as a stage performer, and as a spokesperson for the marginalized, the oppressed, and the disenfranchised - had a less than beneficial impact on her national popularity. Honesty and integrity were Nina's sustaining hallmarks. These four retrospective tribute anthologies contain the sonic dynamite that propelled Nina Simone from small town segregation to international acceptance and fame, from stogy academic rejection to enormous commercial acceptance, and from an isolated focus on elite music to majestic performing capabilities in jazz, blues, pop, and protest songs.

(This commentary was originally published as B. Lee Cooper. "Review of NINA SIMONE: THE DEFINITIVE COLLECTION, 1958-1962 by Nina Simone, FOREVER YOUNG, GIFTED, AND BLACK by Nina Simone, NINA SIMONE SINGS THE BLUES by Nina Simone, and BITTERSWEET by Nina Simone," POPULAR MUSIC AND SOCIETY, 42:3 (July 2019): 392-394.)

Nina Simone by Luigi Di Giammarino

JACKIE WILSON

YOU BETTER KNOW IT: THE U.S. AND U.K. CHART HITS, 1957-1962
Jackie Wilson
Bob Fisher (Comp.)
CD, Jasmine JASCD 918, 2015

NYC, 1961-1966
Jackie Wilson
Bob Hughes (Comp.)
2 CDs, Ace CDTOP2-1428, 2015

New York-based disc jockey Alan Freed nicknamed Jackie Wilson "Mr. Excitement" in 1957. Thirty years later, The Rock And Roll Hall Of Fame inducted him as a member, along with Bo Diddley, Aretha Franklin, Marvin Gaye, Clyde McPhatter, and Big Joe Turner. Ironically, 1987 was also the date when a U.K. record distributor re-issued "Reet Petite (The Finest Girl You Ever Want To Meet)", Jackie Wilson's initial U.S. hit as a single artist. His powerful rendition from the dawn of rock 'n' roll topped the '80s British charts for five weeks and sold over 800,000 units. Unfortunately, Jackie Wilson had died three years earlier, on January 21, 1984. Even more sadly, he had lingered in a semi-coma since September 29, 1975, when he suffered a massive coronary while performing at The Latin Casino in Cherry Hill, New Jersey.

Jackie Wilson was born and raised in the Detroit suburb of Highland Park. He absorbed his initial musical training as a member of The Ever Ready Gospel Singers. He auditioned unsuccessfully for a Johnny Otis talent search in Detroit's Paradise Theatre and finally achieved his first recording hits during the early '50s as the lead singer for Billy Ward's Dominoes. His signature tunes with this group were "Rags To Riches" and "St. Therese Of The Roses". Jackie Wilson's big break as an independent artist came in 1956 when Al Green, the owner of The Flame Show Bar, became his manager. He introduced the young singer to a pair of aspiring songwriters - Tyran Carlo (a.k.aRoquel "Billy" Davis) and Berry Gordy, Jr.. When these two composers crafted "Reet Petite" for their 22-year-old protégé, a Detroit superstar was born. The Carlo/Gordy composing team continued to fuel the Jackie Wilson repertoire with tunes like "To Be Loved", "We Have Love", "Lonely Teardrops", "That's Why (I Love you So)", and "I'll Be Satisfied". Wilson went on to achieve a successful recording career that featured 62 Billboard pop hits. Songwriter Berry Gordy, Jr. invested his new-found composing royalties in a new Michigan business venture. He launched Motown Records.

YOU BETTER KNOW IT and NYC, 1961-1966 explore the initial decade of Jackie Wilson's recording activities. The single-disc Jasmine compilation begins with the six noteworthy Carlo-Gordy compositions that were released between 1957 and 1959. It ends with three less impressive numbers - "Hearts", "I Just Can't Help It", and "Forever And A Day" - that were released in 1962. YOU BETTER KNOW IT contains a total of 29 tunes. Highlights include "Doggin' Around", "Night", "A Woman A Love A Friend", and

"I'm Comin' Back To You". The Ace anthology is much less predictable and in some ways even more rewarding. NYC, 1961-1966 delves more deeply into Wilson's post-Detroit studio work under the directing/arranging/producing leadership of Dick Jacobs, Nat Tarnopol (Jackie's new manager), Alan Lorber, Gil Askey, and Eddie Singleton. With the exceptions of "Baby Workout" from 1963 and "(Your Love Keeps Lifting Me) Higher and Higher" in 1967, Jackie Wilson's greatest pop hits were behind him. But these stimulating New York producers coaxed a variety of fascinating performances on recently composed, highly orchestrated, and musically diverse material. NYC, 1961-1966 delivers 48 songs on two discs. Jackie Wilson performs lively duets with LaVern Baker ("Think Twice") and Linda Hopkins ("Shake A Hand"); he rocks out on "The New Breed", "Twistin' And Shoutin' (Doing The Monkey)", and "Shake! Shake! Shake!"; and he scorches the studio with "No Pity (In The Naked City)" and "Lonely Life". Rob Hughes provides amazingly detailed liner notes outlining the personnel and the production plans behind each anthologized recording.

Jackie Wilson is often categorized as a vocal bridge between '50s R&B and '60s soul music. Undeniably, his gospel roots and black group harmony experiences provided important foundations for his future forays into new audio territory being explored by Jerry Butler, Sam Cooke, and Curtis Mayfield. But Jackie Wilson was never the growling, screaming equivalent of soul giants James Brown, Otis Redding, or Wilson Pickett. His brilliance as a song interpreter is more appropriately linked to the techniques of Al Jolson and Mario Lanza. Audience pleasing (and teasing) and operatic vocalizing were Jackie Wilson's primary talents. On stage, he was peerless. He was a dancer and a showman unmatched by any of his black or white contemporaries. YOU BETTER KNOW IT and NYC, 1961-1966 accurately capture the audio portion of Jackie Wilson's artistic persona. Unfortunately, the brilliant dynamism of his live performances ended tragically - exactly 40 years prior to the release of these two CD tributes.

(This commentary was originally published as B. Lee Cooper. "Review of YOU BETTER KNOW IT: THE U.S. AND U.K. CHART HITS, 1957-1962 by Jackie Wilson and JACKIE WILSON AND NYC, 1961-1966 by Jackie Wilson," POPULAR MUSIC AND SOCIETY, 39:5 (December 2016): 590-591.)

KEY INFLUENCES IN MUSIC ANALYSIS

Roy Brown

LARRY BIRNBAUM

BEFORE ELVIS: THE PREHISTORY OF ROCK 'N' ROLL
Larry Birnbaum
Lanham, Maryland: Scarecrow Press, 2013
ISBN 987-0-8108-8638-4
463pp.   (hb) $85.00

In some ways, Larry Birnbaum seems like an unlikely candidate to explore the roots of rock 'n' roll. This prolific journalist has reviewed classical music and jazz performances for STEREOPHILE and DOWN BEAT; he has served as editor for the world-music and new-music magazines GLOBAL RHYTHM and EAR; he has hosted the world-music radio program "New York International"; and he won the 1988 ASCAP-Deems Taylor Award for a NEW YORK TIMES article on polka music. However, these non-rocking credentials are balanced against Birnbaum's Chicago upbringing, where he encountered large doses of blues, country, R&B, rock 'n' roll, and soul music. In his "Introduction" to BEFORE ELVIS, the author details his long-term curiosity about the origins of rock 'n' roll. For Birnbaum, too many previous studies have depicted rock 'n' roll as an idiosyncratic genie that was miraculously released from upon an unknowing American public in the mid-1950s by raucous rascals like Little Richard, Chuck Berry, and Elvis Presley. This strange and powerful music, with no lyrical legacies, no rhythmic roots, and no performance models, apparently had burst upon the scene out of nowhere. But Birnbaum begs to differ. While he specifically praises two investigations of post-World War II music by Charlie Gillett and Nick Tosches, the author is generally unimpressed by most other studies that greet the dawning of Bo Diddley, Bill Haley and His Comets, and Carl Perkins as unique events. It is undeniable that Birnbaum is a wily, thorough researcher and a music fan broadly familiar with early 20th century recordings. Beyond music, though, he is also a thoughtful and critical reader of not only Gillett and Tosches, but also of the most important analysts of early American music - Tim Brooks, John Broven, Norm Cohen, Rick Coleman, Jim Dawson, Colin Escott, Peter Guralnick, Jeff Hannusch, George Lipsitz, Robert Palmer, Robert Pruter, and Arnold Shaw. Referencing works by this regal clan of music mavens, Birnbaum cuts through a jungle of "lost" musical resources and "little known" performing personnel to uncover previously hidden audio trails. In the five decades before Elvis entered Sam Phillips' Memphis Recording Service studio, rock's roots were sprouting, growing, and thriving. Birnbaum's lengthy tale of this prehistory of rock 'n' roll is a research masterpiece.

BEFORE ELVIS is a complex narrative of American popular music development via cultural interchanges, rhythmic borrowing, lyric stealing, and continuous commercial competition. These activities occurred against a historical backdrop of personal anxiety and national uncertainty. Singers, songwriters, and recording industry personnel faced regional issues of racism, sexism, poverty, and unemployment along with nationwide problems of international warfare, Prohibition, and The Great Depression. Recorded music became an escape for performers and listeners alike. Recordings were also a potential source of profit and fame for singers and instrumentalists. From New York City to Memphis, from Kansas City to Chicago, and from New Orleans to Los Angeles, blues singers, jug bands, jazz artists, chitlin circuit belters, minstrel show performers, vaudeville troupes, swing bands, and folk musicians plied their trades with varying levels of success. Persistence often trumped talent in terms of surviving in the music world. During the Jazz Age and the Swing Era, Tin Pan Alley composers pumped out majestic melodies while unknown pianists bopped their boogies in countless barrelhouses and brothels. Numerous black singers and country artists toiled in the shadows of more famous recording stars like The Andrews Sisters, Cab Calloway, Bing Crosby, Louis Jordan, Glenn Miller, Jo Stafford, Paul Whiteman, and Bob Wills. Yet this cacophony of lowdown, upbeat, crooned, rhythmic, and pop sounds became the sonic sinews of rock 'n' roll.

While Birnbaum acknowledges that easy answers persist (i.e., "...rock 'n' roll is unquestionably an African American invention"), he plunges deeply into the integrated musical pools of jazz, swing, country, and even hokum songs to seek a more comprehensive understanding of rock's roots. The revelations by Birnbaum are plentiful and forceful. His audio evidence is staggering. He examines country yodeling, ragtime rhythms, jive talk, coon songs, and the rampant practice of cover recording (with or without copyright acknowledgements) for examples of the ways that musical patterns were diffused among various listening audiences. In the end, Birnbaum constructs many, many historic bridges to the rock 'n' roll mainland. They include emotive white singers like Ella Mae Morse and Johnnie Ray, comic black performers like Bull Moose Jackson and Louis Jordan, chameleon white-to-black composers like Johnny Otis and Jerry Leiber & Mike Stoller, black doo wop teams like The Orioles and The Ravens, R&B giants like Roy Brown and Wynonie Harris, and numerous early manifestations of Bill Haley's country rock. Despite these years of historical build-up, though, Birnbaum reports that early rock 'n' roll was short-lived compared to its harder rock successor of the '60s, '70s, and beyond. In fact, Birnbaum concludes that the rampant stylistic diversity of rock 'n' roll (ballads, instrumentals, novelty numbers, group harmony tunes, dance crazes, and so on), the public and political backlash to the emergent teenage music and it's howling disc jockeys (Alan Freed and The Payola Hearings), the passing of key recording figures (Buddy Holly, Eddie Cochran, Big Bopper, Ritchie Valens), and the growing corporate control over record production and popular music imagery ("American Bandstand") usurped the dynamism, creativity, and power of the rebellious new sounds. Nevertheless, the author's final observation remains positive. He writes,

> Rock 'n' roll is quintessentially American music, drawing on a wider variety of sources than has been previously acknowledged - not only blues, country, and pop but [also] jazz, hokum, boogie-woogie, mambo, calypso, and more. Besides absorbing external influences - everything from Mexican folk music to grand opera - rock possesses an intrinsic richness born of its diverse formative elements. The rediscovery of these constituents may enhance how rock 'n' roll is perceived and perhaps even how it will evolve in years to come. Much of this music remains to be explored - for example, the mingling of jazz and blues during the swing era, which laid the groundwork for rhythm-and-blues... (p. 380)

There is little to criticize about Larry Birnbaum's extensive, intriguing, elegantly argued presentation. He is particularly convincing as well as enlightening when asserting that as far back as the 1920s that hokum tunes, piano boogies, and jazz-band arrangements offered hints of what would emerge as rock 'n' roll three decades later. Only two things seem strange about the BEFORE ELVIS interpretation. First, the author seems reluctant to trace the continuing lineage of early rock 'n' roll styling from the still-living triumvirate of Chuck Berry, Jerry Lee Lewis, and Little Richard to John Lennon (The Beatles), Keith Richards (The Rolling Stones), John Fogerty (Creedence Clearwater Revival), Bob Seger and The Silver Bullet Band, Dave Alvin (The Blasters), and George Thorogood and The Destroyers. Second, one might have expected Birnbaum to incorporate the cultural insights of Lawrence Levine (from BLACK CULTURE AND BLACK CONSCIOUSNESS - 1977), the extensive genre research of Richard A. Peterson (most recently "Classification Of Culture" - 2008), and the rich history of recorded music styles documented by Phillip Ennis (THE SEVENTH STREAM - 1992). These minor critical observations notwithstanding, Birnbaum's package of ideas, facts, and references is practically flawless. This volume will not end the debates about either the first rock record or the musical roots of rock 'n' roll. However, it will substantially broaden and deepen all future arguments on these subjects.

(This commentary was originally published as B. Lee Cooper. "Review of BEFORE ELVIS: THE PREHISTORY OF ROCK 'N' ROLL by Larry Birnbaum," ROCK MUSIC STUDIES, 1:1 (February 2014): 97-99.)

Ken Burns

KEN BURNS

COUNTRY MUSIC - A FILM BY KEN BURNS: THE SOUNDTRACK
Various Artists
5 CDs, Legacy/Sony/Universal Music LC02361-19075934122, 2019

Documentary filmmaker Ken Burns assembled 16 hours of personal interviews, celebrity photographs, stage performance shots, and cuts from sound recordings to create his enthralling PBS special, COUNTRY MUSIC. It aired in eight episodes during September 2019. This noteworthy production traced the development of recorded country music from studios in Bristol and Nashville, from stages in Austin and Bakersfield, and from various other performing locales. Burns' 70-year, genre-defining journey begins with The Carter Family, Jimmie Rodgers, Uncle Dave Macon, Roy Acuff, and Gene Autry. Next he meanders through commercial music crafted by Bill Monroe, Bob Wills, Hank Williams, Johnny Cash, Loretta Lynn, and Tammy Wynette. This marathon of country classics concludes with the late-20th century sounds of Merle Haggard, Waylon Jennings, Dolly Parton, George Jones, Emmylou Harris, Willie Nelson, and Reba McEntire. During this extended musical salute, numerous songwriters are acknowledged, several prolific pickers are praised, and many clips featuring classic country performances are sampled.

Dayton Duncan's script for Ken Burns' COUNTRY MUSIC is abundant with vignettes depicting rags-to-riches treks by young singers, ingenious orchestral designs by Nashville record production wizards Chet Atkins and Owen Bradley, and discoveries of child music prodigies playing guitars, fiddles, and mandolins. Duncan also highlights the relentless marketing of country music. This occurred via radio stations like WLS (Chicago) and WSM (Nashville), through popular concerts at Ryman Auditorium in Nashville and the Louisiana Hayride in Shreveport, and over television programs like "Hee Haw" and "The Johnny Cash Show." Burns and Duncan seem especially fascinated with the deaths of country stars, both accidental as in the cases of Hank Williams and Patsy Cline, or very late in life like George Jones, Bill Monroe, and Johnny Cash.

Regrettably, the extensive soundtrack for COUNTRY MUSIC adheres too narrowly to the dramatic perspective of the film's script. Although Burns was reportedly assisted by knowledgeable music historians such as Bill Malone and Colin Escott, the audio material selected for the 5-disc soundtrack is far too restricted. The soundtrack seems to follow a path of orthodoxy in respect to traditional artists and commonly accepted country songs. This quest for authenticity and purity minimalizes or excludes many artists who deserve credit for country music's nationwide growth. For example, while Minnie Pearl, Roy Clark, and Roger Miller are identified in the film as humorous stars, more prolific and outrageous country comedians like Homer & Jethro, Sheb Wooley (a.k.a. Ben Colder), and Ray Stevens are totally ignored. So are key country-oriented recording and television stars like Glen Campbell and Tennessee Ernie Ford. It is also unconscionable that the lengthy and influential careers of The Everly Brothers and

Marty Robbins are limited to just two songs - "Bye Bye Love" and "El Paso" - within the *Country Music* soundtrack. Just as shocking are the total lack of recordings by Bobby Bare, Sonny James, Kenny Rogers, and Conway Twitty. Likewise, rockabilly rebels like Elvis Presley, Carl Perkins, and Jerry Lee Lewis are absent from the soundtrack. The list continues with no representation for Brooks & Dunn, Garth Brooks, The Eagles, or Linda Ronstadt. Surely a 5-disc, 105-song anthology of 20th century country music should encompass more than a repetition of songs by Hank, Reba, Dolly, and Waylon. Perhaps fewer versions of "Mule Skinner Blues" (one each by Jimmie Rodgers, Bill Monroe, The Maddox Brothers and Rose, and Dolly Parton) and "Will The Circle Be Unbroken" (one by The Carter Family and two by The Nitty Gritty Dirt Band) would have provided space for Conway, Elvis, Jerry Lee, and Linda. Or maybe the multiple tunes by Jimmie Rodgers (4), Hank Williams (5), Johnny Cash (5), and even Rosanne Cash (3) could have been reduced to foster broader artist representation.

Ken Burns and Dayton Duncan are highly attentive to topical country tunes. Thematically, country recordings are distinctive for producing lyrics about trains, prisons, religion, and romantic regret. The 5-disc COUNTRY MUSIC soundtrack is replete with songs that address these subjects. Illustrations include "Wabash Cannon Ball,""In the Jailhouse Now,""Folsom Prison Blues,""I Saw the Light,""Crazy," and "I Fall to Pieces." However, several other equally important country song topics are overlooked. For example, lyrical laments about smoking, drinking, and carousing were central to blue-collar jukebox music played in Kentucky, Tennessee, and Texas. Yet there is no representation of "Smoke! Smoke! Smoke! (That Cigarette)" by Tex Williams, "Cigarettes and Whiskey and Wild, Wild Women" by The Sons of The Pioneers, or "Another Puff" by Jerry Reed. Similarly, car songs have invariably impressed country music audiences. These folks appreciated the necessity for moonshiners to outrun revenuers during the '20s, '30s, and '40s, the thrills of watching hot rod racing a few decades later, and the excitement generated around NASCAR ovals even today. Yet Burns' COUNTRY MUSIC soundtrack makes no reference to "Hot Rod Race" by Jimmy Dolan, "Hot Rod Lincoln" by Charlie Ryan, or "The Ballad of Thunder Road" by Robert Mitchum. Of course, alcohol abuse and drug addiction undermined both the family lives and the professional careers of many successful country recording artists during the past century. Burns acknowledges this sad reality throughout his film. Yet the extended soundtrack addresses these issues with only two tunes - "Mountain Dew" and "Whiskey River." Burns should have provided additional examples like "The Beer Drinkin' Song" by Mac Davis, "Chug-a-Lug" by Roger Miller, "D.O.A. (Drunk on Arrival)" by Johnny Paycheck, "Drinking Tequila" by Jim Reeves, or "White Lightning" by George Jones.

This $55.00 COUNTRY MUSIC soundtrack of 105 songs contains selected illustrations of bluegrass, cowboy, folk, gospel, Nashville pop, and Bakersfield recordings. It parallels the documentary film's chronology in respect to the song presentations. But there is also a 2-disc, 41-song version of Burns' COUNTRY MUSIC soundtrack that is available for $21.00. Forty country performers are represented on this abbreviated collection. It seems peculiar that the expanded 5-disc anthology doubles down on the narrow artistic representation provided within the smaller 2-disc set. Instead of broadening the range of country songs, vocal styles, and singers, Ken Burns chose to re-emphasize the music from a very limited group of performers. No Alabama or Webb Pierce. No "Elvira" or "He'll Have to Go." No Don Gibson or Hank Snow. No "The Gambler" or "King of the Road." No Wanda Jackson or Skeeter Davis.

While the COUNTRY MUSIC film is informative and the 2-disc soundtrack offers a reasonable representation of the film's artistry, the huge 95-tune, 5-disc soundtrack is a major disappointment. The creative, diverse country music tale championed throughout eight two-hour episodes is inadequately replicated within the expanded soundtrack. For the sake of comparison, check out COUNTRY: THE AMERICAN TRADITION (Sony Music, 1999) for a much more informative and well-represented 2-disc overview of 20th century country singers. The performers anthologized range from Fiddlin' John Carson, Ted Daffan, and Al Dexter to The Charlie Daniels Band, Mary Chapin Carpenter, and The Dixie Chicks. Sadly, none of these artists appear on either of Burns' compilations.

(This commentary was originally published as B. Lee Cooper. "Review of COUNTRY MUSIC - A FILM: THE SOUNDTRACK by Various Artists," POPULAR MUSIC AND SOCIETY, 43:4 (October 2020): 465-467.)

Mark Duffett

MARK DUFFETT

COUNTING DOWN ELVIS: HIS 100 FINEST SONGS
Mark Duffett
Lanham, Maryland: Rowman and Littlefield, 2018.
ISBN 9781442248045
Hb $39.95   293pp.

Elvis Presley has been dead since 1977. Yet he continues to attract the attention of biographers, film critics, music journalists, celebrity tabloid writers, and die-hard Elvis fans. Auburn University scholar George Plasketes detailed this dynamic afterlife phenomenon in IMAGES OF ELVIS PRESLEY IN AMERICAN CULTURE, 1977-1997. SIMILARLY, THE PRINTED ELVIS by Steven Opdyke confirmed that Elvis' demise triggered an avalanche of Presley-related books. Curation of the vast studio and concert audio output by the King of Rock 'N' Roll has been scrupulously assembled by Ernst Jorgensen. His detailed ELVIS PRESLEY - A LIFE IN MUSIC: THE COMPLETE RECORDING SESSIONS documents everything sung and circulated by The King. Finally, music historian Peter Guralnick, in LAST TRAIN TO MEMPHIS and CARELESS LOVE, has produced the most detailed, well-documented biography of Elvis. Despite this mountain of 20th century research and writing, along with the release of innumerable CDs and box sets, 21st century Elvis fans hunger for more. No other celebrity icons, including Johnny Carson, James Dean, Marilyn Monroe, or Hank Williams, continue to elicit such ongoing interest and adoration.

COUNTING DOWN ELVIS: HIS 100 FINEST SONGS is a feast for fans. Mark Duffett is keenly aware of the difference between the relatively objective reception of readers toward critical appraisals of newly released audio material by a contemporary artist and the pre-heated zeal among established fans in regard to judgments about beloved historic recordings by an established celebrity. After all, he is the author of the acclaimed analysis, UNDERSTANDING FANDOM. As a fan himself, though, he simultaneously manifests critical research perspectives and ingrained Elvis loyalties during his thoughtful assessment of the recorded treasury of Elvis Aaron Presley. Full disclosure warrants that I admit my personal biases concerning both the author and the subject of COUNTING DOWN ELVIS. First, I admire Duffett's scholarly explorations into media influences upon popular culture and his skill at defining the motives and behaviors of super-charged pop culture consumers. Yes, I'm predisposed to respect this author. Second, I have been a record-buying fan of The King of Rock 'N' Roll since 1956. I secured a Sun-label 45 r.p.m. copy of "Mystery Train" as a teenager; I purchased the entire 16-volume Time-Life series "The Elvis Presley Collection" as an adult; and I possess more box sets of Presley releases than anyone needs. Yes, I'm particularly fond of Elvis, too. Despite these predispositions, though, I am capable of offering a balanced and fair commentary on this new volume.

COUNTING DOWN ELVIS is part of an ongoing Rowman and Littlefield music series. Previous texts devoted to the recordings of The Beatles, Bob Dylan, The Rolling

Stones, and Bruce Springsteen are already in circulation. This series challenges readers to evaluate their own "Top 100" songs with respect to the selections of authors who are knowledgeable music experts. Mark Duffett is a perfect choice to conduct this reflective exercise with respect to Elvis Presley. Duffett is incredibly well-informed concerning both recording sessions and concert venues. He is also adept at analyzing the distinctions between multiple versions of particular songs. The total Elvis soundscape is his research playground. Better still, Duffett is attuned to the tensions between Elvis' desire to please his fans and those record industry personnel who wished to manipulate and control his song selections. There is no other song-by-song evaluation of Elvis material that seeks to balance commercial success against aesthetic creativity and historic importance. The documentation throughout this volume is massive. The author's attention to detail is impressive. To some, the idea of ranking 100 songs by Elvis Presley may seem like a fool's errand. But in the hands of a gifted analyst like Duffett, the song after song staircase to Presley audio heaven is a valuable learning experience.

Mark Duffett has assembled 100 thoughtful, fact-filled essays in support of his judgments concerning the finest Elvis recordings. No one will agree with all of his listings. But everyone should appreciate his courageous effort to rank this delightful array of tunes. Duffett lionizes expected songs like "Heartbreak Hotel" (#4), "Hound Dog" (#10), and "That's All Right" (#13). He also acknowledges the special meaning of less familiar hits such as "Polk Salad Annie" (#8), "The Wonder of You" (#16), and "(You're So Square) Baby I Don't Care" (#26). He includes several motion picture soundtrack numbers like "Jailhouse Rock" (#7), "King Creole" (#15), and "Bossa Nova Baby" (#39). Finally, he highlights television performances and stage presentations such as "An American Trilogy" (#2), "Tiger Man" (#18), and "I'll Remember You" (#21). Duffett has special enthusiasm for Elvis' most theatrical, operatic, and faith-oriented recordings. The author lauds The King's versions of "If I Can Dream" (#1), "Suspicious Minds" (#3), "Bridge Over Troubled Water" (#5), and "How Great Thou Art" (#9) as extremely important vocal performances. At the far end of this ranking spectrum, Duffett concludes his countdown with "You Don't Have to Say You Love Me" (#98), "Early Mornin' Rain" (#99), and "Reconsider Baby" (#100). As a long-time Elvis fan, I was surprised by the omissions of "Love Me", "Return To Sender", "That's When Your Heartaches Begin", and "Too Much". But why be quarrelsome?

Beyond the issues of signature songs and superior performances, Mark Duffett weaves an insightful, provocative biographical tale of adulation and isolation, confidence and doubt, monetary wealth and spiritual struggle, and on-stage highs followed by dressing room lows. This is an oral history supplemented with song selections, lyrical interpretations, and vocal pyrotechnics. Duffett manifests an almost mystical understanding of the performer's charisma and his fans' receptivity. Elvis was ebullient when he was entertaining. Duffett depicts this boundless joy by crafting vignettes about studio interactions and stage manipulations. While the author treads carefully in categorizing the Elvis sonography, he is clearly in awe of The King's emotional translations, daring adaptations, and idiosyncratic modifications that frequently turn good music into great art.

Simultaneously, the adoring Elvis audiences are spellbound by his stage persona that provides sexual teasing, sartorial splendor, intimate gestures, violent shaking (and rattling and rolling), and melodramatic renderings of song after song. For his fans, Elvis became Adonis, Caruso, Brando, Sinatra, as well as the sweet Southern boy next door. This imagery persisted on LPs, in feature films, and on concert stages. The King unleashed his own stylish interpretations of Roy Hamilton, Clyde McPhatter, and Jackie Wilson. He breathed life into the lyrics of Jerry Leiber & Mike Stoller, Otis Blackwell, and Doc Pomus & Mort Shuman. And the catalyst for the most elegant, most explosive Elvis evenings was always his audience. Sometimes the Elvis observers were just talented session men like Bill Black, James Burton, Floyd Cramer, or Scotty Moore. That's how the Sun and RCA studio performances achieved vitality and verve. But more often it was the insistent urging of screaming fans that elevated The King to mount his sonic throne. They loved Elvis. And he responded in kind. Duffett captures this mutual audio bliss in his thoughtful song narratives.

COUNTING DOWN ELVIS is a fascinating reminder of the 20th century obsession with a man and his music. The King of Rock 'N' Roll was a multi-faceted being, a celebrity with immense vocal talent and seemingly boundless energy and sex appeal. He was somewhat reigned in and controlled by the commercial calculations and machinations of Col. Tom Parker, RCA Victor's executives, and the Hill and Range publishing staff. But throughout his career he retained the vocalizing genius that defied caging or conforming. Duffett doesn't sugarcoat the challenges that Elvis encountered, both personally and professionally. But the author's keen sense of stardom allows him to depict the ritual dance of celebrity brilliance and crowd appreciation. For 21st century readers, meeting Elvis via Duffett's prose is a scintillating treat.

(This commentary was originally published as B. Lee Cooper. "Review of COUNTING DOWN ELVIS: HIS 100 FINEST SONGS by Mark Duffett," ROCK MUSIC STUDIES, 6:3 (October 2019): 173-275.)

Peter Guralnick

PETER GURALNICK

LOOKING TO GET LOST: ADVENTURES IN MUSIC AND WRITING
Peter Guralnick
Boston: Little, Brown and Company, 2020
ISBN 978-0316-41262-9
554 pp   Hb $39.95

Boston-born Peter Guralnick is a persistent, prolific writer. His lifetime of literary zeal is driven by personal determination, professional creative writing training, and an intense love of 20th century popular music. He has succeeded as a short story craftsman, a music critic and journalist, a biographer, a liner notes scribe, a screenwriter and documentarian, a novelist, a bibliographer, and, most recently, an autobiographer. LOOKING TO GET LOST: ADVENTURES IN MUSIC AND WRITING is an author's memoir disguised as a collection of biographical sketches. Along his publishing pathway, Guralnick has been publicly applauded for productivity, diversity in topics, and high quality research. Specifically, he won critical praise and literary prizes for biographies on Elvis Presley (LAST TRAIN TO MEMPHIS and CARELESS LOVE), Sam Cooke (DREAM BOOGIE), and Sam Phillips (THE MAN WHO INVENTED ROCK 'N' ROLL). He also secured several Grammy nominations and two awards for album liner notes and scripts for a documentary on Sam Cooke. Finally, he was inducted into The Blues Hall of Fame for his magnificent enthnomusicological study, SWEET SOUL MUSIC, and for his blues documentary consultation with Martin Scorsese. During the past decade Guralnick has taught graduate-level creative writing classes at Vanderbilt University and assembled essays for his "greatest literary hits" release, LOOKING TO GET LOST.

This book salutes lives committed to music. Artists abound. But the chronicler himself lurks close beside them, diligently documenting and assessing their varying sources of musical distinctiveness. According to Peter Guralnick, all successful musicians surrender to "an inextinguishable drive for self-expression" and are lifted "on the wings of imagination" to create and perform new songs. The author considers American popular music to be unique, although its key elements are hidden in plain sight. The art and genius among musicians is diverse and ever-changing. It exists to be shared with audiences and fellow performers - and to be freely borrowed, adapted, and advanced for future generations. The rhythmic melting pot of America's recorded music allows Ray Charles and Solomon Burke to borrow and personalize songs originated by Hank Williams and John Fogerty. It permits bluegrass giant Bill Monroe to openly acknowledge black bluesman Arnold Schultz as a formative influence. It also lets Peter Guralnick, sans technical musical training, to publicize his own experiences within the "gloriously undifferentiated reality" of popular music as exhibited by Muddy Waters, Chuck Berry, Mississippi John Hurt, and Bo Diddley.

Initially, Guralnick benefitted personally and professionally from earlier fan research on American blues in England and the later emergence of the rock press within the United

States. The sixties successes of fanzines like CRAWDADDY and ROLLING STONE signaled the birth of a new journalistic field. Driven by his belief in "the intrinsic worth of American vernacular culture," the young Boston writer scribbled his way toward greatness. Like many of his journalistic cronies (Lester Bangs, Robert Christgau, Jeff Hannusch, Michael Lydon, Bill Millar, Robert Palmer, and Nick Tosches) and other strong-willed, music-centered writers (John Broven, Colin Escott, Charlie Gillett, and Greil Marcus), Peter Guralnick produced exhortatory essays concerning blues, country, R&B, rock, and soul music. Clearly, he functioned as a cultural historian. Over the years, Guralnick has matured, but not mellowed. He has altered his own opinions about a few specific artists, but never abandoned his trust in their fundamental artistic worth. His commitment to storytelling and truthful analysis still burns brightly. And his admiration for the sonic legends of 20th century recorded music is undiminished.

LOOKING TO GET LOST is an intellectual exercise in research updating and memory checking. The challenge for 77-year-old Peter Guralnick is to present accurate, authentic, exciting, factual, and imaginative profiles of several meritorious musicians. Whether plumbing the myths and majesty of bluesmen Robert Johnson and Skip James or addressing the lyrical gifts of country music stars Johnny Cash and Tammy Wynette, Guralnick is clear-eyed and thoughtful in detailing his perspectives. Unfortunately, he deviates briefly from sonic studies into literary realms when he explores novelists Henry Green and Lee Smith. But even such off-the-road excursions are unexpectedly enjoyable. The remainder of LOOKING TO GET LOST is dedicated to some relatively obscure performers (Dick Curless, Lonnie Mack, Delbert McClinton, and Joe Tex), four mid-century songwriting giants (Willie Dixon, Jerry Leiber & Mike Stoller, and Doc Pomus), a few highly influential recording legends (Chuck Berry, Ray Charles, Eric Clapton, Merle Haggard, and Jerry Lee Lewis), some personal favorites (Solomon Burke, Bill Monroe, and Howlin' Wolf), and three unanticipated characters (Elvis Costello, Col. Tom Parker, and Allen Toussaint). All commentaries are thorough, well-researched, respectful, sensitive, and insightful. After all, this profiler himself is a confident, experienced, reflective, passionate fan of all things musical.

One might wish to quarrel with Guralnick about his boundless fascination over Dick Curless, or his forgiving attitude toward Elvis Presley's self-serving personal manager, or his overly detailed depiction of the unlikely creation of Malaco Records. That's just minor carping, though. It is impossible to overstate the diligence and breath of Guralnick's research into each subject (See "A Fan's Notes," pp. 497-527). LOOKING TO GET LOST is an open admission of musical adultery. Like the incomparable jazz great Duke Ellington, the boyish Boston author has surrendered willingly and joyfully to a fascinating rhythmic mistress. For Guralnick, though, writing about music is a passion not a sin; truth-telling about performers is an honor not a risk of offending social norms; and the musicians themselves are imperfect vessels who magically achieve perfection in phrasing, tone, word choice, beat, and amplification. Recorded music repeatedly generates pleasure, myth, history, and self-knowledge. Peter Guralnick seeks to uncover the human sources behind such audio prestidigitation.

DAVID HAJDU

LOVE FOR SALE: POP MUSIC IN AMERICA
David Hajdu
New York: Farrar, Straus, and Giroux, 2016

This volume is an intriguing rumination on the importance of popular music. Columbia University professor David Hajdu choreographs three dynamic elements that define musical value. These include his personal interactions with pop tunes; his readers' likely encounters with various local and regional soundscapes; and American society's evolution related to music delivery changes and shifts in public audio tastes. While LOVE FOR SALE is ostensibly a chronological narrative, Hajdu often projects the impacts of new rhythmic patterns or novel audio technology forward through several decades. Similarly, he frequently offers retrospective evidence concerning the historic roots of contemporary musical styles or performers' stage behaviors. In this skillful writer's hands, the text is rich and informative, direct and logical. The extensive documentation supporting Hajdu's commentary is detailed in a lengthy "Notes" section (pp. 245-290). Footnotes do not clutter the sterling prose that traces the extended lives of popular songs from 19th century sheet music to 21st century digital circulation via Spotify.

The autobiographical elements in LOVE FOR SALE flow through three generations of the author's extended family. Hajdu himself asserts, "My conception of music as a writer is inextricable from my experience of music as a person." (p. 7) He recounts tales of his mother introducing him to the informative labels of used jukebox discs, his siblings sharing their favorite music with him while often criticizing his peculiar audio choices, and his realization that the transistor radio was a gateway to a wider musical universe. Karen Oberlin, the author's vocalist wife, and Nate, his youngest son, also assume cameo roles throughout the text. She was a punk rocker who became a jazz singer. But her familial roots included generations of vaudevillians, light opera performers, and Tanglewood musicians. The pre-teen Nate, surrounded by literary ethnomusicology and virtuoso vocalizing, persists in assembling Apple Music playlists that feature recordings by Jeremih, Natalie La Rose, and Kid Ink. The Hajdu household is obviously a jumble of tastes, with music from LPs, CDs, and earbuds vibrating from room to room. Music is very, very important in their Manhattan manor.

David Hajdu challenges his readers to reflect upon their own idiosyncratic journeys through music by tracing various potential routes. For instance, he encourages readers to consider their reasons for selecting past and present musical heroes, possibly ranging from Al Jolson and Frank Sinatra to Blondie and Rihanna. He also ponders the importance of musicians who are singer-songwriters vs. those who are non-composing interpreters and song stylists. Does the reader define "authenticity" differently when listening to Bruce Springsteen and Carole King rather than Tony Bennett or Elvis Presley? Hajdu goes on to suggest that individual musical taste is unconsciously yet accurately defined when compiling self-mixed audio tapes or purchasing digitized tunes for personal playlists. One's musical identity, the author speculates, can also be revealed via public comments about favorite artists, songs, or genres. Readers may also elect to listen alone, of course. But most often they gather with like-minded folkies, blues enthusiasts, dance mavens, or punkers. Relationships, both fraternal and sexual, are often deepened by exchanging discs or playlists, by dancing or singing together, or by just following the lyrical advice of Marvin Gaye or Beyoncé. For the reader, musical choice is invariably intimate, relevant, and commercial. Similarly, ethnicity, self-definition, and experience are gathered and lived vicariously through pop recordings. Music, once again, is very important to most individuals.

Finally, David Hajdu addresses the value of music within American society. Clearly, he views music as a change agent as well as a reflection of other socio-political changes. Whether driven by greed and commerce (Tin Pan Alley composers and Brill Building songsmiths), technological advancements (78s, 45s, LPs, CDs, MTV, and so on), patriotism and dissent (World War I, World War II, and Vietnam), national recording heroes (Gene Autry, Roy Rogers, Louis Armstrong, and Ray Charles), or country-wide dance crazes (Fox trot, Charleston, Twist, and cybergrind), the nation's heights and depths are often chronicled via sound recordings. In somewhat hyperbolic style, Hajdu declares, "Popular music is part of the cultural feedback loop through which ideas emerge from all corners of society to be sorted, mixed, enhanced, enlarged, and reintroduced as new ideas." (p. 239) This cycle of renewal underlies the author's belief in social vitality. However, not all audio changes are beneficial. Hajdu seems especially wary, for example, of the new Auto-Tune technology that "de-humanizes" contemporary recording practices by making studio vocalizing...absolutely perfect. He warns that the absolutist musical ideas of Karlheinz Stockhausen and John Cage may be triumphing over the more personalized, energetic, and totally extravagant audio musings of Louis Jordan and Little Richard. The battle for sound's soul persists today and tomorrow. Despite this philosophical carping, though, Hajdu's text unambiguously demonstrates that American society has benefitted enormously from musical change.

LOVE FOR SALE is more than musical history, more than autobiography, and much more than the marriage of instrumental/vocal sound to commerce/technology. This book is a coming-of-age allegory. It acknowledges the simultaneous teenage processes of intellectual awakening, sexual awakening, and musical awakening. David Hajdu shares his own unconventional journey from geeky record label analyst and failing high school band member to small-time concert critic and big-time journalist with THE NATION and NEW YORKER. Yet his message isn't self-congratulatory. He simply acknowledges that like him, most young people initially extend their perspectives through contact with pop music. Whether in church choirs or gospel singing groups, or through public school glee clubs or college pep bands, or through recordings of blues, country, folk, jazz, or hip hop performances, sharing musical experiences enhances maturing and growing. So does criticizing music, your own and recordings admired by others. The author raves, "The miracle of popular music, for me, is that so many songs provide the satisfaction and the surprises that they do." (p. 243) Thus, the excitement of coming-of-age with disco and punk in full flower, and then studying swing, big bands, jump blues, and rock 'n' roll, and finally watching his wife and young son expand their musical horizons has been an uplifting, gratifying experience for this 61-year-old literary scholar. Fortunately for us, Hajdu is upbeat and lyrical in charting this insightful narrative that captures his boundless joy about pop music. As in the life of jazz virtuoso Duke Ellington, music has proven to be a remarkably loving mistress for this professional critic.

(This commentary was originally published as B. Lee Cooper, "Review of LOVE FOR SALE: POP MUSIC IN AMERICA by David Hajdu," POPULAR MUSIC AND SOCIETY, 40:3 (July 2017): 363-364.)

John Lee Hooker

JACK HAMILTON

JUST AROUND MIDNIGHT: ROCK AND ROLL AND THE RACIAL IMAGINATION
Jack Hamilton
Cambridge, Massachusetts: Harvard University Press, 2016
ISBN 9780674416598
340pp.   Hb $29.95

What are the ideal qualifications for analyzing rock music history? Initially, a love of the genre and a breadth of knowledge concerning important songs, influential performers, and significant composers is required. Of course, many fans and most rock critics meet this general standard. Additionally, one ought to be musically adept and trained to assess the structures of songs as well as the impact of varying instrumental arrangements. Such skills are rare among fans and journalists alike. A third important qualification is historical perspective. This would include an understanding of general socio-economic circumstances and specific causation factors that helped generate the rise and expansion of rock. Here acquaintance with artistry, commerce, technology, communication, and fan psychology become essential. Similarly, knowledge of cross-generational rock criticism, both popular and academic, is mandatory. Finally, the ideal analyst of rock music must manifest curiosity. That is, rather than passively accepting repeated music-related myths, conventional wisdom, and standard interpretations, this person should actively assemble and analyze key facts, carefully study specific songs, and critically scan autobiographical and historical works. The skilled analyst would be able to filter multiple ideas and allow logic to determine new judgments and conclusions. The foremost commentators on rock, including gifted observers like John Broven, Simon Frith, Charlie Gillett, and Peter Guralnick, possess most of the aforementioned characteristics. So does the author of this book. Jack Hamilton, a Harvard graduate currently teaching American Studies at the University of Virginia, demonstrates superior analytical facilities in JUST AROUND MIDNIGHT: ROCK AND ROLL AND THE RACIAL IMAGINATION.

This book offers an intriguing, imaginative perspective on rock history. It is a remarkable literary achievement. Jack Hamilton vanquishes the erroneous notion that African-Americans had only a limited, secondary role in the creation and development of rock. The 1960's-based ideology that promoted white rock supremacy is, according to Hamilton, traceable to the convergence of several sources and thought patterns. First, folk mythology surrounding dead bluesmen as the "originators" of rock prompted the corollary idea that white performers were the legitimate "inheritors" and conservators of the blues/rock idiom. Despite ample evidence to the contrary illustrated by the live and lively performances of Albert King, Freddie King, Buddy Guy, and Muddy Waters during the '60s, white rockers claimed to rule. Hamilton exposes the literary collusion among East coast rock critics and ROLLING STONE magazine writers to justify and sustain the myth of African-American absence from '60s rock life. White writers from New York to San Francisco created clipped musical histories that manifested creeping omissions about the continuing influences of Chuck Berry, Bo

Diddley, Little Richard, and Ray Charles. Even the immense popularity and musical vitality of Berry Gordy's Motown Records throughout the '60s was deemed inauthentic and not genuinely black. This allegation ignored the distinctive artistic contributions and music chart dominance of Marvin Gaye, Barrett Strong, Smokey Robinson, and The Marvelettes, supported by the Funk Brothers, featuring James Jamerson. Motown's frequent interactions with The Beatles were also largely ignored by American journalists. Finally, Jimi Hendrix, who didn't fit the anti-black rocker narrative, was labeled "Superspade" and defined by rock critics as the exception that proved the rule. By 1970 no black artist fit the manufactured white rock image attributed to Bob Dylan, The Beatles, The Who, The Rolling Stones, and Creedence Clearwater Revival. Even loud and persistent protestations from Mick Jagger and Keith Richards that living sources of rock still resided at 2120 Michigan Avenue in Chicago were largely silenced in the journalistic whitewash.

While some elements of Jack Hamilton's white-over-black usurpation tale have previously surfaced in other scholarly works, his thoughtful and well-documented chapter-by-chapter vignettes create a strong case for re-calculating the trans-Atlantic, interracial intersections of '60s rock development. His book is structured into six sections. First, Hamilton contrasts the journalistic responses to two important, influential singer-songwriters - Sam Cooke and Bob Dylan. The unequal coverage that they received during the early '60s, with Dylan heralded and Cooke ignored, continued in subsequent journalistic reporting and in later biographical approaches as well. Second, the author highlights the frequent black-and-white trans-Atlantic musical exchanges that occurred between 1950 and 1964. He concludes that the term "British Invasion" is inaccurate. In fact, it is indicative of historical omissions concerning America's "invasion" of the U.K. via U.S. popular recordings between 1955 and 1963. Third, Hamilton examines multiple personal interactions among The Beatles and several Motown artists and concludes that mutual musical benefits were secured through these exchanges. Fourth, he addresses the unanticipated results of the "Who's got soul?" debate in the U.S. in respect to the performing careers of Aretha Franklin, Janis Joplin, and Dusty Springfield. The idea that women, whether black or white, could rock was just as difficult for journalists to rationalize as the concept of contemporary African-American rockers. Fifth, Hamilton introduces Jimi Hendrix as an unclassifiable music-producing figure and a dynamic rock music experimenter who felt trapped in the midst of warring ideologies over soul vs. rock and black vs. white. Finally, Hamilton concludes his book with an assessment of the joyfully black-influenced Rolling Stones. While this abbreviated outline fails to do justice to the complex historical and musicological investigations featured in JUST AROUND MIDNIGHT, it does acknowledge the sweep of Hamilton's interesting commentary.

Jack Hamilton is much more than a racial provocateur or rock revisionist. His thoroughly researched study upends traditional patterns of envisioning popular music as either black (R&B, soul, funk, and hip-hop) or white (pop, folk, and rock). Hamilton isn't simply colorblind. He appears to be totally committed to un-categorizing all music and substituting individual judgments about listening pleasure and sonic complexity for the current fleshtone-based audio segregation. As a musician himself, Hamilton applauds the trading of aesthetic ideas among races, genders, genres, and nationalities as both legitimate and inevitable. He also deems it healthy and creative. Throughout JUST AROUND MIDNIGHT the author also begs for a 21st-century reality check to acknowledge the initial contributions of African-Americans to rock 'n' roll (Wynonie Harris, Roy Brown, Little Richard, Joe Turner, and others) as well as the many black influences on British rock music (Chuck Berry, John Lee Hooker, Big Bill Broonzy, Little Walter, and others). The goal of this slim volume is to undermine several persistent myths that haunt the '60s and extend into the present. Hamilton seeks to promote deeper understanding about musical integration and to end racial/gender segregation within the rock pantheon. Only one thing could have improved this book. The editors at the Harvard University Press should have included a CD featuring illustrations of specific audio products that emerged from black-and-white musical interchanges over the past century. Even the book's author would have appreciated listening to recordings by Johnnie Ray, Taj Mahal, The Crests, Bonnie Raitt, Michael Bolton, Ella Mae Morse, Elvis Presley, Etta James, Angela Strehli, Sly and The Family Stone, Lou Ann Barton, Joe Bonamassa, Joe Cocker, and Gary Moore.

(This commentary was originally published as B. Lee Cooper. "Review of JUST AROUND MIDNIGHT: ROCK AND ROLL AND THE RACIAL IMAGINATION by Jack Hamilton," POPULAR MUSIC AND SOCIETY, 40:2 (May 2017): 239-240.)

Harry Belafonte

JAMES SULLIVAN

WHICH SIDE ARE YOU ON? 20TH CENTURY AMERICAN HISTORY IN 100 PROTEST SONGS
James Sullivan
New York: Oxford University Press, 2019
ISBN 9780190660307
Hb   242 pp. $29.95

The Reverend Martin Luther King, Jr. understood the role of music as an important crowd motivator. Raised in the black church, he experienced jubilee songs and gospel hymns within congregational settings. Later he was exposed to Negro freedom songs as well as inspirational popular music at rallies during the 1950s and 1960s. The civil rights movement rolled forward upon musical wheels. Dr. King cultivated the support of many inspiring vocalists, including Harry Belafonte, Sam Cooke, Mahalia Jackson, Odetta, and The Staples Singers. He also drew personal strength from the popular gospel groups of his day, like The Dixie Hummingbirds, The Soul Stirrers, and The Swan Silvertones. It is likely that he also reveled in the hit recordings of Bob Dylan, Nina Simone, and Curtis Mayfield as well. Dr. King's mission in life was captured in pop hits like "Blowin' in the Wind," "Keep on Pushin'," and "We're a Winner."

As a renowned orator, Dr. King often cited both Scripture and hymn lyrics to support his ideas concerning social justice. But in his famous April 1963 epistolary message "A Letter From A Birmingham Jail," the civil rights icon acknowledged the sad reality that many of his fellow Americans seemed unmoved by the power of "We Shall Overcome,""We Shall Not Be Moved," and similar lyrical calls for change. He bemoaned the cautious neutrality of those who whispered "Wait for the right time" in response to his pleas for immediate racial equality. He worried that white moderates seemed reluctant to actively participate in the cause of freedom. Why were they tone deaf? In essence, Dr. King was confounded by the inaction of persons who proclaimed themselves to be Christians, who lauded the principles of The Declaration of Independence each July 4th, and who could observe the malicious behavior of police toward freedom marchers across the South. It is this same search for civic heroism that motivated James Sullivan to write WHICH SIDE ARE YOU ON?. But the author's scope of concern reaches far beyond the '60s black civil rights struggle. He trumpets the call for action on behalf of climate change, environmental imbalance, and nuclear non-proliferation. He also champions the labor movement, the women's movement, and the gay liberation movement. This experienced, thoughtful, and committed reporter, a frequent contributor to both the SAN FRANCISCO CHRONICLE and THE BOSTON GLOBE, repeatedly poses the key question - Which side are *you* on?

While Martin Luther King, Jr. assumed that Biblical morality and democratic ideals were sufficient to stimulate civil rights activities, the author of WHICH SIDE ARE YOU ON? seems more skeptical about the will and the energy of American citizens to rise up for just causes. Nevertheless, James Sullivan systematically chronicles the history of protestors and their concerns, tracing their tactics and achievements via songs. The lens of protest music is invariably idealistic, caustic, and cataclysmic. Enemies are monstrous; challenges are enormous; battles are onerous; but the goals are glorious - and the victories are sometimes historic. Sullivan tells many lyrical tales. Songwriters and singers are tapped for their commentaries, both spoken and sung. Understandably, opinions vary. Joshua McCarter Simpson, an early 19th century anti-slave song composer, remarks, "You can sing what would be death to speak" (p. xiv). Meanwhile, contemporary artist Neil Young, speculating about the impact of his 1970 composition "Ohio," expressed appreciation for the opportunity to use a message tune to unify a generation and to give them a point of view (p. 119). But Texas songwriter James McMurtry was much more humble about the impact of his 2005 dystopian release "We Can't Make It Here." McMurtry declares that he's always more interested in storytelling than in manifestos (p. 185).

The mixed assessments from composers and vocalists is echoed in James Sullivan's uncertainty about the possibility of generating direct political action through protest music. The power of music, from Sullivan's perspective, is greatest among those already converted. That is, activists who are pursuing freedom of speech, justice for coal miners, and equality for women and minorities are easily motivated by supportive music. Solidarity, conviction, and courage are reinforced when like-minded individuals join voices in familiar protest tunes. But can complacency, apathy, unawareness, or even unknowing complicity be overcome by a powerful lyric or a rousing vocal broadside? Can reluctant minds be swayed? Can hardened hearts be softened? Can courage be summoned? Sullivan is a master of describing the details of oppression and suppression. He tracks assaults on factory workers, immigrant laborers, and black voting rights advocates. He highlights the musical responses to these wicked activities. And he skillfully summarizes the historical progress or frustrated failures experienced by each oppressed group. But the underlying message of his book remains - Which side are *you* on?

This volume is carefully conceived and brilliantly executed. Rather than dissecting just 100 protest songs, though, James Sullivan utilizes more than 300 titles to communicate his audio protest history. This musical story begins during the Revolutionary War era ("The Liberty Tree") and extends to the present decade ("Born This Way"). Sullivan crafts ten chapters that posthole important protest topics. For example, the initial chapter on non-violence surveys anti-war songs. The author highlights tunes ranging from "I Didn't Raise My Boy to Be a Soldier,""With God on Our Side," and "Waist Deep in the Big Muddy." But the book quickly shifts from predictable song selections to more rare and distinctive protest tunes. These numbers speak to the pain and suffering encountered while pressing for organized labor representation, women's pay equality, environmental responsibility, gay pride recognition, and fair immigration policies. Sullivan unearths tunes like "Bread and Roses,""Just Because I'm A Woman,""(Nothing But) Flowers,""I Am What I Am,""Black, Brown, and White," and "Migra." Sullivan's approaches on freedom of speech, nuclear proliferation, the wars in Iraq, Black Lives Matter, and Occupy Wallstreet are fascinating as well. So are his musical references.

They include tunes by Devo ("Clones (We're All)"), Gil Scott-Heron ("We Almost Lost Detroit"), David Crosby and Graham Nash ("They Want It All"), Alicia Keys ("Still I Rise"), and Melissa Etheridge ("I Need to Wake Up").

The confident prose, meaningful song illustrations, and thorough historical coverage featured in WHICH SIDE ARE YOU ON? are invigorating. Frankly, most readers may feel an overwhelming sense of guilt for their failures to become more directly involved in worthy social causes. Obviously, it's much easier to contribute money to a food bank or an animal shelter than to join a picket line at a non-union shop or to march in favor of black voting rights. Complacency and apathy are the targets of James Sullivan's sonic salvos. Of course, a volume like this deserves an accompanying CD tucked into the back cover. Sadly, there is none. The model for such a multi-track protest song supplement might be Colin Escott's magnificent LET FREEDOM SING (Time-Life, 2009) collection. But even without any additional music, Sullivan's work is a gem. It is enlightening to recall how many significant songs of the past century were crafted as reactions to social injustice. There seems to be a Woody Guthrie, a Pete Seeger, a Bob Dylan, a Buffy Sainte-Marie, a Bruce Springsteen, and a Lady Gaga for each new American singing generation. What a wonderful revelation!

(This commentary was originally published as B. Lee Cooper. "Review of WHICH SIDE ARE YOU ON? by James Sullivan," POPULAR MUSIC AND SOCIETY, 43:1 (February 2020): 114-116.)

Gil Scott-heron

STEVE SULLIVAN

ENCYCLOPEDIA OF GREAT POPULAR SONG RECORDINGS
Steve Sullivan
Lanham, Maryland: Scarecrow Press, 2013

In an October 1939 radio broadcast, British Prime Minister Winston Churchill described the foreign policy pursuits of Russia as "...a riddle, wrapped in a mystery, inside an enigma." He concluded, though, that national interest remained the key motivator among Soviet policy planners. Although far less sinister, most assertions about the primacy of particular songs or the greatness of individual recordings tend to be enigmatic as well. Conflicting justifications for such claims invariably create confusion rather than clarity. Over the past century, for instance, disc jockeys, music industry analysts, rock critics, and music magazine editors have identified a strange mixture of recordings as "the best songs ever". But just as Churchill noted the overwhelming influence of national interest in policy-making, one suspects that personal interest or financial interest often drive the conclusions of most musical rankings. It's undeniable that previous audio experience and acquired taste can also impact perceived song hierarchies. For example, tunes that are immensely popular among bluegrass performers might be regarded as nonsensical by hip hop artists. Similarly, a recording that was fundamental in the mind of Mother Maybelle Carter might have seemed either simplistic or antique to Cannonball Adderly.

Even authoritative music scholars often disagree on the meaning, importance, influence, and long-time value of particular recordings. And music historians frequently revisit and revise their original judgments about songs from previous decades, raising the ranks of some while lowering the ranks of others. Clearly, both hindsight and foresight, along with the random appearance of more contemporary cover recordings, make the selection of great songs an ever-moving target. Yet despite these tendencies toward critical disagreement and judgmental fluidity, music historian Steve Sullivan has compiled a thoughtful, well-documented study that identifies 1,000 of the greatest recordings over the past twelve decades. While some of his specific song selections are debatable, his fervor for linking recording practices to cultural development is not. For Sullivan, audio artistry throughout the past century is an integrative, interactive pursuit. The great recordings that he reveals manifest artistic advancement of American musical life.

THE ENCYCLOPEDIA OF GREAT POPULAR SONG RECORDINGS is organized into ten chapters which feature well-written, thoughtfully-researched entries for 1,000 songs. Each chapter highlights 100 different tunes. These recordings are presented in chronological rather than alphabetical order, based either on the original release date or on the initial pop chart debut date. Beginning with music by Scott Joplin, Billy Murray, and John Philip Sousa and ending with tunes by Adele, Alan Jackson, and Alicia Keys, the author lures the reader to critically consider ten different cycles of popular recordings. This cyclical approach is designed to make "old" and "new" music seem more linked and more integrated. Each chapter also intertwines multiple musical genres within the chronological pattern. Sullivan is adept at interfacing blues and folk, jazz and soul, country and gospel, reggae and rock, and numerous forms of world music with traditional American roots tunes. In addition to a lengthy historical narrative, each song entry consists of the full record title, the release date, the performer's name, the composer's name, the record label and number, the recording site and date, the song's pop chart performance, and any professional recognitions of the recording. This latter category includes formal votes of excellence by groups such as the Grammy Hall of Fame, the National Recording Registry (Library of Congress), National Public Radio (NPR), the Recording Industry of America, and Rolling Stone magazine. In his exceptionally thorough and detailed "Bibliography" (pp. 883-912), Sullivan provides hundreds of record lists, discographies, pop charts, and general music guides that feature "top song" categories among bluegrass and country music, ethnic and world music, folk, gospel, jazz and ragtime, movie music and Broadway show tunes, R&B and soul, and rock. An extensive alphabetized song "Title Index" (pp. 913-955), plus a huge alphabetized "Subject And Name Index" (pp. 957-1016), make this encyclopedia amazingly user-friendly.

In the same tradition as Larry Birnbaum's groundbreaking rock and roll roots study BEFORE ELVIS (Scarecrow, 2013), Steve Sullivan's goal is the expand scholarly perspectives on popular music beyond traditional time and stylistic boundaries. "One of the central purposes of this book," writes the author, "is to explore the interconnections between popular music of different eras and genres." He continues, "Pop music is in essence a mighty tree, with roots extending in many directions and going back multiple generations." (p. x) Sullivan illustrates his point in entry after entry of this fascinating sonic history. For example, he traces the development of the definitive barbershop quartet ballad "Sweet Adeline (You're The Flower Of My Heart)" from it's origin in 1896 as "Down Home In England" to it's premiere recording in 1904 by the Haydn Quartet. (pp. 349-350) But elsewhere Sullivan also notes this sentimental ballad's 1904 connection with singers Frederick Wheeler and Albert Campbell (p. 815), with the Haydn Quartet's other 1904 recording "The Old Folks At Home" (p. 265), and with the name-change of the Columbia Male Quartet to the Peerless Quartet shortly after their success with "Sweet Adeline" (p. 436).

Attention to detail - historical, discographic, and musical-- is the hallmark of this encyclopedia. So is breadth of coverage, particularly in respect to the lengthy careers of several popular artists. Sullivan carefully explores the most inspirational and influential recordings by Louis Armstrong, Fred Astaire, James Brown, Bing Crosby, Johnny Mercer, Elvis Presley, and Frank Sinatra. He is equally zealous in examining specific songs of the Beatles, Ray Charles, Miles Davis, Duke Ellington, George Gershwin, Billie Holiday, Mahalia Jackson, and the Rolling Stones. Contemporary artists who receive literary attention include Arcade Fire, Beyonce, Mariah Carey, Coldplay, Eminem, Green Day, John Legend, Rhianna, and Kanye West. But Sullivan's broader cultural objective is clear. He is seeking to identify musical links between Woody Guthrie and Bob Dylan and Bruce Springsteen; he wishes to lay open the hidden connections between blues recordings of the '20s, '30s, and '40s and the updated, electrified versions of these same songs performed by Canned Heat, Eric Clapton, and Johnny Lang; and he desires to demonstrate that country music's often-affirmed songwriting debt to Hank Williams really stretches back to Jimmie Rodgers and even Leadbelly (Huddie Ledbetter). The informative, energizing crosscurrents of recordings - blues to jazz, folk to pop, R&B to soul, country to rockabilly - are documented throughout this insightful compendium.

It is difficult to find fault with any aspect of this complex, informative study. The breadth of musical coverage is astounding; the recordings selected for analysis are ethically diverse yet highly popular; the discographic detail is thorough and accurate; and the multi-paragraph entries are original, lively, and well-documented. Only two points of criticism seem relevant. First, the song distributions among the ten chapters seem arbitrary. Perhaps the author could have reinforced his thesis about chronological evolution and cultural connections in songs by creating a unifying topical format for each chapter. That is, for each 100 recordings presented, he might have arranged them as 1890-to-2010 lyrical essays on "Romance, Marriage, and Divorce", "Travel, Transportation, and Technology", "Social Criticism and Political Protest", "Dance Tunes, Dancing Styles, and Instrumental Music", and so on. The utilization of such persistent social themes would be a vast improvement over the random chapter titles such as "Crazy Blues", "Down Home Rag", and "Memories Of You". Second, there are many important, influential, or culturally significant songs that have been omitted from this compilation. It is predictable that each reader will discover the absence of recordings that he or she considers vital to understanding the American musical tradition. For example, it seems odd that recordings like "Chicago" by Graham Nash, "Slow Down" by Larry Williams/The Beatles, "Toot, Toot, Tootsie (Good'bye)" by Al Jolson, "Speedoo" by The Cadillacs, "Please Come Home For Christmas" by Charles Brown/The Eagles, and "If You Don't Know Me By Know" by Harold Melvin and The Blue Notes/Simply Red are missing from this listing. Perhaps Sullivan is already addressing this issue via a supplementary edition of this study.

Aside from these two concerns, the ENCYCLOPEDIA OF GREAT POPULAR SONG RECORDINGS is a masterful undertaking. It deserves to be read like a collection of short stories rather than just consulted for piecemeal musical information. For instance, the interrelated sections on "Mbube" by Solomon Linda and The Original Evening Birds (pp. 186-187) and "Wimoweh" by The Weavers and "The Lion Sleeps Tonight" by The Tokens (pp. 549-550) are skillfully crafted to highlight cultural borrowing, folk adoption, and pop adaptation in U.S. recording history. This scholarly encyclopedia is a microcosm of Steve Sullivan's broad overview of the integration of melodies and lyrics in American recordings since the invention of the phonograph. Threading the histories of Blind Willie McTell and the Allman Brothers together through songs like "Statesboro Blues", the author weaves a compelling sonic tapestry.

(This commentary was originally published as B. Lee Cooper, "Review of ENCYCLOPEDIA OF GREAT POPULAR SONG RECORDINGS by Steve Sullivan," ROCK MUSIC STUDIES, 2:3 (October 2015): 315-318.)

Blind Willie McTell

AUDIO IMAGES OF AMERICAN CULTURE, 2009-2022

Grand Funk Railroad

PERSONAL MEMOIRS BY MUSICIANS

Autobiographical commentaries are commonplace in the age of the singer/songwriter. However, as in historical novels and poetic self-examinations, singers often intermingle their personal feelings with particular social issues or current political circumstances. This poetic license often shifts documentation from fact to opinion. Of course, some artists elect to sing about their own professional experiences in the limelight. For example, Deep Purple, Creedence Clearwater Revival, The Tractors, and Grand Funk address the perils of rock bands on the road in "Smoke On the Water", "Travelin' Band", "The Tulsa Shuffle", and "We're An American Band". Meanwhile, individual artists like Eddie Vinson, Bobby Bland, Eric Clapton, Kiki Dee, Jerry Reed, Hank Williams, Jr., and Billy Joel depict their distinctive physical characteristics, their peculiar nicknames, and their specific musical preferences in recordings like "Cleanhead Blues", "I'm A Blues Man", "I've Got a Rock 'n' Roll Heart", "I've Got the Music in Me", "Guitar Man", "My Name Is Bocephus", and "Piano Man". Similarly, Fats Domino, Rick Nelson, Jimmy Buffett, Roberta Flack, Jerry Lee Lewis, Chrissie Hynde (with The Pretenders), and Travis Tritt describe their unique performing experiences, their reactions to aging, their responses to the artistry of other singers, and their disgust with urban sprawl in "The Fat Man", "Garden Party", "A Pirate Looks at Forty", "Killing Me Softly with His Song", "Lewis Boogie", "My City Was Gone", and "Put Some Drive in Your Country". Lee Roy Parnell, The Mamas and The Papas, and Jimmy Vaughan explore the training regimen of honky tonk musicians, the formation and evolution of West Coast singing groups during the '60s, and the deaths of guitar giants in "Road Scholar", "Creeque Alley", and "Six Strings Down". Finally, Johnny Cash, Jerry Lee Lewis, and Carl Perkins offer varying perspectives on their magical mid-century musical experiences at Memphis' Sun Studio along with Sam Phillips and Elvis Presley. These autobiographical observations appear in "I Will Rock and Roll with You", "Class Of '55", and "Birth of Rock and Roll".

Discographic Illustrations

"All My Rowdy Friends (Have Settled Down)" (Elektra 47191)
Hank Williams, Jr. (1981)

"The Birth of Rock and Roll" (Spectrum CD 550 838-2)
Carl Perkins (1998)

"Born To Boogie" (Warner Brothers/Curb 28369)
Hank Williams, Jr. (1987)

"Champagne Jam" (Polydor 14504)
The Atlanta Rhythm Section (1978)

"Chicago" (Atlantic 2804)
Graham Nash (1971)

"Class Of '55" (America/Smash 830002)
Jerry Lee Lewis (1986)

"Cleanhead Blues" (Mercury 8023)
Eddie "Cleanhead" Vinson (1946)

"Coal Miner's Daughter" (Decca 32749)
Loretta Lynn (1970)

"Creeque Alley" (Dunhill 4083)
The Mamas and The Papas (1967)

"Dead End Street" (Capitol 5869)
Lou Rawls (1967)

"D. J. Play My Blues" (JSPCD 801)
Buddy Guy (1998)

"Don't Try to Lay No Boogie Woogie on The King of Rock and Roll"
(Stony Plain SPCD 1310)
Long John Baldry (2005)

"Doggy Dogg World" (Death Row 92279)
Snoop Doggy Dogg (1994)

"Dre Day" (Death Row 53827)
Dr. Dre, featuring Snoop Doggy Dogg (1993)

"The Entertainer" (Columbia 10064)
Billy Joel (1974)

"Family Tradition" (Elektra/Curb 46046)
Hank Williams, Jr. (1979)

"The Fat Man" (Imperial 5058)
Fats Domino (1950)

"Fire And Rain" (Warner Brothers 7423)
James Taylor (1970)

"For What It's Worth (Stop, Hey What's That Sound)" (Atco 6459)
Buffalo Springfield (1967)

"Garden Party" (Decca 32980)
Rick Nelson (1972)

"Guitar Man" (RCA Victor 9152)
Jerry Reed (1967)

"Hillbilly Rockin' Man" (Reba RRCD 1008)
Billy Lee Riley (2003)

"I Dig Rock and Roll Music" (Warner Brothers 7067)
Peter, Paul and Mary (1967)

"I Will Rock and Roll with You" (Columbia 10888)
Johnny Cash (1979)

"I Write the Songs" (Arista 0157)
Barry Manilow (1975)

"I'm A Blues Man" (Malaco MCD 7512)
Bobby Bland (2003)

"I've Got a Rock 'n' Roll Heart" (Duck/Warner Brothers 29780)
Eric Clapton (1983)

"I've Got the Music in Me" (Rocket 40293)
The Kiki Dee Band (1974)

"It's Hard Being the Kane" (Cold Chillin' 19536)
Big Daddy Kane (1991)

"Johnny B. Goode" (Chess 1691)
Chuck Berry (1958)

"Keep Playin' That Rock 'n' Roll" (Epic 10788)
The Edgar Winter Group (1971)

"Killing Me Softly with His Song" (Atlantic 2940)
Roberta Flack (1973)

"Lewis Boogie" (Sun 301)
Jerry Lee Lewis (1957)

"My City Was Gone" (Sire 29840)
The Pretenders (1982)

"My Name Is" (Aftermath 95040)
Eminem (1999)

"My Name Is Bocephus" (Warner Brothers/Curb 28581)
Hank Williams, Jr. (1986)

"Ohio" (Atlantic 2740)
Crosby, Stills, Nash, And Young (1970)

"On Broadway" (Warner Brothers 8542)
George Benson (1978)

"Piano Man" (Columbia 45963)
Billy Joel (1974)

"A Pirate Looks at Forty" (Dunhill 15029)
Jimmy Buffett (1975)

"Put Some Drive in Your Country" (Warner Brothers 19715)
Travis Tritt (1990)

"The Real Slim Shady" (Aftermath 497334)
Eminem (2000)

"Road Scholar" (Arista 18684)
Lee Roy Parnell (1992)

"Rock And Roll (I Gave You the Best Years of My Life)" (Columbia 10070)
Mac Davis (1975)

"Rockin' My Life Away" (Elektra 46030)
Jerry Lee Lewis (1979)

"Six Strings Down" (Epic/Legacy EK 86425)
Jimmy Vaughan (2003)

"Smoke On the Water" (Warner Brothers 7710)
Deep Purple (1973)

" Still D.R.E." (Aftermath 497192)
Dr. Dre, featuring Snoop Dogg (1999)

"Streets Of Bakersfield" (Reprise 27964)
Dwight Yoakam and Buck Owens (1988)

"Tears In Heaven" (Duck/Reprise 19038)
Eric Clapton (1992)

"Teen Age Idol" (Imperial 5864)
Ricky Nelson (1962)

"Travelin' Band" (Fantasy 637)
Creedence Clearwater Revival (1970)

"The Tulsa Shuffle" (Arista 18728)
The Tractors (1994)

"We Built This City" (Grunt 14170)
Starship (1985)

"We're An American Band" (Capitol 3660)
Grand Funk (1973)

"Woodstock" (Reprise 0906)
Joni Mitchell (1970)

Print References

Chuck Berry. CHUCK BERRY: THE AUTOBIOGRAPHY. New York: Harmony Books, 1987.

Chris Charlesworth. THE COMPLETE GUIDE TO THE MUSIC OF PAUL SIMON. London: Omnibus Press, 1997.

B. Lee Cooper. "Biographical Studies" and "Rock 'n' Roll Legends" in ROCK MUSIC IN AMERICAN POPULAR CULTURE: ROCK 'N' ROLL RESOURCES by B. Lee Cooper and Wayne S. Haney (New York: Haworth Press, 1995): 27-43 and 231-268.

B. Lee Cooper. "Chuck Berry and the American Motor Car." MUSIC WORLD, No. 86 (June 1981): 18-23.

B. Lee Cooper. "The Coasters - What Was the Secret of Their Success? A Review Essay." POPULAR MUSIC AND SOCIETY, 17 (Summer 1993): 115-119.

David Crosby and David Bender. STAND AND BE COUNTED: MAKING MUSIC, MAKING HISTORY - THE DRAMATIC STORY OF THE ARTISTS AND EVENTS THAT CHANGED AMERICA. New York: HarperCollins, 2000.

John Goldrosen and John Beecher. REMEMBERING BUDDY: THE DEFINITIVE BIOGRAPHY OF BUDDY HOLLY. New York: Penguin Books, 1986.

Peter Guralnick. LOST HIGHWAY: JOURNEYS AND ARRIVALS OF AMERICAN MUSICIANS. Boston: Back Bay Books/ Little, Brown and Company, 1999 (c1979).

George H. Lewis, Matthew Haworth, and Robin Roberts. "Reviews of 'Candle in the Wind 1997' by Elton John." POPULAR MUSIC AND SOCIETY, 22 (Fall 1998): 115-118.

Hank O'Neal. THE GHOSTS OF HARLEM - SESSIONS WITH JAZZ LEGENDS: PHOTOGRAPHS AND INTERVIEWS BY HANK O'NEAL. Nashville, Tennessee: Vanderbilt University Press, 2009.

Jim O'Neal and Amy Van Singel (eds.). THE VOICE OF THE BLUES: INTERVIEWS FROM LIVING BLUES MAGAZINE. New York: Routledge, 2002.

Robert Santelli. "The Rock and Roll Hall of Fame and Museum: Myth, Memory, and History," in STARS DON'T STAND STILL IN THE SKY: MUSIC AND MYTH, edited by Karen Kelly and Evelyn McDonnell (Washington Square, New York: New York University Press, 1999): 237-243.

Nick Talevski. THE UNOFFICIAL ENCYCLOPEDIA OF THE ROCK AND ROLL HALL OF FAME. Westport, Connecticut: Greenwood Press, 1998.

(This commentary was originally published as B. Lee Cooper. "Personal Memoirs by Musicians," in PROMINENT THEMES IN POPULAR SONGS, edited by B. Lee Cooper and Frank W. Hoffmann (Charleston, South Carolina: Paw Paw Press, 2015): 265-270.)

THE PRESIDENCY OF BARACK OBAMA - PART ONE

LIBERAL SHOP OF HORRORS (Capitol Steps CSCD 1030)
The Capitol Steps
Alexandria, Virginia: Capitol Steps Productions, 2010

BARACKIN' AROUND THE CHRISTMAS TREE (Capitol Steps CTL SR 1023)
The Capitol Steps
Alexandria, Virginia: Capitol Steps Productions, 2009

OBAMA MIA! (Capitol Steps CSCD 1029)
The Capitol Steps
Alexandria, Virginia: Capitol Steps Productions, 2009.

CAMPAIGN AND SUFFERING (Capitol Steps CSCD 1028)
The Capitol Steps
Alexandria, Virginia: Capitol Steps Productions, 2008

The Capitol Steps are a political satire ensemble who have attained nationwide cult status over the past three decades. Their stage performances are like Garrison Keillor and his prairie home companions on steroids. This multi-talented, multi-member troupe of singers and comedians was founded by Bill Strauss, Elaina Newport, and Jim Aidala. Initially, they performed in Washington, D.C., at private parties and in local clubs. In November 1983, however, the group's leaders lost their day jobs as political staffers when their boss, Republican Charles Percy, was defeated in the Illinois Senate race by Democrat Paul Simon. With more audacity than musical experience, Strauss and Newport issued their initial live performance recording - THE CAPITOL STEPS: LIVE! AT THE SHOREHAM (1984). Twenty-six years later they have released a total of 30 CDs that have sold over a million copies. More significantly, the Capitol Steps continue to display their zany political commentaries annually before more than 250,000 fans at conferences, conventions, and in theatre settings.

The Capitol Steps develop song parodies that explore the manipulations, mistakes, and missteps of contemporary politicians. Utilizing melodies from well-known pop songs and familiar show tunes, the Capitol Steps lyricists craft caustic, comical, and crazy images of life in America's government. While some might think that this Alexandria, Virginia-based comedy team draws its intellectual roots from the literary works of Jonathan Swift and Voltaire, most modern-day listeners will hear echoes of Tom Lehrer, Stan Freeberg, Vaughn Meader, Rich Little, Mark Russell, Steven Colbert, and Jon Stewart in the mirthful musical tirades of the Capitol Steps. If they were imitating popular literature, they would be either NEW YORKER cartoons or MAD magazine. If they were copying television programs, they would be either Rowan and Martin's "Laugh-In" or "Saturday Night Live". But as a political savvy troupe of merry musical maniacs, they are much more like the incendiary Weird Al Yankovic. Of course, they are lobbing audio

Molotov cocktails at the White House, the Congress, the Supreme Court, and various other wrong-headed city, state, and federal officials.

During the past three years the Capitol Steps have concentrated their lyrical levity on the antics of Barack Obama. They have traced the pitfalls, pranks, and puffery that surrounded his 2008 Presidential campaign and election, plus his initial years in office. Clearly, other current politicians receive their attention, too. So do several blabbering small screen political pundits and a few spoiled big screen celebrities as well. It is particularly fascinating, though, to review the 88 song parodies that depict the early Obama years in CAMPAIGN AND SUFFERING (2008), OBAMA MIA! (2009), BARACKIN' AROUND THE CHRISTMAS TREE (2009), and LIBERAL SHOP OF HORRORS (2010). As a sidelight, it is sad to report that Capitol Steps founder Bill Strauss passed away on December 18, 2007, without even witnessing the Obama inauguration. Nevertheless, it is delightful to note that lyricists Elaina Newport and Mark Eaton are still alive and kicking. They continue to excoriate the fools on The Hill.

CAMPAIGN AND SUFFERING addresses the over-crowded 2008 Presidential primaries, along with the policy-revising campaign styles of the many attention-seeking candidates. Opening with "76 Unknowns" ("76 Trombones"), the Capitol Steps lampoon various weaknesses of several Presidential wannabes. They sharpen their focus on individual candidates in later tunes, jabbing at evangelical literalist Mike "Huckabee" ("Let It Be"); noting that Arizona Senator John "McCain's Campaign" ("Rain in Spain") is slowly going down the drain; having the carefully groomed, self-centered John Edwards croon "I'm So Pretty" ("I Feel Pretty"); featuring Massachusetts Mormon Mitt Romney hiding his moderate political leanings in "Help Me Fake It to The Right"("Help Me Make It Through the Night"); citing New Yorker Rudy Guiliani's political scare tactics of "Relying on Nine-Eleven" ("Stairway to Heaven"); observing that Tennessee's overly talkative Fred Thompson morphed into a law-and-order "Beverly Hills Candidate" (Beverly Hillbillies Theme"); and addressing Bill Clinton's potentially distracting role as a First Husband in "Hilliary's Way" ("My Way"). It's intriguing to discover that only one song - "Obama Meets Osama" ("Black and White") - is directly dedicated to the future President. This tune, much to the dismay of Rush Limbaugh, draws sharp contrasts between the ethnicity, clothing styles, temperaments, and world views of Barack and America's Muslim nemesis, Mr. Bin Laden.

The title tune on OBAMA MIA! ("Mamma Mia") addresses the pro-hope, pro-dream, pro-Barack adoration of the Washington Press corps toward the new President. Following that bouncy number, a less exultant Secretary of State Hilliary Clinton expresses her desire to foster positive chemistry in a new political partnership with Mr. Obama. Her plea is couched in "Ebony and Ovaries" ("Ebony and Ivory"). George W. Bush shuns the prospect of exchanging e-mails with his young Democratic successor, but the former President asks if he can use a Whiteberry rather than a Blackberry in a duet exchange titled "Barackberry" ("You Don't Send Me Flowers"). TV guru and worldly wise women's spokesperson Oprah Windfrey is identified as an unofficial Presidential advisor in "Oprah-bama" ("Oklahoma"). Finally, the linguistically challenged Capitol Steps' Mike

Tilford reviews the results of the recent national election in a nifty, naughty, nutty monologue - "Lirty Dies: 2008 - The Load To The Erection".

Abandoning their standard live audience setting in favor of a studio-produced recording, the Capitol Steps utilize traditional holiday melodies throughout BARACKIN' AROUND THE CHRISTMAS TREE ("Rockin' Around the Christmas Tree"). In the title tune, First Lady Michelle and her liberal-thinking spouse seek a broad, bipartisan coalition to determine the most politically correct ornamentation for their first Yuletide tree. On the next track, Barack's Congressional lady friend Nancy Pelosi is caught inciting right wing holiday wrath by seeking to hire a Santa who is black and gay in "Have Yourself a Very Liberal Christmas" ("Have Yourself a Merry Little Christmas"). President Obama is also urged to "Muzzle Joe" ("Let It Snow! Let It Snow! Let It Snow!") because Vice President Biden continues to make gaffes that are frightful. The Obama decree to close the Guantanamo detention site is addressed in "Stressed Guards Boasting They Will Open Fire" ("The Christmas Song"). Next, in "The Night Before Cambridge" ("The Night Before Christmas") the Capitol Steps revisit the Obama-hosted White House lawn Beerfest that sought to calm the spirits of angry white policeman Sgt. Crowley and irate black professor Henry Louis Gates. Finally, Lou Dobbs and his blogosphere of anti-Democratic buffoons chatter about the questionable citizenship of President Obama in "Do You Hear Who I Smear?" ("Do You Hear What I Hear?").

LIBERAL SHOP OF HORRORS highlights the Obama Administration's mind-boggling health care battles in "Cash For Codgers" ("When I'm Sixty-Four") and the never-ending political clashes over the economic recovery process in "Return to Spenders" ("Return to Sender"). In a spoken tale titled "Obamamania", the President is characterized as a populist huckster selling items including Barack t-shirts, Michelle mouse pads, Yes We Candles, Reverend Wrightguard deodorant, Cherriobamas, and even Oreobamas ("..black enough to make history, but white enough to make Republicand feel safe"). Of course, other anti-Obama looniness is also recognized. CNN's Lou Dobbs continues to lament the absence of an authentic American birth certificate for Obama in "Secret Kenyan Man" ("Secret Agent Man"); Sarah Palin joyfully declares "Everything's Coming Up Roguey" ("Everything's Coming Up Roses"); and the superpatriotic members of the throw-them-all-out-of-office persuasion vocalize their political complaints in "Battle Hymn of the Tea Public" ("Battle Hymn of the Republic"). Finally, the unanticipated Swedish peace award is acknowledged as a contradiction for a President who is directing war efforts in Iraq and Afghanistan, launching drone-directed air strikes into Pakistan, and addressing war-like rhetoric at Iran. The Capitol Steps warn Obama that "You Can't Hide That Nobel Prize" ("Lyin' Eyes").

All four of these recent Capitol Steps CDs contain material that also lambastes non-political figures as well as zany actions by elected officials that are totally unrelated to policy-making. For instance, the recent worldwide flu epidemic is discussed in both "Swine Fever" ("Fever") and "Rudolph, the H1N1 Reindeer" ("Rudolph, the Red-Nosed Reindeer"); the incident of an airline passenger boarding a plane with a drug-resistant strain of tuberculosis is explored on "TB on a Jet Plane" ("Leaving on a Jet

Plane"); public reliance on over-the-counter medications is condemned in "Ten Pills and You're Fine" ("Windmills of Your Mind"); and the airport restroom incident that triggered the arrest of Idaho Senator Larry Craig for soliciting gay sex is recounted in "Tap Three Times" ("Knock Three Times"). Supreme Court Justice Ruth Bader Ginsburg musically decries the behavior of the conservative male majority on the Court and condemns their consistently narrow-minded rulings in "Votin' Four to Five" (Working 9 to 5"). In addition, contradictory immigration policies are confronted in "Taxicab Driver" ("Paperback Writer"), while the multiple sexual liaisons of the world-class golfer Mr. Woods are mocked in "Fly of the Tiger" ("Eye of the Tiger").

The early '80s Republican roots of the Capitol Steps served them especially well as they launched their irreverent, political-bashing careers. Of course, it is their universal penchant for pulling The Wizard's curtain aside, for declaring The Emperor to be without clothes, and for upbraiding the politically powerful throughout Washington, D.C. without regard to party affiliation that has placed them above the current ideological fray. The Capitol Steps have a bipartisan following that includes Democrats, Republicans, Independents, Know-Nothings, Whigs, Bullmooses, and Anarchists alike. The Capitol Steps are not investigative reporters; they are public court jesters. The Capitol Steps are not prosecuting attorneys or hanging judges; rather, they are rowdy revelers and truth-telling troubadours who entertain audiences with never-ending tales of documented scandals, stupidity, and swindles. American Government is an undeniably big target. The Capitol Steps, like all other Americans, often watch the Executive Branch trying to invigorate the muddling Congress under the watchful eye of the Supreme Court. Unlike the rest of us, though, they gain sweet revenge by lyrically pummeling all of the posturing political poohbahs. Just imagine what fun the Capitol Steps will have in 2011 when they record and release their 31st CD! The topics of laughable lyrical lament will probably include: BP oil executives denying responsibility for the Gulf spill and for the accompanying ecological disaster; Republicans Mitch McConnell and John Boehner rationalizing their "Party of No" leadership; the political extremes among Democrats and Republicans opposing both Sonja Sotomeyer and Elena Kagan; the uncertain Treasury Department and Wall Street responses to the Greek economic crisis; Congressional fumbling on the health care bill; the misbehavior of Goldman-Sachs towards its investment clients; the befuddling White House efforts to court the corrupt Hamid Karzai; and the backlash concerning Arizona's new immigration laws. No one could generate this type of laughable political satire material if they tried.

(This commentary was originally published as B. Lee Cooper, "Review of LIBERAL SHOP OF HORRORS (2010) by The Capitol Steps, BARACKIN' AROUND THE CHRISTMAS TREE (2009) by The Capitol Steps, OBAMA MIA (2009) by The Capitol Steps, and CAMPAIGN AND SUFFERING (2008) by The Capitol Steps," POPULAR MUSIC AND SOCIETY, 34 (May 2011), pp. 249-253.)

THE PRESIDENCY OF BARACK OBAMA - PART TWO

TAKE THE MONEY AND RUN FOR PRESIDENT (Capitol Steps CSCD 1032)
The Capitol Steps
Washington, D.C.: Capitol Steps Records, 2012

Political commentary, political drama, and political satire have dominated American airwaves during the past twelve months. Presidential campaigns invariably prompt such media attention. Note the radio tirades from Rush Limbaugh and the televised rants of Chris Matthews. Evening TV programming has been populated by USA's "Political Animals" and HBO's "The Newsroom". Beyond the thoughtful scripts and ideological observations of Aaron Sorkin, Joe Scarborough, and Mike Huckabee, though, there are some very funny audio perspectives on candidate debates, party platforms, and Presidential politics in general. The Capitol Steps regard the quirks of Congressmen and state politicians to be fair game for satire. They listen eagerly to the excessive appeals of evangelical demagogues, Tea Party patriots, big-spending health care advocates, and flat tax simplifiers. Everything they sing about features the same underlying theme: "The Emperor has no clothes!" Actually, they claim, "The opposite of progress is Congress!" For thirty years The Capitol Steps have pilloried politicians - Democrats, Republicans, Libertarians, and Independents as well. TAKE THE MONEY AND RUN FOR PRESIDENT is their latest salute to the persistent silliness of partisan politics in America.

The Capitol Steps are a political satire troupe whose performances are designed to entertain ticked-off taxpayers and perplexed patriots (Strauss and Newport). The same folks who adore Steven Colbert and John Stewart on cable channels are also enamored with The Capitol Steps on stage and on disc. They specialize in performing song parodies that manifest the mannerisms, misadventures, manipulations, and malevolence of contemporary political figures. Stealing melodies from familiar show tunes, traditional American pop standards, and current hit songs, The Capitol Steps construct lethal lyrics that portray culpable Congressman in comedic circumstances of their own making. Listening to The Capitol Steps conjures memories of other grinning storytellers such as Stan Freberg, Tom Lehrer, Vaughn Meader, Weird Al Yankovic, and especially pianist Mark Russell. Beyond these recorded mirth merchants, the shrewd and silly perspectives provided by The Capitol Steps are related to the NEW YORKER's edgy cartoons, MAD magazine's comical articles, Kurt Vonnegut's sly and sarcastic short stories, Dick and Tom Smothers' witty monologues, Rowan and Martin's outrageous "Laugh-In" visuals, and numerous wild "Saturday Night Live" sketches (Cooper).

Borrowing a portion of their CD title from the 1976 hit recording by The Steve Miller Band, The Capitol Steps acknowledge the unprecedented campaign contributions and the incredible spending levels that undergird the 2012 race between Barrack Obama and Mitt Romney. TAKE THE MONEY AND RUN FOR PRESIDENT portrays President Obama as a relentless wealth re-distributor in "If I Tax A Rich Man". Adopting the melody from The Eagles' "Lyin' Eyes" to support lyrics that chastise Obama's Vice President for his verbal gaffes, The Capitol Steps declare "You Can't Hide This Biden Guy". While Democrats Nancy Pelosi and Harry Reid are also mentioned, the majority of this CD is devoted to lambasting Republicans. For example, an over-the-top evangelical preacher lauds the conservative Christian virtues of "Amazing Rick" Santorum. In other songs, Herman Cain markets his new health care elixir as "Love Potion No. 9-9-9"; philandering former House Speaker Gingrich is chided for his cheating heart in "Three Little Wives Of Newt"; former Massachusetts Governor Mitt Romney attempts to hide his liberal-leaning health care history in "Help Me Fake It To The Right"; Tea Party darlings Sarah Palin and Michelle Bachman challenge each other's intellectual bona fides in "Don't Go Fakin' You're Smart"; Texas Governor Rick Perry is depicted as a verbally-obtuse "Bush Cloned Cowboy"; Ron Paul's endorsement of legalized marijuana is lampooned in a tune that suggests smoking that "Green, Green Grass At Home"; and even old-guard Republicans seek to upstage the clownish field of younger candidates by suggesting a 2012 ticket of "McCain And Old Time Bob Dole". Other songs on this disc lash out at Osama Bin Laden, Murimar Khadafy, the Occupy Wall Street participants, Arnold Schwarzenegger, Chris Christie, and a former New York congressman - "Itsy Bitsy Teeny [Anthony] Weiner".

Although creative and irreverent, the 2012 observations and indictments by The Capitol Steps seem incredibly bland and politically naive within the current campaign environment. In fact, the high stakes of this Presidential election seem devalued by The Capitol Steps. For instance, the historical perversions perpetrated by the Tea Party warrant far more ridicule than a casual swipe at Sarah Palin in "Midnight Ride Of Paul, Revised". The debt ceiling debacle orchestrated by Mitch McConnell and John Boehner goes unnoticed by The Capitol Steps. The ideological purity of Grover Norquist and the Scriptural certainty of Rick Santorum also deserve to be painted as antithetical to legitimate political compromise. The Capitol Steps are similarly hesitant to address Paul Ryan's fiscal fabrications or the Koch Brothers financial manipulations. They also bypass the terrible plague of voter suppression laws, the retrograde attacks on women's reproductive rights, the environmental ignorance propagated by anti-science Biblical literalists and anti-evolution cretins, and the cavalier disregard for the nutritional, educational, and medical needs of the very young, the poor, and the elderly. Undeniably,

The Capitol Steps have cultivated a large following by poking fun at uncomplicated political targets. They have sustained a popular 30-year stage act that is universally deemed progressive, non-partisan, and hip. Today, however, this neutral approach deludes more than informs. The particularly serious nature of the 2012 election requires much more than a Gilbert and Sullivan format for launching puns, innuendoes, and giggling remarks. Barack Obama deserves to challenged for his poor legislative leadership tactics and for the tardy economic improvement pattern. But his Republican opponents, who created the Great Recession of 2008, have been both intransigent and irresponsible as political figures throughout the Obama presidency. This CD should condemn such partisan shenanigans. Of course, if The Capitol Steps truly believe that Mitt Romney plans to oversee a transparent, fair reform of the U.S. tax code, then they probably also expect Chris Christie to lead a campaign against childhood obesity in New Jersey. Such optimism is hilarious.

This new Capitol Steps CD is consistent in style and substance with their 31 previous releases. It is funny and fanciful, flippant and farcical. It portrays politicians as flawed characters. The glancing audio blows landed by The Capitol Steps might even make Will Rogers and Woodie Guthrie chuckle. But both men would probably add, "Why are you so easy on these crooks?" TAKE THE MONEY AND RUN FOR PRESIDENT needs to score more direct hits on hypocrisy, hubris, and intellectual dishonesty. The Capitol Steps ought to sharpen their focus on the major political issues of 2012 rather than dumbing down their act to highlight the preposterous antics of Herman Cain, Anthony Weiner, and Michelle Bachman.

Works Cited

B. Lee Cooper. "Review of LIBERAL SHOP OF HORRORS (2010), BARACKIN' AROUND THE CHRISTMAS TREE (2009), OBAMA MIA (2009), and CAMPAIGN AND SUFFERING (2008) by The Capitol Steps," POPULAR MUSIC AND SOCIETY, 34:2 (May 2011): 249-253.

William Strauss and Elainia Newport. SIXTEEN SCANDALS: 20 YEARS OF SEX, LIES, AND OTHER HABITS OF OUR GREAT LEADERS. Naperville, Illinois: Sourcebooks MediaFusion, 2002.

(This essay was originally published as B. Lee Cooper. "Review of TAKE THE MONEY AND RUN FOR PRESIDENT by The Capitol Steps," POPULAR MUSIC AND SOCIETY, 35 (December 2012), pp. 711-713.)

The Capitol Steps

THE DECLINE OF PROTEST SONGS WITHIN AMERICAN POPULAR MUSIC

SONGS OF AMERICA: PATRIOTISM, PROTEST, AND THE MUSIC THAT MADE A NATION
Jon Meacham and Tim McGraw
New York: Random House, 2019
ISBN 9780593132951
302 pp.   Hb $30.00

Not since Yankee sluggers Mickey Mantle and Roger Maris combined to hit 115 home runs during 1961 has praise for an M & M Boys achievement been so enthusiastic. The Random House publication of SONGS OF AMERICA, written by Jon Meacham and Tim McGraw, has been greeted as "a moving and wonderful account" by U.S. Congressman John Lewis, as a "cultural journey" by historian Doris Kearns Goodwin, and as a "glorious celebration of our diversity" by record producer Quincy Jones. These laudatory dust jacket comments are reinforced by the new M & M Boys' exemplary credentials. Jon Meacham is a Pulitzer Prize-winning Presidential historian and a distinguished professor at Vanderbilt University. Tim McGraw, his co-author, is a Grammy Award-winning entertainer with more than a dozen successful country music CDs and scores of BILLBOARD-charted hit singles. McGraw explains that the goal of this volume is to portray "the fact that interwoven into the fabric of our national story were songwriters and performers creating lyrics and melodies at times of great challenge." (p. 233) Over backyard barbeque chats these two Nashville-based M & M Boys conceived a plan to document and analyze the sonic soundscape of the United States. They acknowledge assistance from several highly-regarded colleagues, including Craig Werner, Michael Eric Dyson, and Ken Burns. With Meacham crafting the historical text and McGraw penning side-bar commentaries on nearly 50 tunes, SONGS OF AMERICA strives to be the definitive statement on the music that made the nation.

SONGS OF AMERICA is organized chronologically in eight chapters that address the nation's history from 1768 to 2008. Predictably, the initial sections cover well-known patriotic tunes such as "The Star Spangled Banner", "My Country 'Tis Of Thee", and "The Battle Hymn Of The Republic". There are also examples of early black freedom songs like "Go Down, Moses" and "Swing Low, Sweet Chariot" as well as Confederate anthems such as "I Wish I Was In Dixie's Land". Other lyrics are dedicated to women's voting rights ("Daughters of Freedom, The Ballot Be Yours"), to African-American civil rights ("Lift Every Voice And Sing"), and to the World War I struggle ("Over There"). Meacham and McGraw assess the period from The Great Depression to the election of President Barack Obama in slightly more than 100 pages. Key songs mentioned in this part of the book include "This Land Is Your Land", "We'll Meet Again", "We Shall Overcome", "Blowin' In The Wind", "A Change Is Gonna Come", "Mississippi Goddam", "Okie From Muskogee", "An American Trilogy", and "Born In The U.S.A.". The authors assert that everyone should "... hear the music that lifted us from danger, kept us together amid tragedy, united us anew in triumph, and urged us toward justice." (p. 5).

Assessing lyrical potency in respect to challenging cultural change or motivating political movements is a crapshoot at best. And selecting particular composers or performers as emblematic of the attitudes of specific social groups or defined geographic areas is also a very tricky business. Jon Meacham and Tim McGraw deserve credit for presenting a balanced perspective on music as a driving element in American political thought. However, they must also be held accountable for their errors and omissions, too. There are several. First, it is unimaginable that a dedicated bibliophile like Meacham would fail to identify earlier scholars who have assembled music-focused analyses of American life and times. Yet he fails to acknowledge the groundbreaking works of Richard Barnet, Jacques Barzun, David Brackett, R. Serge Denisoff, Jacqueline Edmondson, Samuel L. Forucci, James Perone, David Pichaske, Jerome L. Rodnitzky, Timothy E. Scheurer, John Anthony Scott, and Nicholas Tawa. Second, Tim McGraw apparently saw no reason to include a detailed discography or list of CDs that would clarify and supplement the songs mentioned within the text. This careless omission lessens the book's value to both music scholars and the general public. Third, and perhaps most important, the two authors ignore the key roles of advancing audio technology and popular communications media in both producing and delivering lyrical messages to the American people. Clearly, the gentle folk singing of the 18th century, the sweet piano playing from sheet music during the 19th century, the raucous blare of jukeboxes during the 20th century, and the worldwide cacophony of digitized tunes during the 21st century manifest starkly different environments for the reception of either inspiring or protesting lyrical messages. Similarly, various segmentations of musical genres over the past three centuries have created diverse popular culture publics for the nationalistic or dissenting ideas being conveyed in blues, country, folk, gospel, heavy metal, hip-hop, R&B, soul, and world music recordings. Meacham and McGraw seem oblivious to these important factors.

I have recently expressed my own concerns about the declining role of popular music as a social information force in two book-length publications. My contention is that lyricists and singers appear to be less willing to risk the market rejection that may result from freely pontificating upon controversial political matters. Similarly, major recording companies tend to resist releasing or marketing socially-charged, politically critical audio material. Thus, recorded calls for change are pre-emptively muted by economic and reputational considerations. Nevertheless, a few independent, non-corporate musicians may seek to generate public debate via extreme lyrical content. In such cases, it is not uncommon for radio airplay bans to block their protest music as well.

Consider the urgency of informed, thoughtful citizenship in today's volatile political climate. Over the past decade, the United States has experienced two transformational presidencies. First, African-American President Barack Obama was elected in 2008. As a Democrat and political liberal, he ended the Great Recession; he heightened domestic concern over the threat of global climate change; he strengthened America's worldwide military alliances; he engaged in multi-lateral international trade agreements; he broadened legal protections for Hispanics and insured the voting rights of black citizens; and he isolated renegade foreign powers like Iran, North Korea, and Russia. Then

Republican President Donald J. Trump was elected in 2016. He has systematically reversed all major policies of the previous administration. Beyond that, he has befriended authoritarian rulers across the globe; he has launched numerous anti-Muslim and anti-immigration actions; he has supported restrictions on women's abortion rights; and he has allowed Cabinet-level corruption on a scale that defies historical parallel. How have 21st century troubadours responded to these two startlingly different presidencies? Which specific recordings illustrate support for Obama or contempt for Trump? Which current singers have championed climate concerns, religious freedom, and protection of voting rights?

Jon Meacham and Tim McGraw elected not to assess any topical recordings released after 2008. This is a colossal error in judgment. It calls the entire SONGS OF AMERICA project into question. Why have unfying patriotic hymns and serious musical dissent ceased to exist among contemporary playlists? Are modern-day composers and vocalists content to ignore the striking political dichotomy exhibited during the past two administrations? Is recorded music no longer relevant as a commentator on social and political change? What appears to be happening today is that composers, singers, and recording companies are consciously self-censoring - perhaps out of fear of FCC retaliation or because they can't abide a Twitter tongue-lashing from the belligerent Commander in Chief. Undeniably, there are issues galore that clamor for courageous audio commentary. It's hard to imagine that Woodie Guthrie, Pete Seeger, and Phil Ochs would have been silent during such an onslaught against traditional American ideals and human rights. Yet Joan Baez, Bob Dylan, John Fogerty, and Bruce Springsteen seem mysteriously tongue-tied today. They have released no recordings expressing personal anger, encouraging defiance, or urging massive protest marches or boycotts. Perhaps, to paraphrase Don McLean, the music really has died. If so, Meacham and McGraw should at least document the appropriate funeral date.

SONGS OF AMERICA features an articulate dash through a multitude of partriotic anthems and protest tunes that have informed and influenced U.S. public opinion from the Revolutionary War to the final days of the George W. Bush Administration. Jon Meacham and Tim McGraw, two Nashville neighbors eager to share their own citizenship voyages and music preferences, present beneficial - but decidedly non-current - viewpoints on songs that provide conflicting images of the American Dream. Sadly, Meacham and McGraw seem unaware of the continuing meaning, power, and providence of timeless recordings like "Black, Brown, and White" by Big Bill Broonzy, "(What Did I So To Be So) Black and Blue" by Louis Armstrong, and "Backlash Blues" by Nina Simone. These sentiments need to echo again today in support of immigrants, poor people, black voters, women seeking access to health care, and seniors relying upon Social Security. Hopefully, the well-credentialed M & M Boys from Nashville will re-think and expand their pilgrimage through the American protest music briar patch. Ideally, they will also unearth and explain the reasons for the strange 21st century silence among previously politically active recording artists.

References

Richard D. Barnet, Bruce Nemerov, and Mayo R. Taylor. THE STORY BEHIND THE SONG: 150 SONGS THAT CHRONICLE THE 20th CENTURY. Westport, Connecticut: Greenwood Press, 2004.

Jacques Barzun. MUSIC IN AMERICAN LIFE. Bloomington, Indiana: Indiana University Press, 1956.

David Brackett (ed.). THE POP, ROCK, AND SOUL READER: HISTORIES AND DEBATES. New York: Oxford University Press, 2005.

B. Lee Cooper and Frank W. Hoffmann. AMERICA IN TRANSITION, 1945-1975: A MUSICAL PERSPECTIVE ON HISTORICAL CHANGE. Columbia, South Carolina: Paw Paw Press, 2017.

B. Lee Cooper and Frank W. Hoffmann. REFLECTION, RESISTANCE, RACISM, AND REBELLION: LYRICAL RESPONSES TO CULTURAL CHANGE. Columbia, South Carolina: Paw Paw Press, 2019.

R. Serge Denisoff. SING A SONG OF SOCIAL SIGNIFICANCE (Second Edition). Bowling Green, Ohio: Bowling Green State University Popular Press, 1983.

Jacqueline Edmondson (ed.). MUSIC IN AMERICAN LIFE: AN ENCYCLOPEDIA OF THE SONGS, STYLES, STARS, AND STORIES THAT SHAPED OUR CULTURE. Santa Barbara, California: Greenwood Press/ABC-CLIO Publishing, 2013.

Samuel L. Forucci. A FOLK SONG HISTORY OF AMERICA: AMERICA THROUGH ITS SONGS. Englewood Cliffs, New Jersey: Prentice-Hall, 1984.

James E. Perone. MUSIC OF THE COUNTERCULTURE ERA. Westport, Connecticut: Greenwood Press, 2004.

David R. Pichaske. A GENERATION IN MOTION: POPULAR MUSIC AND CULTURE IN THE SIXTIES. Granite Falls, Minnesota: Ellis Press, 1989 (c. 1979).

Jerome L. Rodnitzky. MINSTRELS OF THE DAWN: THE FOLK-PROTEST SINGER AS A CULTURAL HERO. Chicago: Nelson-Hall, 1976.

Timothy E. Scheurer. BORN IN THE U. S. A.: THE MYTH OF AMERICA IN POPULAR MUSIC FROM COLONIAL TIMES TO THE PRESENT. Jackson, Mississippi: University Press of Mississippi, 1991.

John Anthony Scott. THE BALLAD OF AMERICA: THE HISTORY OF THE UNITED STATES IN SONG AND STORY. Carbondale, Illinois: Southern Illinois University Press, 1983 (c1966).

Nicholas Tawa. SUPREMELY AMERICAN: POPULAR SONG IN THE 20th CENTURY - STYLES AND SINGERS AND WHAT THEY SAID ABOUT AMERICA. Lanham, Maryland: Scarecrow Press, 2005.

Jon Meacham and Tim McGraw

THE GREAT WALL OF AMERICAN MUSIC

Old music warms my soul. I heed Bob Seger's mandate. Old records jump off of my shelves and leap upon my turntable daily. CD re-issues of classic tunes are also frequently revisited. Chuck Berry, Jerry Lee Lewis, and Little Richard remain constants in my weekly music listening regimen. Of course, I also enjoy female vocalists. Bonnie Raitt, Aretha Franklin, Nina Simone, and The Shirelles still hold my attention. My zeal for newer music by artists like Joe Bonamassa, Warren Haynes, Christone "Kingfish" Ingram, and Keb' Mo' is fueled by my lifetime devotion to blues, R&B, soul, and rock music. Clearly, my large vinyl record and CD collection represents a significant financial investment in music that continues to bring me pleasure. It's certainly worth it. Why would anyone dare to suggest that greater availability and increased public interest in old music poses a threat to the future of the American recording industry?

In January 2022 jazz pianist-turned-music historian Ted Gioia attempted to shock the record industry out of lethargy by speaking truth to power. He issued a thought-provoking essay in THE ATLANTIC titled "Is Old Music Killing New Music?" The iconoclastic Gioia assembled CD and vinyl sales statistics, music streaming data, and other historical evidence - including the decline of public interest in viewing annual TV Grammy Award presentations - to demonstrate waning support for contemporary recordings. Twenty-first century BILLBOARD "Hot 100" songs are becoming like audio dreams that appear for a very short time and quickly vanish from cultural memory. Gioia also notes that record company conglomerates have been padding their music catalogs by purchasing the recorded remnants of smaller disc-producing operations along with the composing properties and previously-vocalized hits of classic superstars. Thus wealthy old performers like Bob Dylan, Bruce Springsteen, and Paul Simon have become even richer by selling commercial rights to their ample bundles of signature songs. The future seems to guarantee that Sony, Universal Music, and other huge audio-focused corporations will be recycling even more music from the '60s, '70s, '80s, and '90s to compete against the newest 21st century releases.

Clearly, hip-hop, country, urban black, international ethnic, and electronic music of post-2020 creation will continue to be authored, produced, and marketed. New styles, new singers, and new songwriters will still populate the contemporary recording scene. But Ted Gioia is predicting, and actually tracing the ongoing pathway of, a growing dominance of older music as the preferred type of listening throughout the United States. Listeners vote with their ears on a daily basis. This trend will continue. The flood of recycled music, either as "golden oldies" or as cover recordings of previous hits, will thrive. Repackaging material as "greatest hits" or as multi-disc packets of re-issued songs will become an even more commonplace practice. For example, consider the 2021 release of a 6-disc tribute to Ray Charles. It is titled TRUE GENIUS. This is a sign of the times. This retrospective on Brother Ray's lifetime of hits encourages 21st century listeners to ponder a remarkable diversity of rhythms and musical genres -- all produced by an artist who died in 2004. This gigantic album will be attracting new fandom, opening a broader marketplace, creating a new Ray Charles product, and allowing the entire playlist of Ray Charles hits to recycle again commercially.

Granted, Ray Charles is a unique, seminal figure in American popular music history. And his renditions of classic tunes deserve to live on for generations. "Georgia On My Mind" is now a state anthem. "America The Beautiful" is a national treasure. But Ray Charles is a stalking horse for the preservation and redistribution of a million other wonderful old tunes by thousands of 20th century recording artists. Ray lets a listener sample R&B with "I've Got a Woman." He shows the magical melding of country and R&B with "I Can't Stop Loving You." He raises the tempo to rock 'n' roll levels with "What'd I Say." He reverts to his jazz roots with "One Mint Julep." He cries the blues with "Drown in My Own Tears." He presents topical soul music in "Living for The City." Then he turns back in time to a pop classic like "Come Rain or Come Shine." Ray Charles even highlights other old singers during his duets with Norah Jones, Billy Joel, and Willie Nelson. In one compilation of old music, the dangers of drowning out new music have been realized. TRUE GENIUS makes the case for Ted Gioia. Who can possibly compete with Brother Ray for sensitive vocalizing, innovative keyboard work, tight orchestration, and the selection of memorable, melodic songs?

The essence of the "current recording crisis" depicted by Ted Gioia is not just that new music is being overtaken by old music within the contemporary marketplace. It is that the best music recorded in the 20th century overmatches the best music produced during the 21st century. As noted earlier, listeners vote with their ears - and also with their pocketbooks. Quality is always the issue. And the singing, playing, and creative elements within the total recorded music phenomenon are standing the test of time. When a new music product emerges, it initially competes with other new music. But as generation after generation filters the totality of American popular songs, the very best recordings rise to the top. They are memorable. They are repeatable. They are often unforgettable. Nothing is wrong with valuing and honoring past hits. However, Ted Gioia is worried that the future may be robbed of good new music if good old music crushes the creative urges, commercial opportunities, and financial incentives for 21st century singers and songwriters.

What's happening today isn't just the recognition of the commercial triumph of old music over new music. It's the continuing technological expansion of audio availability and the consequences of aesthetic choices being stretched over a full century of recorded music. The past is still prelude to the future. Past hits are forever. They are a constant in public judgment of new music as well as in the listening patterns among multiple generations. And the past isn't just several old songs. It's also an accumulation of overt and subtle marketing techniques, audio technology advancements, improvements in radio/television/digital communications, and the sonic hindsight exercised by music critics and music fans alike. Past recordings are no longer history or memory only. They constitute building blocks for future recordings that will help to expand America's aesthetic "Wall of Songs". Most new recordings hit this "Wall of Songs" and immediately collapse into cinders. Some new recordings echo off of the "Wall of Songs", but eventually fade into obscurity. But truly great new recordings adhere to the "Wall of Songs", becoming part of the vast American musical treasury and tradition.

This non-Phil Spector "Wall of Songs" currently drives streaming services like Pandora, Spotify, and YouTube as they seek to identify individual patterns of audio interest and appreciation. Rhythms, lyrics, vocal styles, and melodies are translated into specific songs performed by specific artists. The great American "Wall of Songs" extends from the 1920s to the present day. Whether songs were originally released in 78, 45, or 33 1/3 r.p.m. formats or during the CD age of digitized music, they are currently fodder for recall and replay. Bessie Smith, Ruth Etting, Ella Fitzgerald, Billie Holiday, Jo Stafford, Doris Day, Patsy Cline, Etta James, Aretha Franklin, Carole King, Madonna, Beyonce, Alicia Keyes, and Taylor Swift are instantly contemporaries via modern streaming technology. So are Louis Armstrong, Bing Crosby, Al Jolson, Frank Sinatra, Louis Jordan, Perry Como, Elvis Presley, Pat Boone, Nat King Cole, James Brown, Solomon Burke, Wilson Pickett, Prince, John Legend, Drake, and Jay-Z.

The years 1955 to 1975 constitute two foundation decades in the assembly of the great American "Wall of Songs". Music across the United States changed dramatically during this 20-year period. Audio technology exploded; music radio thrived; "American Bandstand" and "Soul Train" rocked TV-watching teenagers; roots tunes and other music sub-culture songs secured pop chart traction; young artists wrote and performed their own compositions; lyrics entered the culture-defining currency and took sides in political conflicts; regional music companies attained both national and international attention; and visionary record label leaders created million-dollar enterprises from scratch.

All of this aesthetic/technological/capitalistic activity provided the groundwork for the assembly and expansion of a magical and majestic great American "Wall of Songs". Each audio brick in the wall (with apologies to Pink Floyd, of course) was an outstanding hit song. Not just any recording, though. Only the most memorable, influential, and significant renditions were enshrined. During 1955 to 1975 releases like "(We're Gonna) Rock Around the Clock" and "Hound Dog" were joined by tunes like "Respect," "Satisfaction," and "Let It Be." The artistic fingerprints on the "Wall of Songs" can be traced to Hank Williams, Fats Domino, Chuck Berry, Muddy Waters, Jackie Wilson, The Beach Boys, The Beatles, The Four Seasons, Diana Ross and The Supremes, Jimi Hendrix, B. B. King, Steppenwolf, Joe Cocker, John Fogerty and CCR, and The Jackson 5. From 1976 to the present, many new artists and many new songs have increased the breadth and height of this "Wall of Songs".

When Ted Gioia views the current impact of the great American "Wall of Songs", he worries. Will the existence of such a strong recorded musical tradition deter the enthusiasm of new songsters? Will it overwhelm future singer-songwriters to compete with the established songbooks of Bob Dylan, Elton John, and Bruce Springsteen? Will the magnificent history of old music literally drive new music out of existence? Is it fair to force contemporary recording stars to deal with the recorded legacies of Ray Charles and Aretha Franklin? Can current artists like Tim McGraw, Drake, Rihanna, Lil' Wayne, and Adele take on the likes of Bonnie Raitt, Stevie Wonder, Paul McCartney, John Lennon, and Smokey Robinson? Time will tell. But the reality is clear. American popular music is a linear flow that is no longer segregated into seldom heard "golden oldies" and often-played new music. From Cole Porter and Duke Ellington to Leadbelly and Bo Diddley to Tim McGraw and Beyonce, singers, songsmiths, and their tunes are much more than just passing fancies. Music is available from all decades at all times of the day upon listener request. The forever nature of old hits, whether from 1925, 1965. 1985, or 2015, should inspire, challenge, energize, and provoke new artists to flourish. Don't worry so much, Ted.

Contrary to Ted Gioia's dystopian projections about the decline and possible death of American popular music, music fans should openly celebrate 1955-to-1975 as the golden age of sonic growth and innovation. Many contemporary recording achievements still feed off of this two-decade base. It is the legacy and treasury of America's audio relevance. Not unlike the literary heritage grounded in Nathaniel Hawthorne, Edgar Allan Poe, and Mark Twain or the rich film history grounded in "Casablanca," "Psycho" and "Star Wars," there is a solid cultural basis of artistic and commercial success found in old songs performed by old artists. This is the great American "Wall of Songs". More than a century in the making, this recorded history is currently available for everyone to enjoy, sample, cover, and utilize in crafting new creative models. It is simultaneously a reflective, progressive, and forward-thinking concept.

(This commentary was originally published as B. Lee Cooper. "Introduction," for THE GREAT AMERICAN WALL OF SONGS, edited by B. Lee Cooper and Frank W. Hoffmann (Monee, Illinois: Paw Paw Press, 2022): 7-10.)

CELEBRATING AUDIO JOYS OF YESTERYEAR – CHRISTMAS SONGS

HERE COMES SANTA CLAUS: 29 SWINGING CHESTNUTS
Various Artists
CD, Bear Family Records BCD 17619, 2021

CHRISTMAS WAY BACK HOME: JOINT SESSIONS AND RARITIES
Various Artists
2 CDs, Jasmine Records JASCD 846, 2017

HERE WE COME A-CAROLING: THE GROUPS CELEBRATE THE HOLIDAYS
Various Artists
2 CDs, Jasmine Records JASCD 832, 2015

SNOWBOUND FOR CHRISTMAS: FUN SONGS, CLASSICS, & RARITIES
Various Artists
2 CDs, Jasmine Records JASCD 803, 2014

Popular Christmas songs live forever. Like audio zombies, they return year-after-year during December to haunt Yuletide revelers. The notion that historic Christian figures must dominate holiday music evaporated more than a century ago. Granted, "O Holy Night" and "Silent Night" remain church choir staples and radio favorites. But since the Second World War the sacred trio of Jesus, Mary, and Joseph have shared annual Christmas jukebox time with the secular trio of Jolly Old St. Nick, a red-nosed reindeer named Rudolph, and Frosty the Snowman. Of course, novelty characters aren't the only non-religious elements that have broadened sonic perspectives on the Christmas season. Prompted by Irving Berlin, Americans universally dream of a joyous "White Christmas." They also plead with absent loved ones - "Please Come Home for Christmas." And they frequently encourage their boyfriends or girlfriends to join them on a cuddly "Sleigh Ride." Romance blooms again and again each December.

There are also powerful youth-oriented motives behind many popular Christmas tunes. For instance, teenage dance interests are clearly articulated in "Jingle Bell Rock." More selfish financial concerns are voiced in adult terms in songs like "Five Pound Box of Money." There are also laughable novelty numbers like "The Happy Reindeer," warmly vocalized invitations to stroll through the "Winter Wonderland," and rich praise for cold weather and seasonal foliage in "Let It Snow! Let It Snow! Let It Snow!" and "Mistletoe and Holly." Holiday joy can even be found in classical orchestrations such as "The Nutcracker Suite."

Many of the aforementioned tunes appear in Bear Family's HERE COMES SANTA CLAUS: 29 SWINGING CHESTNUTS. Numerous mid-20th century pop performers - including Pearl Bailey, Les Brown, Bing Crosby, Ella Fitzgerald, Mahalia Jackson, Peggy Lee, and Frank Sinatra - offer upbeat renditions of familiar sacred and secular holiday songs. The term "chestnuts" extends well beyond Nat King Cole's hit version of "The Christmas Song." In fact, this collection encompasses a wide realm of well-known gospel, inspirational, and pop recordings. With the exceptions of "Happy Birthday To You" and "Auld Lang Syne," no yearly-repeated celebratory tunes are more frequently performed than America's Christmas songbook.

The remaining three holiday collections - CHRISTMAS WAY BACK HOME (2017), HERE WE COME A-CAROLING (2015), and SNOWBOUND FOR CHRISTMAS (2014) - offer a sleigh-full of multi-voiced renditions of popular December ditties. These three compilations feature spirited performances by M-O-R artists appearing in duets, trios, quartets, and larger vocal ensembles. It is harmonic caroling on cut after cut. It is a cavalcade of traditional Christmas music designed for family consumption. It combines traditional Christian imagery with Yuletide commercialism, old hymns with new novelty hits, and adult romantic interests and childhood nostalgia expressed with seasonal sincerity.

CHRISTMAS WAY BACK HOME is a two-disc, 57-song holiday extravaganza. It contains duets by Jo Stafford & Gordon MacRae ("O Holy Morning"), Martha Tilton & Harry Babbit ("'Twas The Night Before Christmas"), Connee Boswell & Russ Morgan ("Let It Snow! Let It Snow! Let It Snow!"), and Kitty Kallen & Richard Hayes ("Silver Bells"). Other tracks offer pop artists backed by small vocal ensembles. These include Johnny Mercer & The Pied Pipers ("Winter Wonderland"), Dick Haymes & The Ken Darby Singers ("Santa Claus Is Ridin' the Trail"), Dick Haymes & The Andrews Sisters ("There's No Man Like a Snowman"). Alvino Rey & The King Sisters ("Santa Claus Is Comin' To Town"), Perry Como & The Ray Charles Singers ("Home for The Holidays"), and Jerry Gray & The Andrews Sisters ("I've Got My Love to Keep Me Warm"). This extensive collection is also chocked full of orchestral arrangements by Billy May ("Joy to The World"), Glenn Miller ("Jingle Bells"), Leroy Anderson ("Sleigh Ride"), and Vaughn Monroe ("A Marshmallow World"). A few of the big band numbers are supplemented with brief vocal interludes as well.

HERE WE COME A-CAROLING is a two-disc, 71-song anthology of Yuletide recordings performed by harmonizing duets, larger brother or sister acts, and other bigger vocal groups. Artists presented include The Everly Brothers ("God Rest Ye Merry Gentlemen"), The Ames Brothers ("What Child Is This"), The Mills Brothers ("I'll Be Home For Christmas"), The DeJohn Sisters ("The Only Thing I Want For Christmas"), The Lennon Sisters ("Every Night When You Say A Prayer"), The McGuire Sisters ("Frosty The Snowman"), The Song Spinners ("The Toymaker's Dream"), and The Ray Charles Singers ("Angels We Have Heard On High").

SNOWBOUND FOR CHRISTMAS is a two-disc, 58-song tribute to traditional holiday melodies. Orchestral groups, individual performers, and vocal ensembles share the playbill on this assembly of re-issued recordings. Lawrence Welk ("Merry Christmas Polka"), Fred Waring ("Jingle Bells"), and Guy Lombardo ("White Christmas") offer particularly bouncy tunes. Dinah Shore ("I Wish You a Merry Christmas"), Red Foley ("Rudolph, The Red-Nosed Reindeer"), and Ernest Tubb ("Blue Christmas") present stylistically predictable material. And The Andrews Sisters & Bing Crosby ("Twelve Days of Christmas"), Les Paul & Mary Ford ("Santa Claus Is Comin' To Town"), and The DeCastro Sisters ("Snowbound for Christmas") are uniformly peppy and preppy. This songfest is drawn from holiday LP vinyl releases that were originally issued during the 1940s and 1950s.

These four Christmas collections are entertaining, but not historically enlightening. They are illustrative of both sacred and secular holiday tunes, but far from indicative of the madcap variety of 1940-1965 American Yuletide releases. They offer beautiful harmonizing and skillful orchestration, yet they fail to exhibit the lyrical creativity, bizarre story lines and song parodies, and zany vocalizations that typified mid-20th century pop Christmas recordings. For 21st century listeners, these Bear Family and Jasmine anthologies narrow the boundaries of America's seasonal music jamboree. At best, the European compilers cherry-pick the most publicly acceptable, least offensive examples of pop holiday numbers. At worst, the compilers censor the sounds of the '40s, '50s, and early '60s by omitting key original performers, wild comic observations about Santa Claus, and sexually suggestive lyrics about Christmas-time dating and mating.

Let's get specific. Precisely what has been left out of these song-stuffed 21st century holiday retrospectives. First, classic versions of important Christmas tunes are strangely overlooked. This includes releases by Chuck Berry ("Run Rudolph Run"). Bobby Helms ("Jingle Bell Rock"), Eartha Kitt ("Santa Baby"), Mario Lanza ("Ave Maria"). Brenda Lee ("Rockin' Around the Christmas Tree"), Roy Orbison ("Pretty Paper"), Elvis Presley ("Blue Christmas"), The Harry Simeone Choral ("The Little Drummer Boy"), and Mel Torme ("The Christmas Song"). Second, holiday humor is largely ignored. No representation is offered for Mel Blanc ("The Hat I Got for Christmas Is Too Beeg"), Bill Buchanan & Dickie Goodman ("Santa and The Satellite"), Art Carney ("Santa and The Doddle-Li-Bop"), Jerry Lewis ("I've Had A Very Merry Christmas"), David Seville ("The Chipmunk Song -- Christmas Don't Be Late"), and Ray Stevens ("Santa Claus Is Watching You"). Third, foreign language titles are ignored. There is no acknowledgement of Trini Lopez ("El Nino Del Tambor"), Augie Rios ("Donde Esata Santa Claus"), and the hilarious Yogi Yorgesson ("Yingle Bells"). Fourth, holiday song parodies are skipped over altogether. No fun tracks are offered by Dorothy Collins ("Mr. Santa"), Stan Freberg & Daws Butler ("Christmas Dragnet"), Homer & Jethro ("All I Want For Christmas Is My Upper Plate"). Spike Jones and His City Slickers ("I Saw Mommy Kissing Santa Claus"), and Fred Waring & His Pennsylvanians ("Rudolph, The Red-Nosed Reindeer").

And there's more. Fifth, children's perspectives on comical holiday happenings are unexplainably black-balled. This eliminates performances by Jimmy Boyd ("I Say Mommy Kissing Santa Claus"), Buck Owens ("Santa Looked A Lot Like Daddy"), and Gayla Peevey ("I Want a Hippopotamus For Christmas"). Sixth, hipster tales of holiday pranks are shelved. This action eliminates recordings by Louis Armstrong ("Zat You, Santa Claus"), Edd "Kookie" Byrnes ("Yulesville"), Oscar McLollie ("Dig That Crazy Santa Claus"), and Phil Moore ("Blink Before Christmas"). Seventh, influential Afro-American R&B renditions of traditional Christmas hits are slighted. There are no illustrations of songs by The Cadillacs ("Rudolph, The Red-Nosed Reindeer"), The Drifters ("White Christmas"), The Orioles ("O Holy Night"), or The Ravens ("Silent Night"). Eighth, no bluesmen are included. This means the omission of songs by Charles Brown ("Please Come Home For Christmas"), Detroit Junior ("Christmas Day"), Gatemouth Brown ("Christmas Blues"), Johnny Otis and Friends ("Far Away Xmas Blues"), and Joe Turner ("Christmas Date Boogie"). Finally, all sorts of sexually suggestive holiday tunes are forbidden. This censorship covers numbers by Jimmy Butler ("Trim Your Tree"), Thelma Cooper ("I Want A Man For Xmas"), Ella Fitzgerald and Louis Jordan ("Baby, It's Cold Outside"), Amos Milburn ("Let's Make Christmas Merry, Baby"), Johnny Moore's Three Blazers ("Merry Christmas, Baby"), Elvis Presley ("Santa Claus Is Back in Town"), and Titus Turner ("Christmas Morning").

Christmas songs remain an annual American obsession. All four holiday anthologies examined in this review focus on mid-20th century pop recording artists and their distinctive takes on sacred/secular holiday songbooks. Unfortunately, this highly selective approach reflects only a portion of the holiday music mania that thrived in the United States between 1945 and 1965. The audio material presented in the Bear Family and Jasmine compilations is predictable, but not bland. Established singing stars perform widely-recognized Yuletide hits with appropriate zeal. What's especially problematic, though, is the under-representation of black recording artists, humorous and suggestive holiday tunes, and classic hit versions of well-known Christmas songs within these four anthologies. Perhaps it is the compilers' desire to depict mid-20th century American holiday music as less pluralistic, non-controversial, and untainted by either the teenage rebellion of the '50s and '60s or the black musical ascendency during the same period. Of course, that is creating an even bigger social myth than the one concerning a Jolly Old Fat Man who dwells at the North Pole and delivers gifts worldwide via a reindeer-pulled sleigh each December 25th.

CELEBRATING AUDIO JOYS OF YESTERYEAR – HALLOWEEN AND HORROR TUNES

THE SHADOW KNOWS MORE: 35 SCARY TALES FROM THE VAULTS OF HORROR
Various Artists
CD, Bear Family BCD 17545, 2020

THE MOJO MAN'S HALLOWEEN PARTY: 28 SPOOKY SONGS FROM THE CRYPT
Various Artists
CD, Koko-Mojo KM-CD 81, 2019

Joyous shouts of "Trick or Treat!" were absent. So were little ones disguised as cowboys, Ninja Turtles, princesses, or pirates. October 31, 2020 was depressing. There were fewer carved Jack-O-Lanterns; there was less candy circulating; and there were fewer lighted porches welcoming small strangers. The coronavirus manifested itself during Halloween as if it was the viral embodiment of the Grinch who stole Christmas. The potential magic of an October night was dramatically diminished. Ironically, facial coverings were more prevalent than ever before. Adults joined children in mask wearing, but not for the fun of fooling anybody. No matter how gayly colored, COVID-19 face protectors could not substitute for the former plastic visages of Snow White, Darth Vader, or Mickey Mouse. Across the United States, children and parents longed for the return of celebratory normalcy - and for tales of The Great Pumpkin as well.

The sad experience of October 31, 2020 notwithstanding, most scholarship on traditional Halloween celebrations depicts that evening as a cosmic clash of dualities. That is, angelic children threaten to perpetrate devilish acts if sweet treats are withheld. Likewise, pagan rituals of human sacrifice are memorialized in recited stories of ghosts and graveyards while popular culture characters like Wonder Woman, Batman, and Superman are lauded in fancy costumes. The wicked world of witches and warlocks collides with child-centered playfulness and innocent masquerading. Fascinating documentations of late October high jinks include: HALLOWEEN: AN AMERICAN HOLIDAY, AN AMERICAN HISTORY (Pelican, 1998) by Lesley Pratt Bannatyne; HALLOWEEN: FROM PAGAN RITUAL TO PARTY NIGHT (Oxford U. P., 2002) by Nicholas Rogers; HALLOWEEN AND OTHER FESTIVALS OF DEATH AND LIFE (U. of Tennessee P., 1994) by Jack Santino; and HALLOWEEN: THE HISTORY OF AMERICA'S DARKEST HOLIDAY (Dover, 2016) by David J. Skal. Even fastidious hostess Martha Stewart has internalized the sweet-dominated annual October celebration in HALLOWEEN: DELICIOUS TRICKS AND WICKED TREATS FOR YOUR SCARIEST HALLOWEEN EVER (Clarkson N. Potter, 2001).

THE SHADOW KNOWS MORE and THE MOJO MAN'S HALLOWEEN PARTY are additions to the ever-expanding audio menagerie of ghosts, goblins, ghouls, and gremlins. Rare recordings abound in these two collections. Both anthologies skip over frequently referenced recordings like: "Dead Man's Stroll," "Dinner with Drac," "Eye of

The Zombie," "Frankenstein," "Ghostbusters," "Haunted House," "I Put a Spell on You," "(It's A) Monsters' Holiday," "Monster Mash," "Morgus the Magnificent." "Nightmare On My Street," "The Purple People Eater," "Superstition," "Thriller," "Werewolves of London," and "Witch Doctor." Instead, these new collections delve deeply into instrumental representations of discomfort, fear, and uncertainty. Finally, both the Bear Family set and the Koko-Mojo compilation depict classic horror characters ranging from Dr. Frankenstein's Monster, Dracula, and The Werewolf to Jack the Ripper, Dr. Jekyll and Mr. Hyde, and a multitude of zombies and other creatures of the night. There are three duplications within the two releases - "Experiment in Terror," "Frankie and Igor at A Rock & Roll Party," and "The Voodoo Walk." But the remainder of recordings are distinctive, diabolical, and valuable additions to the realm of anthologized Halloween tunes.

THE SHADOW KNOWS MORE features 35 cunning, comical, crypt-shaking cuts originally issued between 1930 and 1966. Among these tracks is a 1930 radio transcription of actor/director Orson Welles introducing "The Detective Story Hour." His words are still familiar today. Welles drones, "Who knows what evil lurks in the hearts of men? The Shadow knows." Next, singer-guitarist Paul Peek warns his fickle female partner that he is aware of every questionable romantic move she makes. Peek's 1966 Columbia recording is titled "The Shadow Knows." Beyond these two CD title-affirming commentaries, instrumental releases are dominant. These tunes include: "The Creep" by Ted Heath, "El Vampiro" by Los Gibson Boys, "Hell's Bells" by David Carroll, and "The Raven" by Freddy Countryman. There are also several tributes to '50s and '60s TV hosts of late-night horror movie shows. They include audio salutes to Bob Guy's "Jeepers Creepers Theater" on KCOP-TV in Los Angeles, to Baron Daemon's night-time program on WNYS-TV in Syracuse, New York; and to John "Roland" Zacherle's "Shock Theater" broadcast on WCAU-TV in Philadelphia. Other interesting tunes assembled for THE SHADOW KNOWS MORE are: "Don' Meet Mr. Frankenstein" by Carlos Casal, Jr., "Dr. Jekyll and Mr. Hyde" by The Crossfires, "The Ghost Song" by Salty Holmes, "The Naughty Ghost" by Jan August, "Skeleton In The Closet" by Putney Dandridge, "Split Personality (Jekyll and Hyde)" by Jim Burgett, and "Spooks!" by Louis Armstrong.

THE MOJO MAN'S HALLOWEEN PARTY consists of 28 recordings that were first released between 1950 and 1962. This haunting horror compilation highlights happy social activities - dining, dancing, drinking, and other party-related pursuits. Of course, monsters and mayhem are interspersed with music and midnight hour shenanigans. Songs presented include: "At the House of Frankenstein" by Big Bee Kornegay, "Happy Halloween" by John Zacherle, "Igor's Party" by Tony and The Monstrosities, "Monster Party" by Bill Doggett, "The Monster Twist" by Tyrone A'Saurus and His Cro-Magnons, "The Mummy's Ball" by The Verdicts, "Screamin' Ball (At Dracula Hall)" by The Duponts, and "Zombee Jamboree" by Calypso Carnival, featuring King Flash. Considerable attention is also paid to cemetary plots and tombstones. These spooky subjects are explored in "Graveyard" by The Blenders, "Graveyard Boogie" by Little Victor, "Graveyard Cha Cha" by The Three D's, "Graveyard Giggle" by Frank N. Stein and The Tombstones, and "Walking Through a Cemetary" by Claudine Clark. Many other scary cuts are also fascinating. Check out "Gwendolyn and The Werewolf" by Hutch Davie and The Honky Tonkers, "Haunted House" by Oscar Hamod and His Majestics, "Little Demon" by Screamin' Jay Hawkins, "Voodoo Doll" by The Interiors, and "Zombie" by The Harlem Wildcats.

The unanticipated, unthinkable moratorium on 2020 Halloween festivities was regrettable. I'm still bummed out about missing out on all of those leftover trick-or-treat chocolates. But individual memories of earlier Halloween treats, pranks, and frights can be rekindled. Individual sonic pleasures are reasonable alternatives to mandated social distancing. THE SHADOW KNOWS MORE and THE MOJO MAN'S HALLOWEEN PARTY offer familiar paths to future October enjoyment. These two discs feature raucous screams and chilling howls, inventive tales of graveyard mischief and malevolence, and rocking rhythms loud enough to raise the dead. Rather than just curling up with a short story by Edgar Allan Poe or a novel by either Bram Stoker or Mary Shelley, just insert one of these CDs into your Bose player, turn up the volume, and enjoy an audio voyage to Transylvania and beyond.

David Carroll

ACKNOWLEDGING PERSONAL MORTALITY

David Frizzell

TRIBUTE RECORDINGS AS LYRICAL EULOGIES

The passing of a popular music performer often prompts public sympathy and career-assessing recorded eulogies. Tribute songs offer commentaries on the lifestyles, the achievements, and the influences of special musicians. From Enrico Caruso to Jimmy Hendrix, from Billie Holiday to Janis Joplin, feelings of loss experienced by friends and by fans alike are represented in rhythm and verse. Occasionally, the death of a star will trigger an even broader salute concerning the potential end of a particular musical era. This enlarged tribute scope is demonstrated in "American Pie", "I Dreamed of A Hill-Billy Heaven", "Nightshift", "Reflections", "R.O.C.K. In The U.S.A. (A Salute To 60s Rock)", "Rock and Roll Heaven", "The Rock Stops Here", "Sir Duke", "Sweet Soul Music", and "Teenage Heaven".

Some tribute tunes are intensely personal, as when David Frizzell eulogizes his older brother "Lefty" or when Jimmy Vaughan leads a tribute to his brother Stevie Ray in "Six Strings Down". More standard tribute acknowledgements are performed by stylistic admirers, by fellow band members, or by future admirers. For example, songs hailing Hank Williams - "The Death of Hank Williams", "From Hank to Hendrix", "Hank, It Will Never Be the Same Without You", and "Hank Williams, You Wrote My Life"; or Bob Wills - "Bob Wills Is Still the King", "Bob's Got a Swing Band In Heaven", and "Lone Star Beer and Bob Wills Music"; or Elvis Presley - "Big Train (From Memphis)", "Blue Christmas (Without Elvis)", "E.P. Express", "From Graceland to The Promised Land", "The King Is Gone", and "We Remember the King" illustrate typical approaches to tribute recordings.

Discographic Illustrations

"American Pie" (United Artists 50856)
Don McLean (1971)

"Angel Of Harlem" (Island 99254)
U2 (1988)

"Are You Sure Hank Done It This Way" (RCA Victor 10379)
Waylon Jennings (1975)

"Big Train (From Memphis)" (Warner Brothers 29100)
John Fogerty (1984)

"Blue Christmas (Without Elvis)" (Appaloosa 112)
Leigh Grady (1977)

"Bob Wills Is Still the King" (RCA Victor 10379)
Waylon Jennings (1975)

"Bob's Got a Swing Band in Heaven" (ABC 12337)
Red Steagall (1978)

"A Bottle of Wine and Patsy Cline" (MCA 53762)
Marsha Thornton (1990)

"Buddy Holly Tribute" (Romar 715)
Micky Dolenz (1974)

"Buddy's Song" (EMI 81128)
Bobby Vee (1992)

"Cole, Cooke, And Redding" (Atlantic 2722)
Wilson Pickett (1970)

"The Death of Hank Williams" (King 1172)
Jack Cardwell (1953)

"Down In New Orleans" (Oahu CD 404)
Ray Fuller and The Blues Rockers (1997)

"E.P. Express" (Mercury 55009)
Carl Perkins (1977)

"Elvis Is A Legend" (Dee Bee 20)
B.F. Snow (1977)

"Free Bird" (MCA 40328)
Lynyrd Skynyrd (1974)

"From Graceland to The Promised Land" (MCA 40804)
Merle Haggard And The Strangers (1977)

"From Hank to Hendrix" (Reprise CD 45057)
Neil Young (1992)

"Gene And Eddie" (EMI CD 53728)
The Stray Cats (1996)

"Goodbye King of Rock 'n' Roll" (True 107)
Leon Everette (1977)

"Hank" (MGM 14550)
Hank Williams, Jr. (1973)

"Hank, It Will Never Be the Same Without You" (Decca 28630)
Ernest Tubb (1953)

"Hank Williams, You Wrote My Life" (Columbia 10265)
Moe Bandy (1975)

"(He's Just a Runaway) Bob Marley Tribute" (Cotillion 46017)
Sister Sledge (1981)

"I Dreamed of a Hill-Billy Heaven" (Capitol 4567)
Tex Ritter (1961)

"I Was with Red Foley (The Night He Passed Away)" (MGM 14002)
Luke the Drifter, Jr. (1968)

"In Memory of Johnny Horton" (J&J 003)
Johnny Hardy (1961)

"In the Quiet Morning (For Janis Joplin)" (A&M 1362)
Joan Baez (1972)

"Johnny Ace's Last Letter" (Hollywood 1031)
Johnny Moore And The Three Blazers (1955)

"Johnny Has Gone" (Savoy 1153)
Varetta Dillard (1955)

"Johnny's Still Singing" (King 4778)
The Five Wings (1955)

"The King Is Gone" (Scorpion 135)
Ronnie McDowell (1977)

"Lefty" (Viva 49778)
David Frizzell (1981)

"(Life To Legend) Bob Wills Tribute" (Starday 904)
Gene Henslee (1970)

"Lone Star Beer and Bob Wills Music" (ABC/Dot 17610)
Red Steagall (1976)

"Missing Stevie" (Inak CD 9017)
Bernard Allison (1993)

"Missing You" (RCA 13966)
Diana Ross (1984)

"Nightshift" (Motown 1773)
The Commodores (1985)

"Nightshift" (MCA 1333737)
Nashville Nightshift (1985)

"Ode To Otis Redding" (Diamond 237)
Mark Johnson (1968)

"The Real Buddy Holly Story" (Elektra 46616)
Sonny Curtis (1980)

"Reflections" (Sony AK 66394)
Charlie Daniels (1995)

"Rock And Roll Heaven" (Haven 7002)
The Righteous Brothers (1974)

"R.O.C.K. In The U.S.A. (A Salute To 60s Rock)" (Riva 884455)
John Mellencamp (1986)

"The Rock Stops Here" (Cool 101)
Eric Carmen (n.d.)

"Sir Duke" (Tamla 54281)
Stevie Wonder (1977)

"Six Strings Down" (Epic EK 67599)
Jimmy Vaughan, Eric Clapton, Bonnie Raitt, Robert Cray, B.B. King, Buddy Guy, Dr. John, and Art Neville (1996)

"A Song for Hank Williams" (Scepter 12389)
John Edward Beland (1973)

"Sweet Soul Music" (Atco 6463)
Arthur Conley (1967)

"Teenage Heaven" (Sony AK 66394)
Johnny Cymbal (1995)

"Thanks E.T. Thanks A Lot" (SCR 162)
Billy Parker (1979)

"They Needed a Song Bird in Heaven (So God Took Caruso Away)" (Cardinal 2040)
Anthony Urato (1921)

"Three Stars" (Crest 1057)
Tommy Dee, with Carol Kay and The Teen-Aires (1959)

"A Tribute to A King" (Stax 248)
William Bell (1968)

"Tribute To Buddy Holly" (Rollercoaster RCCD 6002)
Mike Berry And The Outlaws (1998)

"Tribute To Freddie" (Bullseye Blues BB 9588)
Andrew "Jr. Boy" Jones (1997)

"Tribute To Hound Dog" (Ruf CD 51416 1354)
Luther Allison (1995)

"Tribute To Luther Allison" (Blue Thumb CD 314 547 433-2)
Lucky Peterson (1999)

"Walking In Memphis" (Atlantic 87747)
Marc Cohn (1991)

"We Remember the King" (Spectrum CD 550 838-2)
Johnny Cash (1998)

Print References

B. Lee Cooper. "Audio Musicology: A Discography of Tributes to Musical Styles and Recording Artists." INTERNATIONAL JOURNAL OF INSTRUCTIONAL MEDIA, 26:4 (1999): 459-467.

B. Lee Cooper. "From Johnny Ace to Frank Zappa: Debating the Meaning of Death in Rock Music - a Review Essay." POPULAR CULTURE IN LIBRARIES, 3:1 (1995): 51-75.

B. Lee Cooper. "A Taxonomy of Tributes on Compact Disc." POPULAR MUSIC AND SOCIETY, 20 (Summer 1996): 204-217.

B. Lee Cooper. "Tribute Discs, Career Development, and Death: Perfecting the Celebrity Product from Elvis Presley to Stevie Ray Vaughan." POPULAR MUSIC AND SOCIETY, 28 (May 2005): 229-248.

B. Lee Cooper. "Tribute Recordings as Teaching Tools: Recommended Audio Resources." INTERNATIONAL JOURNAL OF INSTRUCTIONAL MEDIA, 34:2 (2007): 1-11.

Bill Griggs. "'American Pie : Was It a Tribute to Buddy Holly? Was It a Protest Song?" ROCKIN' 50s, No. 20 (October 1989): 22-23.

Charles Reinhart. "John Lennon Tribute Records." GOLDMINE, No. 70 (March 1982): 15-16.

George Plasketes. "Like a Version: Cover Songs and The Tribute Trend in Popular Music." STUDIES IN POPULAR CULTURE, 14:1 (1992): 1-18.

George Plasketes. "Look What They've Done to My Song: Covers and Tributes - An Annotated Discography, 1980-1995." POPULAR MUSIC ANDSOCIETY, 19 (Spring 1995): 79-106.

(This commentary was originally published as B. Lee Cooper. "Tribute Recordings as Eulogies," in PROMINENT THEMES IN POPULAR SONGS, edited by B. Lee Cooper and Frank W. Hoffmann (Charleston, South Carolina: Paw Paw Press, 2015): 350-355.)

AGING AND DEATH

Death is a somber subject. Yet it is a common topic in song lyrics. Popular recordings often address the passing of soldiers ("Billy and Sue" and "War"), the execution of criminals ("Green, Green Grass of Home" and "Tom Dooley"), and even incidents of murder ("Mack the Knife" and "Stagger Lee") and suicide ("Ode to Billy Joe" and "A Well Respected Man"). Of course, most individuals experience death as an unfortunate accident or as the natural result of old age. Numerous singers and composers address stages of physical decline, personal feelings about the passing of elderly parents, friends, or loved ones, and the inevitable conclusion of the personal life cycle.

Although Little Milton contends that "Age Ain't Nothin' But A Number", The Beatles express genuine concern about the impact of aging on a romantic relationship in "When I'm Sixty-Four". Jerry Lee Lewis, Ray Price, Bruce Springsteen, and David Bowie address varying perspectives on growing older in "39 And Holding", "Forty and Fadin'", "Glory Days", and "Golden Years". In 1980, the 83-year-old comedian George Burns asserted "I Wish I Was Eighteen Again". Ray Bolger and Ethel Merman tease each other about the problems of aging in "Dearie", while Peggy Lee reflects on the end of life existentially by singing "Is That All There Is?" Frank Sinatra was a particularly skillful and insightful commentator on the nature of a life well-lived. He addressed later life in "It Was a Very Good Year", "My Way", and "That's Life".

The passing of a loved one may be experienced in childhood ("Patches"), at mid-life ("Honey"), or during old age ("He Stopped Loving Her Today"). Frankie Laine capsules the feelings of those left behind because of a death in "You Gave Me A Mountain". The accidental death of a young person is always quite shocking - and generally less comprehensible than the passing of an elderly individual. Lyrical illustrations of unanticipated deaths include references to car crashes, airplane disasters, and motorcycle accidents. Recordings featuring these topics are "Dead Man's Curve", "Ebony Eyes", "Last Kiss", "Leader Of the Pack", and "Seasons In The Son".

Discographic Illustrations

"Age Ain't Nothin' But A Number" (MCA 52184)
Little Milton (1983)

"And When I Die" (Columbia 45008)
Blood, Sweat and Tears (1969)

"Alone Again (Naturally)" (Mam 3619)
Gilbert O'Sullivan (1972)

"Autumn Of My Life" (United Artists 50318)
Bobby Goldsboro (1968)

"Beautiful Girl" (Brunswick 6694)
Bing Crosby (1933)

"A Beginning From An End" (Liberty 55849)
Jan And Dean (1966)

"The Bells" (Federal 12114)
Billy Ward And The Dominoes (1952)

"Billy And Sue" (Hickory 1395)
B.J. Thomas (1966)

"Car Crash" (Jan-Lar 102)
Cadets (1960)

"Daisy A Day" (MGM 14463)
Jud Strunk (1973)

"Dead Man's Curve" (Liberty 55672)
Jan And Dean (1964)

"Dearie" (Decca 24873)
Ray Bolger And Ethel Merman (1950)

"Ebony Eyes" (Warner Brothers 5199)
The Everly Brothers (1961)

"Fire And Rain" (Warner Brothers 7423)
James Taylor (1970)

"Forty And Fadin'" (Dimension 1031)
Ray Price (1982)

"Games People Play" (Capitol 2248)
Joe South (1969)

"Give Us Your Blessings" (Red Bird 10030)
The Shangri-Las (1965)

"Glory Days" (Columbia 04924)
Bruce Springsteen (1985)

"Goin' Down Slow" (Dunhill 4379)
Bobby "Blue" Bland (1974)

"Golden Years" (RCA 10441)
David Bowie (1975)

"Green, Green Grass Of Home" (Parrot 40009)
Tom Jones (1966)

"He Stopped Loving Her Today" (Epic 50867)
George Jones (1980)

"Honey" (United Artists 50283)
Bobby Goldsboro (1968)

"I Feel That Old Age Coming On" (King 4276)
Wynonie Harris (1949)

"I Wish I Was Eighteen Again" (Mercury 57011)
George Burns (1980)

"In My Eyes" (MCA 52282)
John Conlee (1983)

"Is That All There Is?" (Capitol 2602)
Peggy Lee (1969)

"It Was A Very Good Year" (Reprise 0429)
Frank Sinatra (1966)

"The Last Game Of The Season (Blind Man In The Bleachers)" (Big Tree 16052)
David Geddes (1975)

"Last Kiss" (Josie 923)
J. Frank Wilson And The Cavaliers (1964)

"Leader Of The Pack" (Red Bird 014)
The Shangri-Las (1964)

"Live Your Life Before You Die" (Blue Thumb 262)
The Pointer Sisters (1975)

"Mack The Knife" (Atco 6147)
Bobby Darin (1959)

"My Way" (Reprise 0817)
Frank Sinatra (1969)

"No Headstone For My Grave" (Mercury 73402)
Jerry Lee Lewis (1973)

"O Death, Where Is Thy Sting?" (Columbia 2652)
Bert Williams (1919)

"Ode To Billy Joe" (Capitol 5950)
Bobbie Gentry (1967)

"Old And Wise" (Arista 1048)
The Alan Parsons Project (1983)

"Old Doc Brown" (Columbia CL 1464)
Johnny Cash (1960)

"Patches" (Atlantic 2748)
Clarence Carter (1962)

"Seasons In The Sun" (Bell 45532)
Terry Jacks (1974)

"Stagger Lee" (ABC-Paramount 9972)
Lloyd Price (1958)

"Teen Angel" (MGM 12845)
Mark Dinning (1959)

"Tell Laura I Love Her" (RCA 7745)
Ray Peterson (1960)

"That's Life" (Reprise 0531)
Frank Sinatra (1966)

"39 And Holding" (Elektra 47095)
Jerry Lee Lewis (1981)

"Too Young to Be A Widow" (Coed 586)
Cobey Carson (1964)

"War" (Gordy 7101)
Edwin Starr (1970)

"The Way We Were/ Try To Remember" (Buddah 463)
Gladys Knight And The Pips (1975)

"When I Grow Too Old To Dream" (Capitol 4048)
Ed Townsend (1958)

"When I'm Dead And Gone" (MGM 14206)
Bob Summers (1971)

"A Well Respected Man" (Reprise 0420)
The Kinks (1965)

"When I'm Sixty-Four" (Capitol 2653)
The Beatles (1967)

"Yes" (Epic 03917)
Billy Swan (1983)

"Yesterday, When I Was Young" (Dot 17246)
Roy Clark (1969)

"You Gave Me A Mountain" (ABC 11174)
Frankie Laine (1969)

Print References

Robert A. Armour and J. Carol Williams. "Death in Popular Culture," in THE HANDBOOK OF AMERICAN POPULAR CULTURE - VOLUME TWO, edited by M. Thomas Inge (Westport, Connecticut: Greenwood Press, 1980): 79-104.

Alan Clayson. DEATH DISCS: AN ACCOUNT OF FATALITY IN POPULAR SONG. London: Sanctuary, 1997.

B. Lee Cooper. "Death", in A RESOURCE GUIDE TO THEMES IN CONTEMPORARY AMERICAN SONG LYRICS, 1950-1985 (Westport, Connecticut: Greenwood Press, 1986): 49-63.

Donald M. Davis. "Rock 'n' Roll and Death: Nihilism in Music Videos." FEEDBACK, 27 (Fall 1986): 9-13.

R. Serge Denisoff. "'Teen Angel': Resistance, Rebellion, and Death - Revisited." JOURNAL OF POPULAR CULTURE, 16 (Spring 1983): 116-122.

George E. Dickinson, Michael R. Leming, and Alan C. Mermann (eds.). DYING, DEATH, AND BEREAVEMENT (Second Edition). Guilford, Connecticut:Dushkin Publishing Group, 1994.

Aaron A. Fox. "The Jukebox of History: Narratives of Loss and Desire in the Discourse of Country Music." POPULAR MUSIC, 11 (January 1992): 53-72.

Richard A. Kalish (ed.). DEATH AND DYING: VIEWS FROM MANY CULTURES. New York: Baywood Press, 1980.

Elisabeth Kubler-Ross. ON DEATH AND DYING. New York: Macmillan, 1969.

Katie Letcher Lyle. SCALDED TO DEATH BY THE STEAM: AUTHENTIC STORIES OF RAILROAD DISASTERS AND BALLADS THAT WERE WRITTEN ABOUT THEM. Chapel Hill, North Carolina: Algonquin Books of Chapel Hill, 1991.

Jon Newlin. "Those Great Old Death Songs." WAVELENGTH, No. 33 (July 1983): 19-20.

Bruce L. Plopper and M. Ernest Ness. "Death as Portrayed to Adolescents Through Top 40 Rock and Roll Music." ADOLESCENCE, 28 (Winter 1993): 793-807.

Michael Roos. "Fixin' to Die: The Death Theme in the Music of Bob Dylan." POPULAR MUSIC AND SOCIETY, 8:3-4 (1982): 103-116.

Nick Talevski. TOMBSTONE BLUES: THE ENCYCLOPEDIA OF ROCK OBITUARIES. New York: Omnibus Press, 1999.

Dave Thompson. BETTER TO BURN OUT: THE CULT OF DEATH IN ROCK 'N' ROLL. New York: Thunder's Mouth Press, 1999.

DeLoris Von Nordheim. "Vision of Death in Rock Music and Musicians." POPULAR MUSIC AND SOCIETY, 17 (Summer 1993): 21-31.

Avery D. Weisman. ON DYING AND DENYING: A PSYCHIATRIC STUDY OF TERMINALITY. New York: Behavioral Publications, 1972.

Sean Wilentz and Greil Marcus. THE ROSE AND THE BRIAR: DEATH, LOVE, AND LIBERTY IN THE AMERICAN BALLAD. New York: W.W. Norton and Company, 2005.

Charles Reagan Wilson. "Digging Up Bones: Death in Country Music", in YOU WROTE MY LIFE: LYRICAL THEMES IN COUNTRY MUSIC, edited by Melton A. McLaurin and Richard A. Peterson (Philadelphia, Pennsylvania: Gordon and Breach, 1992): 113-129.

(This commentary was originally published as B. Lee Cooper. "Aging and Death," in PROMINENT THEMES IN POPULAR SONGS, edited by B. Lee Cooper and Frank W. Hoffmann (Charleston, South Carolina: Paw Paw Press, 2015): 7-12.)

OBITUARY - KATHLEEN M. COOPER (1921-2008)

Kathleen Marie Kunde Cooper, the oldest daughter of Walter and Helen Kunde, died of a heart attack on Friday, September 12th. She was a loving wife, a caring mother, a giving nurse, and an unconditional friend to everyone she met. Married to Charles Albert Cooper for 67 years, she was his lifetime partner, his confidant, and his protector. They determined together that sacrificing and vigilance in raising, caring for, educating, and supporting their three children would be their highest parental priority. Mrs. Cooper worked at several jobs throughout her life, but found her professional calling in 1973 when she earned her LPN and began her 12-year nursing career. As a liberal Catholic dedicated to respect for all individuals, social justice, and freedom of opinion, Mrs. Cooper befriended neighbors, fellow churchgoers, and other acquaintances. She never met a stranger.

Mrs. Cooper was dedicated to cooking, gardening, cheering for Chicago sports teams, and watching classic television programs. She prepared homemade soups, fresh salads, and exceptional coffee cakes. Her children and grandchildren adored her desserts, as did her ever-hungry husband. Flowering plants always decorated Mrs. Cooper's yard, front porch, and front room. She loved mums, begonias, and African violets. Mrs. Cooper was a diehard Chicago White Sox fan, but also supported the Bears, the Blackhawks, and even the Cubs (on behalf of her youngest sister). An avid television viewer, Mrs. Cooper enjoyed watching re-runs of classic dramas such as "Perry Mason" and "Quincy", along with courtroom TV shows. She was full of life, always ready for fun, and politically active as a vigorous, life-long Democrat.

A highlight in Mrs. Cooper's life was the joy of music. She and her husband appreciated the special music presentations provided each week at St. Mary's Assisted Living Center. With the encouragement and assistance of her family, she developed a large collection of albums and compact discs. Her favorite artists were Jo Stafford, Margaret Whiting, Perry Como, Bing Crosby, and Connie Boswell. Mrs. Cooper and her husband shared their enjoyment of music with family and friends.

Born on May 29, 1921 in Hammond Indiana, Mrs. Cooper is survived by her 88-year-old husband, by her youngest sister, Dorothy, by three children - Lee, Patty, and Larry, by two daughters-in-law - Jill and Marianna, by five grandchildren - Michael, Laura, Julie, Sabine, and Mieke, and by five great grandchildren - Dustin, Nicholas, Lauren, Sam, and Kiano.

A Mass of Christian burial will be celebrated on Monday September 15, 2008 at 11 AM at the Our Lady of the Rosary Chapel at Morris Hall, 1 Bishops Drive, Lawrenceville. Friends may call on Sunday (this evening) from 7 to 8 PM and Monday (tomorrow) from 10 to 11 AM at the chapel. Burial will be private.

Mr. Cooper has requested that friends wishing to commemorate his wife's life send donations to Holy Rosary Chapel at Morris Hall, One Bishops Drive, Lawrenceville, New Jersey 08648.

Arrangements are under the direction of Poulson & Van Hise Funeral Directors, Lawrenceville (www.poulsonvanhise.com).

OBITUARY - CHARLES A. COOPER (1920-2009)

Charles Albert Cooper was unconditionally dedicated to his wife, to his children and extended family, and to his country. Married to Kathleen Marie (Kunde) Cooper for 67 years, he benefited from her loving support while he provided strength, energy, and financial resources throughout their life together. Mr. Cooper joined his wife, who passed away on September 12, 2008, in enthusiastically encouraging their three children to achieve excellence in academic pursuits and in athletic competition. An exemplary member of what has been labeled "America's greatest generation", he served in the U.S. Marine Corps in the Pacific theatre during World War II, surviving the battle for Iwo Jima. Mr. Cooper was a loyal and loving husband, a caring and supportive father, and a patriotic American citizen.

Born in Lawrenceville, Illinois on February 5, 1920, Mr. Cooper was the second son of William Luther Cooper and Minnie Pauline Cooper. A 1938 graduate of Hammond High School in Hammond, Indiana, Mr. Cooper served in various supervisory roles and quality control capacities in the steel industry in Indiana, Ohio, and Michigan for the majority of his working years. He retired in 1985 from the Michigan-based Fundimensions Corporation, a company that produced Lionel model trains. Mr. Cooper and his wife lived in Rochester, Michigan until 2005 when they relocated to St. Mary's Assisted Living Center in Lawrenceville, New Jersey. Mr. Cooper died of heart failure on January 17, 2009. He was 88 years old.

Mr. Cooper was admired and respected by his friends and fellow-workers for his warm personality, gentle manner, boyish wit, and kind-heartedness. He was an avid reader of spy novels and detective fiction. He enjoyed following his favorite professional football, hockey, and basketball teams and was a particularly strong fan of the Chicago White Sox. He also enjoyed watching television re-runs, especially "Quincy", "Perry Mason", and "Columbo". Dining was a particular highlight for Mr. Cooper, who loved everything his wife cooked as well as commercially prepared pizza, bacon, ham, ice cream, and a myriad of pies and cakes. He also loved to read jokes, hear jokes, and tell jokes. His sense of humor was infectious.

Mr. Cooper is survived by three children - Lee, Patty Jo, and Larry, by two daughters-in-law - Jill and Marianna, by five grandchildren - Michael, Laura, Julie, Sabine, and Mieke, and by six great-grandchildren - Dustin, Nicholas, Lauren, Sam, Katarina, and Kiano. The Cooper Family requests that friends and family members who wish to honor Mr. Cooper's life and memory send donations to the Chapel Fund at St. Mary's Assisted Living Center at One Bishops Drive in Lawrenceville.

Lee and Jill Cooper's children: Michael, Laura & Julie

A HEALTH CRISIS AND MEMORYCARE ASSISTANCE

The Beatles were right. Everybody needs "Help!" at some point in their lives. Being independent, competent, and confident may have been the norm for "Yesterday." But today, with the unexpected onset of Alzheimer's, Parkinson's, or some other debilitating health problem, assistance is mandatory. If a couple hopes to get by with "A Little Help From My Friends," then it is obligatory to establish new medical friendships. Help must be enlisted from highly skilled, empathetic, experienced professionals. MemoryCare filled this vital role for us.

Jill and I retired from our educational positions in 2008. She was a pre-school teacher. I was a history professor and university provost. We moved to Asheville. In 2017 Jill began manifesting cognition loss. In 2018 she was diagnosed with mild Alzheimer's and Parkinson's. We immediately signed on as MemoryCare clients. The "Blue Skies" of our long-time marriage were suddenly being darkened by "Stormy Weather." The progressive nature of Jill's illness demanded careful monitoring and skillfully applied delaying tactics. My role as chief caregiver required definition and guidance. We both sought MemoryCare help to better understand the unwanted journey we were taking.

My avocational interest in popular music has aided me in reflecting upon our medical predicament. Song titles and lyrical images abound as life descriptors. Dealing with dementia necessitates mutual trust and personal determination. The patient can't just concede that it's "Funny How Time Slips Away." Similarly, the caregiver can't casually remark "Don't Worry," everything will be fine. Sustaining the highest possible quality of life for an Alzheimer's patient requires effort and planning. Our marriage vows have "Always" reminded us that our love would be present "Come Rain Or Come Shine." Our unspoken pledge was "You Are My Sunshine" and "I Can't Stop Loving You."

We formally enrolled with MemoryCare in February 2019. There were constant temptations to claim "It's Only Make Believe" about new signs of dementia, or to feel as if we were compelled to dwell alone in "Heartbreak Hotel," Fortunately, Dr. Amy Cohen and her assistant Carly Woods emerged as our "Bridge Over Troubled Water" team. They carefully analyzed Jill's current condition, drafted prescriptions for necessary medications, provided personal counseling about caregiving techniques, and even offered advice about life-time medical and financial planning. Put succinctly, they answered our desperate cries for "Help!" Without fanfare, these two MemoryCare employees communicated "You've Got A Friend" and "Lean On Me."

MemoryCare administrators, doctors, nurses, and staff members demonstate "Amazing Grace" daily. They are experts in dealing with cognitive challenges. They are sympathetic listeners, knowledgeable medical professionals, and empathetic advisors. They live the philosophy "He Ain't Heavy, He's My Brother." Beyond that, they say "Let's Work Together" to dementia patients and their caregivers. The unpredictable and unforgiving nature of Alzheimer's is confronted with the best medical treatment possible.

Cooperative measures and thoughtful counseling allows couples to sense "We Shall Overcome" this unwanted personal challenge.

MemoryCare offered even more learning formats of superior medical consultation. I participated in the six-session Caregiver College program that suggested best practices in dealing with the progressive stages of Alzheimer's disease. Other Zoom session lectures concerning the mixed manifestations of vocal, physical, and emotional changes brought on by dementia were also extremely enlightening. Rather than just advising caregivers "Don't Be Cruel," these supplementary educational activities stressed "Try A Little Tenderness" and "Put A Little Love In Your Heart" as guiding principles of care. MemoryCare coaching is clear and direct. Don't succumb to a "19th Nervous Breakdown" or the lament "It's Too Late" to do anything. A loved one's journey with Alzheimer's merits the supportive pledge "Stand By Me".

The nature of my life-time journey with Jill has not been diminished by her battle with dementia. In fact, my admiration for my cute spouse has grown and deepened as we have struggled together with her mental and physical decline. She's brave. She's involved. She appreciates help. MemoryCare has been a constant helpmate during our time of need. The people we have encountered there resonate with energy, bristle with ideas, and foster hope that enables us to "Imagine" a fulfilled life together. They demonstrate "Respect". They offer genuine concern. And they counsel a balanced perspective in the face of unknowable future challenges.

Last June Jill and I celebrated our 57th wedding anniversary. She couldn't remember the exact date. She couldn't recall the state where we were wed. But she still knew with certainty that I was her husband and her chief caregiver. Her warm smile and her ongoing delight at being with her three children made me think of the soaring devotion voiced by Whitney Houston in "I Will Always Love You."

OBITUARY - JILL E. COOPER (1942-2022)

Jill Cooper assembled memories for more than seven decades. These included the childhood joys of sledding and jumping rope, family trips to the St. Lawrence Seaway in New York and to Oregon, marriage and motherhood, teaching pre-schoolers, and celebrating anniversaries, birthdays, and holidays. It was sad to watch those memories disappear during her final three years of life. Photographs, conversations, and sing-alongs helped postpone the inevitable loss of familiar names, friendly faces, and happy events. But Alzheimer's is unforgiving. To the end, Jill knew she was loved. She will be remembered fondly.

Jill Elizabeth (Cunningham) Cooper died at the age of 80 on July 25, 2022. She bravely battled the mental and physical ravages of Alzheimer's and Parkinson's diseases for several years. She is survived by her husband Lee, three children - Michael, Laura, and Julie, son-in-law - Vivek, two grandsons - Dustin and his wife Katelyn, and Nicholas and his finacee Samantha, and a great grandson - Emmett.

Jill was a loving wife, a devoted mother, and a talented educator. A graduate of Berea (Ohio) High School (1960) and Bowling Green State University (1964), she taught pre-school and kindergarten students across Michigan, Ohio, South Carolina, Georgia, Montana, and Kansas for 50 years. She demonstrated her love for God and for the United Methodist church through volunteer work, as a choir member, and as a Sunday school teacher. Jill was a tireless homemaker, avid gardener, Brownie troop and Cub Scout leader, walking enthusiast, and collector of glass rabbits and Hummel figurines. Following her 2008 retirement to the scenic Blue Ridge Mountains of North Carolina, she attended classes at the Osher Lifelong Learning Institute (OLLI) at UNC Asheville and toured western North Carolina with her husband. Her evening and weekend television interests focused on Michigan State University basketball, major league baseball, and quiz programs like "Jeopardy!" and "Wheel of Fortune."

Jill was beloved by family and friends alike. Caring, selfless, and soft-spoken, she embodied the values of empathy, honesty, and kindness. Her husband treasured her enthusiasm for new adventures in life, her support of his professional career and post-retirement teaching and writing, and her household management skills. Her three children benefited from her constant support, nourishment, and loving advice. Jill's teaching colleagues appreciated her love of children, her eagerness to assist, and her expertise in early childhood education.

Those wishing to honor Jill's life should forward memorial contributions to MemoryCare / 100 Far Horizons Lane/Asheville, North Carolina 28803. Or, visit https://memorycare.org/ to donate online and to learn more about this organization's mission to support families affected by Alzheimer's.

Jody Reynolds

DEATH AND DYING

DEAD GOOD: ETERNAL CLASSICS FROM THE GRIM REAPER'S JUKEBOX
Various Artists
Lucky Parker, compiler
CD, Fantastic Voyage FVCD 177, 2013

GROOVING WITH THE GRIM REAPER: SONGS OF DEATH, TRAGEDY, AND MISFORTUNE, 1954-1962
Various Artists
Groper Odson, compiler
2 CDs, Jasmine JASCD 256, 2013

STILL DEAD! THE GRIM REAPER'S JUKEBOX
Various Artists
Brian Nevill, compiler
CD, Ace CDCHD 1205, 2008

DEAD! THE GRIM REAPER'S GREATEST HITS
Various Artists
Brian Nevill and Roger Armstrong. compilers
CD, Ace CDCHD 1100, 2006

Songs about death are common in American popular music. Commercial recordings often contain references to aging and dying, to military casualties and prison executions, as well as to suicides and homicides. During the early 20th century, for instance, several 78 rpm discs featured lyrics addressing deaths related to railroad accidents, gunfighting, and love triangles. In 1919 singer/comedian Bert Williams issued a Shakespearean-sounding challenge in "O Death, Where Is Thy Sting?". Twelve years later jazz giant Louis Armstrong expressed his frustration with an annoying romantic competitor in "I'll Be Glad When You're Dead, You Rascal You". Other popular crooners addressed the aging process in tunes like "Dearie", "Beautiful Girl", and "Too Old to Cut the Mustard".

More frequently, though, early audio commentaries about death were featured in tales about bad men and bad women. From "Stack O' Lee Blues" and "Frankie and Johnny" to "Pretty Boy Floyd" and "Miss Otis Regrets (She's Unable to Lunch Today)", murder ranked high on lyrical agendas. Death themes were also recounted in western tunes like "Billy the Kid", "Jesse James", "The Streets Of Laredo", and the prophetic "Riders in The Sky (A Cowboy Legend)". Similarly, runaway trains and other dangers associated with railroading constituted a particularly rich field of recorded tales about death and destruction. These songs focused on individual heroism ("John Henry"), attempted suicides ("Trouble in Mind"), engineer bravery ("Casey Jones"), funeral coaches ("Death's Black Train Is Coming"), and train crashes ("The Wreck of Old 97", "The Wreck of The Virginian Train", and "The Wreck on The C&O").

Prior to 1950 relatively little lyrical attention was devoted to automobile accidents, teenage suicides, motorcycle crashes. This changed dramatically as mid-century recordings began to dramatize teenage troubles on 45 rpm releases. By the 1960s there was an identifiable genre of recordings that linked love and death with romantic sincerity. Teenage coffin songs depicted Romeo and Juliet-type tragedies as everyday events. Young lovers suffered lyrically from parental misunderstandings, from socio-economic disparities, from peer criticism, and from the most terrible twists of fate. Pop music composers and singers willingly melded devotion and death. Record sales soared. Coffin songs flourished.

DEAD GOOD is an eclectic collection featuring 30 recordings released between 1955 and 1962. Compiler Lucky Parker capsules his compilation as an audio escapade through the "...heartbreak world of teen tragedy, graveyard grooves, and crypt lickin' classics from the rock 'n' roll era". Signature songs from the teenage coffin genre abound. These include "Ebony Eyes" by the Everly Brothers, "Endless Sleep" by Jody Reynolds, "Patches" by Dickey Lee, "Teen Angel" by Mark Dinning, "Tell Laura I Love Her" by Ray Peterson, and "Tell Tommy I Love Him" by Skeeter Davis. Beyond this expected doomsday material, Dead Good also plumbs planned executions ("The Ballad Of Caryl Chessman (Let Him Live, Let Him Live, Let Him Live)" and "(Why Must I Die) The Girl On Death Row"), tribute tunes ("Three Stars", "Marilyn", and "The Great Tragedy"), cemetery chants ("Dead Man's Stroll", "The Ghost Of Mary Meade", and "Graveyard Giggle"), and suicide songs ("Don't Jump" and "Moody River"). Automobile accidents are also examined in "The Ballad Of Thunder Road", "The Prom", and "Tragic Honeymoon". Compiler Parks extends his net of deadly ditties to capture the over-powering gloom of The Fleetwoods' "Tragedy" and the drunken nuttiness of Nervous Norvus' "Transfusion".

GROOVING WITH THE GRIM REAPER surveys 56 tear-drenched tunes from the 1954-to-1962 period. British compiler Groper Odson anthologizes several popular, readily recognizable death songs performed by Pat Boone, Del Shannon, the Everly Brothers, and Mark Dinning. But he also steps into more interesting audio territory by exploring gun-fighter ballads ("El Paso" and "Big Iron" by Marty Robbins), Native American love tragedies ("Running Bear" by Johnny Preston), folk tunes about murder and capital punishment ("Tom Dooley" by the Kingston Trio"), R&B revenge tales ("There's Something On Your Mind" by Bobby Marchan), country music retrospectives on children's deaths ("The Drunken Driver" by Ferlin Husky, "No School Bus In Heaven" by the Statler Brothers, and "Tragedy On School Bus 27" by Ralph Bowman), and eulogies to dead celebrities ("Message From James Dean" by Bill Hayes and "I Miss You Jimmy" by Varetta Dillard). There are also several novelty numbers represented in this collection. Among the most off-beat death descriptions provided are "Don't Go Near the Indians" by Rex Allen, "A Thousand Feet Below" by Terry Tyler, and "Big Bad John" by Jimmy Dean. This double-disc anthology is loaded with lurid lyrical descriptions of murders and suicides, car wrecks, and plane crashes.

DEAD! and STILL DEAD! combine to create a 48-song, two-disc focus on teenage tragedy. These Ace compilations cover death-related recordings that were released between 1952 and 1974. Compilers Brian Nevill and Roger Armstrong dive into the teen coffin tune tradition with illustrations such as "Give Us Your Blessings" by the Shangri-Las, "Last Kiss" by J. Frank Wilson, "Too Young to Be A Widow" by Cobey Carson, and "Death of An Angel" by Donald Woods and the Vel-Aires. While these two discs also acknowledge such death-song stalwarts as Mark Dinning, the Everly Brothers, Ray Peterson, and Jody Reynolds, they break new ground in terms of devilish deeds and murderous mayhem with "Psycho" by Jack Kittrel, "The Dream" by The Fox [Ike Turner], "A Beginning from An End" by Jan and Dean, and "Goodbye Baby" by Little Caesar. In addition to "The Drunken Driver" and several other auto-related death tunes, this collection highlights hearses and hotrods with "Long Black Limousine" by Vern Stovall and "Dead Man's Curve" by Jan and Dean. Not unexpectedly, airline disasters and motorcycle accidents are also featured in "Flight 1203" by the Beverly Sisters and "Leader of The Pack" by the Shangri-Las. The Dominoes weeping version of "The Bells" and Thomas Wayne's emotion-laden reading of "Tragedy" are typical of the tear-stained tunes in this compilation.

DEAD GOOD, GROOVING WITH THE GRIM REAPER, DEAD!, and STILL DEAD! offer fascinating audio overviews of a two-decade period of teenage angst and personal tragedy. These four anthologies of death songs demonstrate how popular and how genre-jumping these tunes were from the mid-'50s to the mid-'70s. Regrettably, though, these collections are too redundant and too narrowly focused. Death stalked mid-century record-buyers in many, many ways that are omitted in these four CDs. While teenage coffin songs were ubiquitous, so too were other important songs about drug overdoses and violent crimes, about political assassinations and military-related body counts. The Kennedy/Johnson/Nixon years featured fierce singles and thought-provoking album cuts that addressed animal deaths ("Old Rivers" and "Old Sheep"), assassinations ("Abraham, Martin, and John", "Too Many Martyrs", and "Why (The King Of Love Is Dead)"), cannibalism ("Timothy"), comical passings ("Mr. Custer"), drug-related deaths ("Amphetamine Annie", "Freddie's Dead", "Once You Understand", and "The Pusher"), funerals ("Danny Boy" and "Eleanore Rigby"), lynchings ("The Death Of Emmett Till" and "Smackwater Jack"), homocides ("Born In Chicago", "Folsom Prison Blues", "I Shot Mr. Lee", "I Shot The Sheriff", "Mack The Knife", "Maxwell's Silver Hammer", "Mississippi Murderer", "Stagger Lee", and "Swamp Witch"), passings of loved ones and close friends ("Daisy A Day", "He Stopped Loving Her Today", "Honey", "Old Doc Brown", "Patches" [by Clarence Carter], "Ruben James", "The Three Bells (The Jimmy Brown Story)", and "You Gave Me A Mountain"), romantic revenge ("Frankie and Johnny" and "Over You"), suicides ("If You Don't Come Back", "A Most Peculiar Man", "Richard Cory", "Trouble in Mind", and "A Well Respected Man"), tributes and eulogies ("American Pie", "Cole, Cooke, and Redding", "The Death of Hank Williams", "I Dreamed Of A Hill-Billy Heaven", "Ohio", "Rock And Roll Heaven", and "Vincent"), and war-time casualties ("The Battle Hymn Of Lt. Calley", "Billy and Sue", "Billy, Don't Be A Hero", "Blowin' In The Wind", "I-Feel-Like-I'm-Fixin'-To-Die Rag", "The Night They Drove Old Dixie Down", "2 + 2 = ?", "The Universal Soldier", "The Unknown Soldier", "War", and "Where Have All The Flowers Gone"). While these four retrospectives on teenage coffin songs are very interesting, the 1952-1974 period cannot be accurately depicted in terms of death songs without addressing the lyrical legacies of drugs, racism, domestic violence, and international warfare.

(This commentary was originally published as B. Lee Cooper, "Review of DEAD GOOD by Various Artists, GROOVING WITH THE GRIM REAPER by Various Artists, DEAD! by Various Artists, and STILL DEAD! by Various Artists," POPULAR MUSIC AND SOCIETY, 38:4 (October 2015): 539-542.)

PROFESSIONAL RESUME OF B. LEE COOPER

B. LEE COOPER, Ph.D.
Popular Music Research, Ltd.
4 Grey Goose Court
Biltmore Lake, North Carolina 28715
(316) 734-5509 (Cell)
(828) 633-6152 (Home)
ashevillecats1@charter.net (E-mail)

Educational Institutions and Degrees

    D.H.L. (2009) – Academic Excellence (Honorary)
    Newman University – Wichita, Kansas

    Institute for Educational Management (1980)
    Harvard University – Cambridge, Massachusetts

    Ph.D. (1971) – History
    Ohio State University – Columbus, Ohio

    M.A. (1965) – History
    Michigan State University – West Lansing, Michigan

    B.S. cum laude (1964) – History and English
    Bowling Green State University – Bowling Green, Ohio

Teaching and Administrative Experience

2010 - President and CEO of Popular Music Research, Ltd.

2009 - Lecturer in Popular Music for The College For Seniors at the Osher Life-Long Learning Institute at U.N.C. – Asheville

2007 - 2008 Provost and Vice President for Academic Affairs at Newman University

2006 - 2007 Interim President and Provost at Newman University

2002 - 2005 Provost and Vice President for Academic Affairs and Professor of History and American Culture at Newman University

2000 – 2002 Vice President for Academic Affairs/Dean of the College and Professor of History and American Culture at Reinhardt College

1993 – 2000 Provost and Vice President for Academic Affairs and Professor of History at the University of Great Falls

1986 – 1992 Academic Vice President/Dean of the College and Professor of History at Olivet College

1976 – 1986 Academic Dean and Professor of History at Newberry College

1974 – 1976 Academic Dean and Professor of History at Urbana College

1973 – 1974 Dean of Student Affairs at Urbana College

1968 – 1973 Associate Professor of History (tenured) and Chair of the Social Science Division at Urbana College

1967 – 1968 Graduate Instructor and Supervisor of Social Studies Student Teachers at Ohio State University

1965 – 1967 Instructor of History at Urbana College

1964 – 1965 Graduate Instructor in American History at Michigan State University

Scholarly Publications and Professional Presentations

Print Books

Academic Reviews of Rock Writings: A Topical Presentation of Critical Commentaries (Charleston, South Carolina: Paw Paw Press, 2015), 136 pp. (with Frank W. Hoffman)

America in Transition, 1945-1975: A Musical Perspective on Historical Change (Charleston, South Carolina: Paw Paw Press, 2017, 581 pp. (with Frank W. Hoffmann)

Answer Songs: A Reference Guide to Response Recordings, 1900-2015, two volumes (Charleston, South Carolina: Paw Paw Press, 2015), 614 pp. (with Frank W. Hoffmann, Stephen D. Briggs, David A. Milberg, William L. Schurk, and Debbie Edens)

Baseball and American Culture (Jefferson, North Carolina: McFarland and Company, 1995), 257 pp. (with Donald E. Walker)

Cover Recordings, 1900-2016 (Charleston, South Carolina: Paw Paw Press, 2016), 378 pp.

Dawn of the Singer-Songwriter Era, 1944-1963: Bibliographic Profiles of the Performer-Composers (Charleston, South Carolina: Paw Paw Press, 2015), 451 pp. (with Frank W. Hoffmann)

Discs of Distinction: Essays on Remarkable Recordings by Exceptional Artists (Charleston, South Carolina: Paw Paw Press, 2015), 164 pp. (with Frank W. Hoffmann and Debbie Edens)

The Doo-Wop Decades, 1945-1965 (Columbia, South Carolina: Paw Paw Press, 2017), 354 pp.

Images of American Society in Popular Music (Chicago: Nelson-Hall, 1982), 282 pp.

The Keyboard Kingdom: A Resource Guide to Rock, Pop, Blues, and Country Keyboard Players and Their Music (San Bernadino, California: Paw Paw Press, 2015), 126 pp. (with Michael L. Cooper, Frank Hoffmann, and William L. Schurk)

The Literature of Rock, 1984-1990 (Metuchen, New Jersey: Scarecrow Press, 1995), 1003 pp. (with Frank W. Hoffmann)

Lyrical Legacies: Essays on Topics in Rock, Pop, and Blues Lyrics … and Beyond (Charleston, South Carolina: Paw Paw Press, 2015), 171 pp. (with Frank W. Hoffmann and Debbie Edens)

More Discs of Distinction: Additional Essays on Remarkable Recordings by Exceptional Artists (Charleston, South Carolina: Paw Paw Press, 2015), 220 pp. (with Frank W. Hoffmann and Debbie Edens)

More Than Just the Music: Essays in Lyrical Analysis and Topical Identification, (Charleston, South Carolina: Paw Paw Press, 2015), 260 pp. (with Frank W. Hoffmann, Stephen D. Briggs, William L. Schurk, and Debbie Edens)

New Orleans Rhythm & Blues (Columbia, South Carolina: Paw Paw Press, 2017), 223 pp. (with Debbie Edens and Frank W. Hoffmann)

Novelty Records: Selected Subjects and Artists (Charleston, South Carolina: Paw Paw Press, 2015), 257 pp. (with Frank W. Hoffmann and Debbie Edens)

Novelty Records: A Topical Discography, 1900-2015 (Charleston, South Carolina: Paw Paw Press, 2015), 497 pp. (with Frank W. Hoffmann)

Persistent Themes in South Recordings – Seven Volumes (Charleston, South Carolina: Paw Paw Press, 2016), (with Frank W. Hoffmann)

Popular Music Perspectives: Ideas, Themes, and Patterns in Contemporary Lyrics (Bowling Green, Ohio: Bowling Green State University Popular Press, 1991), 213 pp.

Popular Music Research (Charleston, South Carolina: Paw Paw Press, 2015), 284 pp. (with Frank W. Hoffmann)

Popular Music Scholarship (San Bernadino, California: Paw Paw Press, 2015), 323 pp. (with Frank W. Hoffmann)

Popular Music Teaching Handbook (Westport, Connecticut: Libraries Unlimited, 2004), 371 pp. (with Rebecca A. Condon)

Prominent Themes in Popular Songs: An Exploration of 54 Persistent Lyrical Themes (Charleston, South Carolina: Paw Paw Press, 2015), 392 pp. (with Frank W. Hoffmann, Debbie Edens, Matthew J. Masters, and William L. Schurk)

A Resource Guide to Themes in Contemporary Song Lyrics, 1950-1985 (Westport, Connecticut: Greenwood Press, 1986), 435 pp.

Response Recordings: An Answer Song Discography, 1950-1990 (Metuchen, New Jersey: Scarecrow Press, 1990), 272 pp. (with Wayne S. Haney)

Revisiting Rock's "Lost Years", 1959-1963 (Middleton, Delaware: Paw Paw Press, 2017), 378 pp. (with Frank W. Hoffmann)

The Rise Of Rock 'n' Roll, 1950-1959 (Charleston, South Carolina: Paw Paw Press, 2016), 363 pp. (with Frank W. Hoffmann)

Rock Music in American Popular Culture – Three Volumes (New York: Haworth Press, 1995, 1997, and 1999) (with Wayne S. Haney)

Rockabilly: A Bibliographic Resource Guide (Metuchen, New Jersey: Scarecrow Press, 1990), 352 pp. (with Wayne S. Haney)

Rockabilly! The Artists, the Music, the Heritage (Charleston, South Carolina: Paw Paw Press, 2016), 342 pp. (with Frank W. Hoffmann)

Soul Music Ascending, 1961-1970 (Columbia, South Carolina: Paw Paw Press, 2017), 492 pp. (with Frank W. Hoffmann)

Three of a Kind: The Rolling Stones, John Fogerty, and Male/Female Recording Duos (Charleston, South Carolina: Paw Paw Press, 2015), 137 pp. (edited by Frank W. Hoffmann)

The Triumph of Rhythm & Blues, 1945-1960 (Columbia, South Carolina: Paw Paw Press, 2017), 385 pp. (with Frank W. Hoffmann)

Visions of Axemen: A Resource Guide to Guitarists and Their Recordings (Charleston, South Carolina: Paw Paw Press, 2015), 196 pp. (with Michael L. Cooper, Frank W. Hoffmann, and William L. Schurk).

Doctoral Dissertation

"The Objectives of Teaching Survey History Courses in American High Schools and Colleges: A Content Analysis of Articles from Selected Periodicals, 1939-1969" (Columbus, Ohio: Unpublished Doctoral Dissertation at Ohio State University, 1971), 206 pp.

Essays in Anthologies

"My Music, Not Yours: Ravings of a Rock 'n' Roll Fanatic," in Fan Identities and Practices in Context: Dedicated to Music, edited by Mark Duffett (Oxford: Routledge, 2016), pp. 99-112.

"The Hyperbolic Hit Parade: Extravagant Lyrical Assertions in Popular Recordings," in Popular Music Scholarship, edited by B. Lee Cooper, Frank W. Hoffmann, Debbie Edens, and William L. Schurk (San Bernadino, California: Paw Paw Press, 2015), pp. 7-45.

"Play With Fire: Tracking the Promethean Rolling Stones and Their African-American Musical Inspirations – A Discographic Study," in Three of a Kind, edited by Frank W. Hoffmann (Charleston, South Carolina: Paw Paw Press, 2015), pp 5-40.

"John Fogerty and America's Three Rock Generations," in Finding Fogerty: Interdisciplinary Readings of John Fogerty and Creedence Clearwater Revival, edited by Thomas M. Kitts (Lanham, Maryland: Lexington Books/Rowman and Littlefield Publishing, 2013), pp. 151-173 (with William L. Schurk).

"Contemporary Christmas Recordings," "Fools and Foolish Behavior," "Halloween and Horror Recordings," "Matrimony in Music," "Nonsense Lyrics," "Obesity in Song," "Personal Appearance and Clothing Styles on Disc," and "Technology in Lyrics" in Music in American Life: An Encyclopedia of the Songs, Styles, Stars, and Stories that have Shaped Our Culture, edited by Jacqueline Edmondson (Santa Barbara, California: ABC/ CLIO Publishers, 2013), pp. 215-217, 231-322, 462-463, 536-537, 695-696, 807-809, 2145-216, and 1132-1137.

"Good Time Rollers: Little Richard and Huey 'Piano' Smith" and "Midnight in Memphis with the Wicked Pickett," in Please Allow Me to Introduce Myself: Essays on Debut Discs, edited by George Plasketes (Burlington, Vermont: Ashgate Publishing Company, 2013), pp. 29-34 and 49-52 (with William L. Schurk)

"Charting Cultural Change, 1953-1997: Song Assimilation Through Cover Recording," in Play It Again: Cover Songs in Popular Music, edited by George Plasketes (Burlington, Vermont: Ashgate Publishing Company, 2010), pp. 43-76.

"Right Place, Wrong Time: Discography of a Disaster," in New Orleans Music: Legacy and Survival, edited by B. Lee Cooper (Oxford, England: Routledge, 2008), pp. 263-268.

"The Pendulum of Cultural Imperialism: Popular Music Interchanges Between the United States and Britain, 1943-1967," in The American Impact on European Popular Culture Since 1945, edited by Sabrina P. Ramet and Gordana P. Crnovic (Lanham, Maryland: Rowman and Littlefield, 2003), pp. 69-82 (with Laura E. Cooper).

"Formal Education as a Lyrical Target: Images of Schooling in Popular Music, 1955-1980," in Images of Youth: Popular Culture as Educational Ideology, edited by Michael A. Oliker and Walter P. Krolikowski (New York: Peter Lang, 2001), pp. 73-95.

"Popular Music's Dilemma during the Vietnam War: Presumed Patriotism versus Democratic Dissent," in Proceedings from The University of Great Falls Vietnam War Symposium, edited by William Furdell (Great Falls, Montana: University of Great Falls Press, 2000), pp. 79-107.

"Reveille, Riveting, and Romance Remembered: Popular Recordings of the World War II Era," in Proceedings of the University of Great Falls World War II Symposium (October 2-6, 1995), edited by William Furdell (Great Falls, Montana: University of Great Falls, 1996), pp. 43-73.

"Rumors of War: Lyrical Continuities, 1914-1991," in Continuities of Popular Culture, edited by Ray B. Browne and Ronald J. Ambrosetti (Bowling Green, Ohio: Bowling Green State University Popular Press, 1993), pp. 121-142.

"A Resource Guide to Studies in the Theory and Practice of Popular Culture Librarianship," in Popular Culture and Acquisitions, edited by Allen Ellis (Binghamton, New York: Haworth Press, 1992), pp. 131-147.

"Popular Music: A Creative Teaching Resource," in Nonprint in the Secondary Curriculum: Readings for Reference, edited by James L. Thomas (Littleton, Colorado: Libraries Unlimited, 1982), pp. 78-87.

"An Opening Day Collection of Popular Music Resources: Searching for Discographic Standards," in Twentieth-Century Popular Culture in Museums and Libraries, edited by Fred E. H. Schroeder (Bowling Green, Ohio: Bowling Green State University Popular Press, 1981), pp. 226-255.

"William L. Schurk: Audio Center Director – A Close Encounter with a Librarian of a Different Kind," in Twentieth Century Popular Culture in Museums and Libraries, edited by Fred E. H. Schroeder (Bowling Green, Ohio: Bowling Green University Press, 1981), pp. 210-225.

"Social Change, Popular Music, and the Teacher," Ideas for Teaching Gifted Students: Social Studies, edited by Jackie Mallis (Austin, Texas: Multi Media Arts, 1979), pp. 9-19.

"Images of the Future in Popular Music: Lyrical Comments on Tomorrow," Ideas for Teaching Gifted Students: Social Studies, edited by Jackie Mallis (Austin, Texas: Multi Media Arts, 1979), pp. 97-108.

"Popular Culture Teaching: Problems and Challenges," in Popular Culture and the Library, edited by Wane A. Wiegand (Lexington: University of Kentucky, 1978), pp. 10-26.

Selected Articles

"The Hyperbolic Hit Parade: A Discographic Study of Extravagant Lyrical Assertions in Romantic Recordings," Popular Music and Society, XXXVIII, No. 5 (December 2015), pp. 611-624.

"My Music, Not Yours: Ravings of a Rock-and-Roll Fanatic," Popular Music and Society, 36 (July 2013), pp. 397-410.

"From Cement Mixers to Personal Computers: Images of Technology in Commercial Recordings, 1910-2010," Popular Music and Society, 36 (February 2013), pp. 40-75.

"Seasonal Music: Heat Up the Holidays With This Playlist, Goldmine, No. 808 (November 2011), pp. 11-15.

"Bumble Boogie: 100 Years of Bee Imagery in American Sound Recordings," Popular Music and Society, XXXIV, No. 4 (October 2011), pp. 493-502 (with William L. Schurk).

"Odes to Obesity: Images of Overweight Men and Women in Commercial Sound Recordings – A Discography," Popular Music and Society, XXXIV, No. 2 (May 2011), pp. 237-246 (with William L. Schurk).

"Blue-Eyed Soul Performers Before and After the Wicked Pickett and Lady Soul: A Bio-Bibliography and Discography," Popular Music and Society, XXXIII, No 5 (December 2010), pp. 663-693.

"Contemporary Blueswomen: A Bibliography of Female Blues Singers, Composers, and Instrumentalists, 1955-2005," Popular Music and Society, XXXIII, No. 3 (July 2010), pp. 395-414.

"Charting the Success of Male Recording Duos: Billboard Recognition of Country, Pop, R&B/Rap Pairs, 1944-2004," Popular Music and Society, XXXIII, No. 2 (May 2010), pp. 237-257.

"Rock Journalists and Music Critics: A Selected Bibliography," Popular Music and Society, XXXIII, No. 1 (February 2010), pp. 75-101.

"Honky Tonks, Jukeboxes, and Wild, Wild Women: Audio Images of Blue Collar Night Life – A Selected Discography," Popular Music and Society, XXXI, No. 5 (December 2008), pp. 663-383.

"Architects of the New Orleans Sound, 1946-2006: A Bio-Bibliography," Popular Music and Society, XXXI, No. 2 (May 2008), pp. 221-261.

" 'Do You Know What It Means to Miss New Orleans?': Discovery, Dominance, and Decline of the Crescent City's Popular Music Influence, 1946-2006," Popular Music and Society, XXXI, No. 2 (May 2008), pp. 151-190.

"From the Bunny Hop to the Funky Chicken: An American Dance Song Discography, 1945-1975," Popular Music and Society, XXX, No. 5 (December 2007), pp. 651-666.

"Apple and Atlantic, Stax and Sun: Teaching About Contemporary Music from a Record Label perspective," International Journal of Instructional Media, XXX, No. 4 (2007), pp. 457-467.

"American Disc Jockeys, 1945-1975: A Bibliographic and Discographic Survey," Popular Music and Society, XXX, No. 3 (July 2007), pp. 401-423.

"Before the Beatles: International Influences on American Popular Recordings, 1940-1963," Popular Music and Society, XXX (May 2007), pp. 227-266 (with William L. Schurk).

"Good Timin': Searching for Meaning in Clock Songs," Popular Music and Society, XXX (February 2007), pp. 03-106.

"From 'Mystery Train' to 'Cyberspace Sadie': References to Technology in Blues Recordings, 1923-2003," International Journal of Instructional Media, XXXIII, No. 3 (2006), pp. 1-9.

"Tribute Discs, Career Development, and Death: Perfecting the Celebrity Product from Elvis Presley to Stevie Ray Vaughan," Popular Music and Society, XXVIII (May 2005), pp. 229-248.

"The Sky is Crying: Tales Told in Tearful Tunes, Popular Music and Society, XXVII (Winter 2004), pp. 107-115.

"Accordions, Banjos, Cornets…and Zithers: Sound Recordings Archives and Musical Instruments," Popular Music and Society, XXVI (October 2003), pp. 387-398 (with Patty Falk and William L. Schurk).

"'A' – You're Adorable: Abbreviations, Acronyms, and Other Alphabetical Arrangements in Popular Recordings, 1920-2000, International Journal of Instructional Media, XXX, No. 3 (2003), pp. 1-8.

"Why Don't You Write Me? A Letter Song Discography, 1945-1995," Rock and Blues News, No. 12 (October/November 2000), pp. 37-39.

"From Lady Day to Lady Di: Images of Women in Contemporary Recordings, 1938-1998," International Journal of Instructional Media, XXVI, No. 3 (1999), pp. 353-358.

"The Life of the Mind: A Personal Perspective," Delta Epsilon Sigma Journal, XLIII (Winter 1998), pp. 32-33.

"Teaching with Popular Music Resources: A Bibliography of Interdisciplinary Instructional Approaches," Popular Music and Society, XXII (Summer 1998), pp. 85-115.

"Terror Translated into Comedy: The Popular Music Metamorphosis of Film and Television Horror, 1956-1991," Journal of American Culture, XX (Fall 1997), pp. 31-42.

"Wise Men Never Try: A Discography of Fool Songs, 1945-1995," Popular Music and Society, XXI (Summer 1997), pp. 115-131.

"It's Still Rock and Roll to Me: Reflections on the Evolution of Popular Music and Rock Scholarship," Popular Music and Society, XXI (Spring 1997), pp. 101-108.

"From 'Love Letters' to 'Miss You': Popular Recordings, Epistolary Imagery, and Romance During War Time, 1941-1945," Journal of American Culture, XIX (Winter 1996), pp. 15-27.

"From Johnny Ace to Frank Zappa: Debating the Meaning of Death in Rock Music – A Review Essay," Popular Culture in Libraries, III, No. 1 (1995), pp. 51-75.

"Smokin' Songs: Examining Tobacco Use as an American Cultural Phenomenon Through Contemporary Lyrics," International Journal of Instructional Media, XXI, No. 3 (1994), pp. 261-268.

"Processing Health Care Images from Popular Culture Resources: Physicians, Cigarettes, and Medical Metaphors in Contemporary Recordings," Popular Music and Society, XVII (Winter 1993), pp. 105-124.

"Popular Songs, Military Conflicts, and Public Perceptions of the United States at War," Social Education, LVI (March 1992), pp. 160-168.

"Lyrical Commentaries: Learning from Popular Music," Music Educator's Journal, LXXVII (April 1991), pp. 56-59.

"Black Players and Baseball Cards: Exploring Racial Integration with Popular Culture Resources," Social Education, LV (March 1991), pp. 169-173, 204 (with Donald E. Walker).

"Christmas Songs as American Cultural History: Audio Resources for Classroom Investigation, 1940-1990," Social Education, LIV (October 1990), pp. 374-379.

Popular Records as Oral Evidence: Creating an Audio Time Line to Examine American History, 1955-1987," Social Education, LIII (January 1989), pp. 34-49.

"Perceptions of Education in the Lyrics of American Popular Music, 1950-1980," American Music, V (Fall 1987), pp. 31-41 (with Ronald E. Butchart).

"Controversial Issues in Popular Lyrics, 1960-1985: Teaching Resources for the English Classroom," Arizona English Bulletin, XXIX (Fall 1986), pp. 174-187.

"Mick Jagger as Herodotus and Billy Joel as Thucydides? A Rock Music Perspective, 1950-1985," Social Education, XLIX (October 1985), pp. 596-600.

"Oral History, Popular Music, and American Railroads, 1920-1980," Social Studies, LXXIV (November/December 1983), pp. 223-231.

"Present at the Creation: The Legend of Jerry Lee Lewis on Record, 1956-1963," JEMF Quarterly, XIX (Summer 1983), pp. 122-129 (with James A. Creeth).

"The Music Magazine Reader's 'Hot 100': Popular Music Periodicals, 1950-1982," JEMF Quarterly, XIX (Spring 1983), pp. 32-48 (with Frank W. Hoffmann and William L. Schurk).

"Music and the Metropolis: Lyrical Images of Life in American Cities, 1950-1980," Teaching History, VI (Fall 1981), pp. 72-84.

"Popular Music in the Classroom: Audio Resources for Teachers (How To Do It – Series 2, No. 13)." Washington, D.C.: National Council for the Social Studies, 1981.

"Information Services, Popular Culture, and the Librarian: Promoting a Contemporary Learning Perspective," Drexel Library Quarterly, XVI (July 1980), pp. 24-42.

"Nothin' Outrun My V-8 Ford: Chuck Berry and the American Motorcar, 1955-1979," JEMF Quarterly, XVI (Spring 1980), pp. 18-23.

"Popular Music: An Untapped Resource for Teaching Contemporary Black History," Journal of Negro Education, XLVIII (Winter 1979), pp. 20-36.

"The Image of the Outsider in Contemporary Lyrics," Journal of Popular Culture, XII (Summer 1978), pp. 168-178.

"Women's Studies and Popular Music: Using Audio Resources in Social Studies Instruction," The History and Social Science Teacher, XIV (Fall 1978), pp. 29-40.

"Oral History, Popular Music, and Les McCann," Social Studies, LXVII (May/June 1976), pp. 115-118.

"Rock Music and Religious Education: A Proposed Synthesis," Religious Education, LXX (May-June 1975), pp. 289-299.

Selected Book Reviews

"Review of Blue Monday: Fats Domino and the Lost Dawn of Rock 'n' Roll by Rick Coleman," Popular Music and Society, XXX (May 2007), pp. 294-295.

Review of Risky Business: Rock in Film by R. Serge Denisoff and William D. Romanowski," Michigan Academician, XXIV (Winter 1992), pp. 413-415.

"Review of When the Music's Over: The Story of Political Pop by Robin Denselow," Notes: Quarterly Journal of The Music Library Association, XLIX (March 1992), pp. 889-890.

"Review of The Seventh Stream by Phillip H. Ennis," Popular Music and Society, XVII (Winter 1993), pp. 136-137.

"Review of Performing Rites: On the Value of Popular Music by Simon Frith," Journal of American Culture, XXI (Fall 1998), pp. 103-104.

"Review of She's a Rebel: The History of Women in Rock and Roll by Gillian G. Gaar," Journal of American Culture, XVII (Spring 1994), pp. 99-100.

"Review of The United States and the End of the Cold War by John Lewis Gaddis," Popular Culture in Libraries, II, No. 2 (1994), pp. 81-83.

"Review of Sweet Soul Music by Peter Guralnick," Popular Music and Society, XI (Spring 1987), pp. 88-90.

"Review of The Vietnam Experience: A Concise Encyclopedia of American Literature, Songs, and Film by Kevin Hillstrom and Laurie Collier Hillstrom," Popular Music and Society, XXIV (Summer 2000), pp. 170-172.

"Review of Visions of War by M. Paul Holsinger and Mary Anne Schofield," Popular Culture in Libraries, II, No. 4 (1994), pp. 103-104.

"Review of Recorded Music in American Life: The Phonograph and Popular Memory, 1890-1945 by William Howland Kenney," Notes: Quarterly Journal of the Music Library Association, LVII (March 2000), pp. 733-734.

"Review of All That Glitters: Country Music in America by George H. Lewis," American Culture Association Newsletter (Spring 1994), pp. 3-4.

"Review of Born in the U.S.A.: The Myth of America in Popular Music From Colonial Times to the Present by Timothy E. Scheurer," Journal of American Culture, XV (Summer 1992), pp. 91-92.

"Review of The History of Texas Music by Gary Hartman," Popular Music and Society, XXXIII, No. 3 (July 2010), pp. 421-422.

"Review of Old Rare New: The Independent Record Store by Emma Pettit and Kathe Monem," Popular Music and Society, XXXIII, No. 3 (July 2010), pp. 425-427.

Selected Audio Reviews

"Review of Ray Charles – Genius and Soul: The 50th Anniversary Collection," Popular Music and Society, XXI (Winter 1997), pp. 134-136.

"Review of Doctors/Professors/Kings and Queens: The Big Ol' Box of New Orleans," Popular Music and Society, XXIX (May 2006), pp. 259-260.

"Review of Leading Ladies: The Best of the Great Ladies of Song from Reader's Digest Music," Popular Music and Society, XXI (Winter 1997), pp. 136-144.

"Review of Johnny B. Goode: His Complete '50s Recordings by Chuck Berry," Popular Music and Society, XXXII, No. 1 (February 2009), pp. 127-128.

"Review of Hall of Fame (2012), The Fame Studios Story (2011), Take Me to the River (2008), and The Muscle Shoals Sound (1993) by Various Artists," Popular Music and Society, 36 (May 2013), pp. 293-295.

"Review of 45 RPM Answer/Parody Songs: A Reference Guide to Response Songs by Ron Davis and Brenda Davisk" Popular Music and Society, 36 (July 2013), pp. 417-420.

"Review of Love Me Do (2012), Beatles Beginnings (2009, 2010, 2011), and The Hamburg List (2010) by Various Artists," Popular Music and Society, 36 (October 2013), pp. 550-554.

"Review of This Could be the One (2013), Secret Agent Man (2006), Last Train to Memphis (1998), and The Memphis Sun Recordings (1991) by Johnny Rivers," Popular Music and Society, 36 (December 2013), pp. 715-718.

Professional Conference Presentations

American Culture Association

"Another Brick in the Wall: Perceptions of Education and Schooling in American Popular Music" (April 1983)

"Christmas Songs as American Cultural History: An Update of Holiday Hits, 1991-2001" (March 2002)

American Historical Association

"The Audio Image of the Black Man: Lyrical Resources for Historical Instruction" (December 1977)

American Library Association

"Information Services, Popular Culture, and the Librarian" (June 1980)

American Psychological Association

"Introducing Historical Concepts Through Science Fiction Stories" (August 1977)

Association of Recorded Sound Collections

"Little Red Riding Hood Meets Sam The Sham and The Pharoahs: Popular Recordings Featuring Nursery Rhyme and Fairy Tale Themes, 1950-1985" (May 1988)

Duquesne History Forum

"The Historian as a Freelance Writer" (October 1989)

Kansas Council for the Humanities

"Technology References in Blues Recordings: A Preliminary Lyric Analysis" (April 2004)

Michigan Academy of Science, Arts, and Letters

"Cultural Imperialism and Contemporary Music: Recorded Interchanges Between the United States and Great Britain, 1943-1967" (March 1991)

Michigan College English Association

"Monsters, Movies, and Music: The Meandering Path from Literature to Popular Culture" (October 1993)

Midwest Popular Culture Association

"The Record(s) of American at War, 1941-1991: An Audio Perspective" (October 1991)

"Where Have You Gone Joe DiMaggio? The Decline of Heroic Baseball Images in Contemporary American Recordings" (October 1989)

Missouri Valley History Conference

"Popular Music and American History: Exploring Unusual Audio Teaching Resources" (March 1981)

Montana Committee for the Humanities

"Cross Over the Bridge: Images of Bridges in Popular Recordings" (May 1999)

Music Library Association

"I'm a Hog for You, Baby: Problems of Thematic Classification in Popular Music" (February 1988)

National Council for the Social Studies

"Music and the Metropolis: Lyrical Images of Life in American Cities, 1950-1980" (November 1981)

Ohio Council for the Social Studies

"Social Change, Popular Music, and the Teacher" (April 1973)

Phi Alpha Theta Regional Convention

"Oral History, Popular Music, and American Railroads" (March 1985)

Popular Culture Association

"Just Seven Numbers Can Straighten Out My Life: Lyrical Images of Human Relations in Telephone Songs" (September 1985)

"Somewhere Between Theory and Trivia: Library Service and Information Requests from Popular Culture Researchers" (March 1991)

Reinhardt College Colloquia Series

"Women and PMS (Popular Music Stereotypes): A Politically Incorrect Analysis" (January 2001)

Southwestern Historical Association

"Popular Music in the Classroom: The Case of Vietnam" (March 2002)

Utah History Academy

"Teaching Social Studies with Popular Music Resources" (June 1993)

Scholarships and Professional Acknowledgements

Presidents Club at Bowling Green State University (2015)
Friends Award from the Bowling Green State University Library System (2013)
Newman Medal for Outstanding Leadership (2008)
Who's Who in America – 62nd Edition (2008)
Who's Who in American Education – 7th Edition (2006-2007)
Who's Who in the World – 24th Edition (2007)
Contemporary Authors (2002)
Dictionary of International Biography (1998)
Phi Delta Kappa (1995)
International Who's Who in Music – 14th Edition (1994)
International Authors and Writers Who's Who (11th Edition)
Contemporary Authors (1986)
ASCAP-Deems Taylor Award for Literary Excellence (1983)
South Carolina Foundation of Independent College Council of Academic Deans (1982) – President
Outstanding Young Men of America (1976, 1977, 1978)
Dictionary of American Scholars (6th Edition)
Outstanding Educators in America (1970, 1973, 1975)
"Teacher of the Year" Award at Urbana College (1967)
Phi Alpha Theta Scholarship for Graduate Study (1965)
University President's Distinguished Service Award (1964)
Sidney Frohman Senior Scholarship (1964)
Phi Kappa Phi (1964)
Phi Alpha Theta (1963) – President
Omicron Delta Kappa (1964)
Who's Who Among Students in American Universities and Colleges (1963-64)
Phi Eta Sigma (1962)

Other Professional Activities

Coordinated Self-Study development and successful ten-year accreditation from the Higher Learning Commission of the North Central Association at Newman University.

Directed "Teaching Strategies" Workshop for the Utah History Academy at Brigham Young University.

Chaired Carl Bode Literary Award Committee for the American Culture Association (1986); elected for four-year term as Vice President of the Academic Culture Association (1987-91); elected to four-year term on the Governing Board of the American Culture Association (1991-95); and appointed to R. Serge Denisoff Literary Award Committee (2001-2004).

Appointed to Editorial Advisory Boards of Popular Music and Society (1990-present), Journal of American Culture (1991-1998), and Popular Culture in Libraries (1992-1998).

Served as institutional Accreditation Liaison Officer to the North Central Association (NCA), the Northwest Association of Schools and Colleges (NWASC), and the Southern Association of Colleges and Schools (SACS).

Worked as Senior Editor of the Popular Culture Book Division for Haworth Press in Binghamton, New York (1998-2007).

Drafted grant proposals and secured external funding resources from the National Endowment for the Humanities (NEH) and the NDEA Title III and Title IV programs.

Current Memberships

Biltmore Lake Homeowners Association
Bowling Green State University Alumni Association
Central United Methodist Church of Asheville
Enka-Candler Friends of the Library
National Baseball Hall of Fame and Museum at Cooperstown
Newman University Alumni Association
North Carolina Arboretum Society
Osher Lifelong Learning Institute (OLLI) at UNC – Asheville
Presidents Club at Bowling Green State University

References

Dr. Gary Burns
Department of Communication
Northern Illinois University
DeKalb, Illinois 60115
(815) 753-7108
gburns@niu.edu

Dr. Noreen Carrocci
Office of the President
Newman University

3100 McCormick Avenue
Wichita, Kansas 67213
(316) 942-4291
carroccin@newmanu.edu

Dr. Jacqueline Edmondson
Chancellor and Chief Academic Officer
Penn State Greater Allegheny
4000 University Drive
McKeesport, Pennsylvania 15132
(412) 675-9080
jxe117@psu.edu

Dr. Shirley M. Erickson
Executive Director
Maine Educational Loan Authority
One City Center
11th Floor
Portland, Maine 04101
(207) 6791-3600
serickson@mela.net

Dr. Catherine Frank
Executive Director
Osher Life-Long Learning Institute
U.N.C. – Asheville
One University Heights
Asheville, North Carolina 28804
(828) 251-6873
cfrank@unca.edu

Dr. Thomas Kitts
Division of English and Speech
St. John's University
8000 Utopia Parkway
Jamaica, New York 11439
kittst@stjohns.edu

Dr. George M. Plasketes
Department of Communication
Auburn University
Auburn University, Alabama 36849
(334) 844-2727
plaskgm@mail.auburn.edu

Mr. William L. Schurk
Sound Recordings Archive
Jerome Library
Bowling Green State University
Bowling Green, Ohio 43403
(419) 372-2308
wschurk@bgnet.bgsu.edu

A CHRONOLOGICAL PROFILE OF BOOKS AND ARTICLES BY B. LEE COOPER, 1971-2016

1971

"The Objectives of Teaching Survey History Courses in American High Schools and Colleges: A Content Analysis of Articles from Selected Periodicals, 1939-1969," (Columbus, Ohio: Ph.D. Dissertation at Ohio State University, 1971), 206 pp.

1972

"Using Popular Music in Social Studies Instruction," Audiovisual Instruction, XVII (November 1972), pp. 86-88 (with Larry S. Haverkos).

1973

"Examining Social Change Through Contemporary History: An Audio Media Proposal," The History Teacher, VI (August 1973), pp. 623-634.

"The Image of American Society in Popular Music: A Search for Identity and Values," Social Studies, LSIV (December 1973), pp. 319-322 (with Larry S. Haverkos).

"Social Change, Popular Music, and the Teacher," Social Education, XXXVII (December 1973), pp. 776-781, 793.

1974

"Review of the 'American Graffiti' Soundtrack," The History Teacher, VII (February 1974), pp. 283-284.

1975

"Popular Music and Academic Enrichment in the Residence Hall," NASPA Journal, XI (Winter 1975), pp. 50-57.

"Images of the Future in Popular Music: Lyrical Comments on Tomorrow," Social Education, XXXIX (May 1975), pp. 276-285.

"Rock Music and Religious Education: A Proposed Synthesis," Religious Education, LXX (May-June 1975), pp. 289-299.

1976

"Futurescope," Audiovisual Instruction, XXI (January 1976), pp. 42-48.

"Resources for Teaching Popular Music: A Checklist," Popular Culture Methods, III (Spring 1976), pp. 37-38.

"Exploring the Future Through Popular Music," Media and Methods, XII (April 1976), pp. 32-35ff.

"Oral History, Popular Music, and Les McCann," Social Studies, LXVII (May/June 1976), pp. 115-118.

"Popular Music, Science Fiction, and Controversial Issues: Sources for Reflective Thinking," The History and Social Science Teacher, XII (Fall 1976), pp. 31-45.

"Teaching American History Through Popular Music," AHA Newsletter, XIV (October 1976), pp. 3-5.

1977

"An Error in Punctuation," in Stellar #3: Science Fiction Stories, edited by Judy-Lynn del Rey (New York: Ballantine Books, 1977), pp. 108-115 (with Larry S. Haverkos).

"Folk History, Alternative History, and Future History," Teaching History: A Journal of Methods, II (Spring 1977), pp. 56-62.

"The Traditional and Beyond: Resources for Teaching Women's Studies," Audiovisual Instruction, XXII (December 1977), pp. 14-18ff.

1978

A Science Fiction Perspective on Contemporary Issues (Dayton, Ohio: Occasional Paper Series of the Ohio Council for the Social Studies, 1978), 16 pp.

"Popular Culture: Teaching Problems and Challenges," in Popular Culture and the Library, edited by Wayne A. Wiegand (Lexington: University of Kentucky, 1978), pp. 10-26.

"Images of the Black Man: Contemporary Lyrics as Oral History," Journal of the Interdenominational Theological Center, V (Spring 1978), pp. 105-122.

"Beyond Flash Gordon and 'Star Wars': Science Fiction and History Instruction," Social Education, XLII (May 1978), pp. 392-397.

"The Image of the Outsider in Contemporary Lyrics," Journal of Popular Culture, XII (Summer 1978), pp. 168-178.

"Women's Studies and Popular Music: Using Audio Resources in Social Studies Instruction," The History and Social Science Teacher, XIV (Fall 1978), pp. 29-40.

1979

"Social Change, Popular Music, and the Teacher," Ideas for Teaching Gifted Students: Social Studies, edited by Jackie Mallis (Austin, Texas: Multi Media Arts, 1979), pp. 9-19.

"Images of the Future in Popular Music: Lyrical Comments on Tomorrow," Ideas for Teaching Gifted Students: Social Studies, edited by Jackie Mallis (Austin, Texas: Multi Media Arts, 1979), pp. 97-108.

"Popular Music: An Untapped Resource for Teaching Contemporary Black History," Journal of Negro Education, XLVIII (Winter 1979), pp. 20-36.

"Popular Music: A Creative Teaching Resource," Audiovisual Instruction, XXIV (March 1979), pp. 37-43.

"Establishing Rock Standards – The Practice of Record Revivals in Contemporary Music, 1953-1977," Goldmine, No. 36 (May 1979), pp. 37-38 (with Verdan D. Traylor).

"Rock Discographies: Exploring the Iceberg's Tip," JEMF Quarterly, XV (Summer 1979), pp. 115-120.

"Beyond Lois Lane and Wonder Woman: Exploring Images of Women Through Science Fiction," Library-College Experimenter, V (November 1979), pp. 7-15.

"The Song Revival Revolution of the Seventies: Tapping the Musical Roots of Rock," Goldmine, No. 42 (November 1979), p. 126.

"Liberal Education and Technology in Small Colleges: Popular Music and the Computer," International Journal of Instructional Media, VII (1979-80), pp. 25-35 (with Verdan D. Traylor).

1980

"Popular Music: An Untapped Resource," in Ideas for Teaching Gifted Students: Music, edited by Jackie Mallis (Austin, Texas: Multi Media Arts, 1980), pp. 217-221.

"Les McCann, Elvis Presley, Linda Ronstadt, and Buddy Holly: Focusing on the Lives of Contemporary Singers," Social Education, XLIV (March 1980), pp. 217-221.

"A Popular Music Perspective: Challenging Sexism in the Social Studies Classroom," Social Studies, LXXI (March/April 1980), pp. 71-76.

"Nothin' Outrun My V-8 Ford: Chuck Berry and the American Motorcar, 1955-1979," JEMF Quarterly, XVI (Spring 1980), pp. 18-23.

"Rock Discographies Revisited," JEMF Quarterly, XVI (Summer 1980), pp. 89-94.

"Information Services, Popular Culture, and the Librarian: Promoting a Contemporary Learning Perspective," Drexel Library Quarterly, XVI (July 1980), pp. 24-42.

"Discographies of Contemporary Music, 1965-1980: A Selected Bibliography," Popular Music and Society, VII (Fall 1980), pp. 253-269.

1981

"William L. Schurk: Audio Center Director – A Close Encounter With a Librarian of a Different Kind," in Twentieth Century Popular Culture in Museums and Libraries, edited by Fred E. H. Schroeder (Bowling Green, Ohio: Bowling Green University Press, 1981), pp. 210-225.

"An Opening Day Collection of Popular Recordings: Searching for Discographic Standards," in Twentieth Century Popular Culture in Museums and Libraries, edited by Fred E. H. Schroeder (Bowling Green, Ohio: Bowling Green University Press, 1981), pp. 228-255.

"Popular Music in the Classroom: Audio Resources for Teachers (How to Do It – Series 2, No. 13)." Washington, D.C.: National Council for the Social Studies, 1981.

"Audio Images of the City," Social Studies, LXXII (May/June 1981), pp. 130-136.

"Examining a Decade of Rock Bibliographies, 1970-1979," JEMF Quarterly, XVII (Summer 1981), pp. 95-101.

"Music and the Metropolis: Lyrical Images of Life in American Cities, 1950-1980," Teaching History, VI (Fall 1981), pp. 72-84.

"Jerry Lee Lewis: Rock 'N' Roll's Living Legend," Music World, No. 90 (October 1981), pp. 28-36.

1982

Images of American Society in Popular Music: A Guide to Reflective Teaching (Chicago: Nelson-Hall, 1982), 282 pp.

"Popular Music: A Creative Teaching Resource," in Nonprint in the Secondary Curriculum: Readings for Reference, edited by James L. Thomas (Littleton, Colorado: Libraries Unlimited, 1982), pp. 78-87.

"Johnny Rivers and Linda Ronstadt: Rock 'N' Roll Revivalists," JEMF Quarterly, XVII (Fall 1982/Winter 1983), pp. 166-177.

"Huntin' for Discs with Wild Bill: William L. Schurk – Sound Recordings Archivist," ARSC Journal, XIV (1983), pp. 9-19.

1983

"The Music Magazine Reader's 'Hot 100': Popular Music Periodicals, 1950-1982," JEMF Quarterly, XIX (Spring 1983), pp. 32-48 (with Frank W. Hoffmann and William L. Schurk).

"Present at the Creation: The Legend of Jerry Lee Lewis on Record, 1956-1963," JEMF Quarterly, XIX (Summer 1983), pp. 122-129 (with James A. Creeth).

"Oral History, Popular Music, and American Railroads, 1920-1980," Social Studies, LXXIV (November/December 1983), pp. 223-231.

"Just Let Me Hear Some of That…: Discographies of Fifty Classic Rock Era Performers," JEMF Quarterly, No. 74 (Fall 1983/Winter 1984), pp. 100-116.

1984

The Popular Music Handbook: A Resource Guide for Teachers and Media Specialists (Little, Colorado: Libraries Unlimited, 1984), 415 pp.

"Dr. Rock on Little Richard: Speculating on a Long-Awaited Biography," R.P.M., No. 4 (February-March 1984), pp. 21-22, 25.

"The Fats Domino Decades, 1950-1969," R.P.M., No. 5 (May 1984), pp. 56-58, 71.

"'It's a Wonder I Can Think At All': Vinyl Images of American Public Education, 1950-1980," Popular Music and Society, IX (1984), pp. 47-65.

"Foreword," in Popular Culture and Libraries, compiled by Frank W. Hoffmann (Hamden, Connecticut: Library Professional Publications/Shoe String Press, 1984), pp. vii-xv.

1985

"Mick Jagger as Herodotus and Billy Joel as Thucydides? A Rock Music Perspective, 1950-1985," Social Education, XLIX (October 1985), pp. 596-600.

1986

A Resource Guide to Themes in Contemporary American Song Lyrics, 1950-1985 (Westport, Connecticut: Greenwood Press, 1986), 458 pp.

The Literature of Rock II, 2 volumes (Metuchen, New Jersey: Scarecrow Press, 1986), I, 114 pp. (with Frank Hoffmann).

"Human Relations, Communication Technology and Popular Music: Audio Images of Telephone Use in the United States, 1950-1985," International Journal of Instructional Media, XIII (1986), pp. 75-82.

"Controversial Issues in Popular Lyrics, 1960-1985: Teaching Resources for the English Classroom," Arizona English Bulletin, XXIX (Fall 1986), pp. 174-187.

1987

"Perceptions of Education in the Lyrics of American Popular Music, 1950-1980," American Music, V (Fall 1987), pp. 31-41 (with Ronald E. Butchart).

"Response Recordings as Creative Repetition: Answer Songs and Pop Parodies in Contemporary American Music," OneTwoThreeFour: A Rock 'N' Roll Quarterly, No. 4 (Winter 1987), pp. 79-87.

"Food for Thought: Investigating Culinary Images in Contemporary American Recordings," International Journal of Instructional Media, XIV (1987), pp. 251-262 (with William L. Schurk).

1988

"Social Concerns, Political Protest, and Popular Music," Social Studies, LXXIX (March/April 1988), pp. 53-60.

"Bear Cats, Chipmunks, and Slip-In Mules: The Answer Song in Contemporary American Recordings, 1950-1985," Popular Music and Society, XII (Fall 1988), pp. 57-77.

"Christmas Songs: Audio Barometers of Tradition and Social Change in America, 1950-1987," Social Studies, LXXXIX (November/December 1988), pp. 278-280.

1989

"Popular Records as Oral Evidence: Creating an Audio Time Line to Examine American History, 1955-1987," Social Education, LIII (January 1989), pp. 34-40.

"From 'I Saw Mommy Kissing Santa Claus' to 'Another Brick in the Wall': Popular Recordings Featuring Pre-Teen Performers, Traditional Childhood Stories, and Contemporary Pre-Adolescent Perspectives, 1945-1985," International Journal of Instructional Media, XVI (1989), pp. 83-90 (with William L. Schurk).

"Rhythm 'N' Rhymes: Character and Theme Images from Children's Literature in Contemporary Recordings, 1950-1985," Popular Music and Society, XIII (Spring 1989), pp. 53-71.

"Repeating Hit Tunes, A Cappella Style: The Persuasions as Song Revivalists, 1967-1982," Popular Music and Society, XIII (Fall 1989), pp. 17-27.

"Rick Nelson: A Review Essay," Popular Music and Society, XIII (Winter 1989), pp. 77-82.

"Promoting Social Change Through Audio Repetition: Black Musicians as Creators and Revivalists, 1953-1978," Tracking: Popular Music Studies, II (Winter 1989), pp. 26-46.

1990

Response Recordings: An Answer Song Discography, 1950-1990 (Metuchen, New Jersey: Scarecrow Press, 1990), 272 pp. (with Wayne S. Haney).

Rockabilly: A Bibliographic Resource Guide (Metuchen, New Jersey: Scarecrow Press, 1990), 353 pp. (with Wayne S. Haney).

"Teaching American History Through Major League Baseball and Popular Music: A Resource Guide," International Journal of Instructional Media, XVII (1990), pp. 83-87 (with Donald E. Walker).

"Baseball, Popular Music, and Twentieth-Century American History," Social Studies, LXXXI (May-June 1990), pp. 120-124 (with Donald E. Walker).

"Exploring Cultural Imperialism: Bibliographic Resources for Teaching About American Domination, British Adaptation, and the Rock Music Interchange, 1950-1967," International Journal of Instructional Media, VII (1990), pp. 167-177 (with Laura E. Cooper).

"Christmas Songs as American Cultural History: Audio Resources for Classroom Investigation, 1940-1990," Social Education, LIV (October 1990), pp. 374-379.

"From Anonymous Announcer to Radio Personality, From Pied Piper to Payola: The American Disc Jockey, 1950-1970," Popular Music and Society, XIV (Winter 1990), pp. 89-95.

1991

Popular Music Perspectives: Ideas, Themes, and Patterns in Contemporary Lyrics (Bowling Green, Ohio, Bowling Green State University Popular Press, 1991), 216 pp.

"Black Players and Baseball Cards: Exploring Racial Integration with Popular Culture Resources," Social Education, LV (March 1991), pp. 169-173, 204 (with Donald E. Walker).

"Lyrical Commentaries: Learning from Popular Music," Music Educator's Journal, LXXVII (April 1991), pp. 56-59.

"Dancing: The Perfect Educational Metaphor," Garfield Lake Review, (Spring 1991), pp. 14-15.

"Having a Screaming Ball at Dracula's Hall," Popular Music and Society, XV (Spring 1991), pp. 103-105.

The Decline of Contemporary Baseball Heroes in American Popular Recordings," Popular Music and Society, XV (Summer 1991), pp. 49-62 (with Donald E. Walker and William L. Schurk).

1992

"Popular Songs, Military Conflicts, and Public Perceptions of the United States at War," Social Education, LVI (March 1992), pp. 160-168.

"Commercial Recordings and Cultural Interchanges: Studying Great Britain and the United States, 1943-1967," International Journal of Instructional Media, XIX, No. 2 (1992), pp. 183-189 (with Laura E. Cooper).

"A Review Essay and Bibliography of Studies on Rock 'N' Roll Movies, 1955-1963," Popular Music and Society, XVI (Spring 1992), pp. 85-92.

"Popular Culture Research and Library Services: A Selected Bibliography," Popular Culture Association Newsletter, XIX (May 1992), pp. 5-7.

"I'll Fight for God, Country, and My Baby: Persistent Themes in American Wartime Songs," Popular Music and Society, XVI (Summer 1992), pp. 95-111.

"Examining the Audio Images of War: Lyrical Perspectives on America's Major Military Crusades, 1914-1991," International Journal of Instructional Media, XIX, No. 3 (1992), pp. 277-287.

"A Resource Guide to Studies in the Theory and Practice of Popular Culture Librarianship," in Popular Culture and Acquisitions, edited by Allen Ellis (Binghamton, New York: Haworth Press, 1992), pp. 131-146.

"Dracula and Frankenstein in the Classroom: Examining Theme and Character Exchanges in Film and Music," International Journal of Instructional Media, XIX, No. 4 (1992), pp. 339-347.

1993

"Rumors of War: Lyrical Continuities, 1914-1991," in Continuities of Popular Culture, edited by Ray B. Browne and Ronald J. Ambrosett. (Bowling Green, Ohio: Bowling Green State University Popular Press, 1993), pp. 121-142.

"Popular Culture Materials in Libraries and Archives," Popular Culture in Libraries, I, No. 1 (1993), pp. 5-35 (with Michael Marsden, Barbara Moran, and Allen Ellis).

"From the Outside Looking In: A Popular Culture Researcher Speaks to Librarians," Popular Culture in Libraries, I, No. 1 (1993), pp. 37-46.

"Sultry Songs as High Humor," Popular Music and Society, XXVII (Spring 1993), pp. 71-85.

"Searching for the Most Popular Songs of the Year…with Menomonee Joe, Big Al, Louisiana Jim, and Bayou Barry," Popular Culture in Libraries, I, No. 2 (1993), pp. 125-130.

"From American Forces Network to Chuck Berry, From Larry Parnes to George Martin: The Rise of Rock Music Culture in Great Britain, 1943-1967 and Beyond – A Biblio-Historical Study," Popular Culture in Libraries, I, No. 2 (1993), pp. 33-64 (with Laura E. Cooper).

"Sultry Songs and Censorship: A Thematic Discography for College Teachers," International Journal of Instructional Media, XX, No. 2 (1993), pp. 181-194.

"The Coasters – What is the Secret of Their Success? A Review Essay," Popular Music and Society, XVII (Summer 1993), pp. 115-119.

"Jackie Wilson – Mr. Excitement? Mr. Musical Diversity? Mr. Song Stylist? Or Mr. Stage Show? A Review Essay," Popular Music and Society, XVII (Summer 1993), pp. 119-122.

"A Haunting Question: Should Sound Recordings Archives Promote the Circulation of Horror Material?" Popular Culture in Libraries, I, No. 3 (1993), pp. 45-58 (with William L. Schurk).

"Baseball Cards, Hispanic Players, and Public School Instruction," Popular Culture in Libraries, I, No. 3 (1993), pp. 85-104 (with Donald E. Walker).

"Can Music Students Learn Anything of Value by Investigating Popular Recordings?" International Journal of Instructional Media, XX, No. 3 (1993), pp. 273-284.

"Awarding an 'A' Grade to Heavy Metal: A Review Essay," Popular Music and Society, XVII (Fall 1993), pp. 99-102.

"The Pendulum of Cultural Imperialism: Popular Music Interchanges Between the United States and Britain, 1943-1967," Journal of Popular Culture, XXVII (Winter 1993), pp. 61-78 (with Laura E. Cooper).

"Tapping a Sound Recording Archive for War Song Resources to Investigate America's Major Military Involvements, 1914-1991," Popular Culture in Libraries, I, No. 4 (1993), pp. 71-93.

"Processing Health Care Images from Popular Culture Resources: Physicians, Cigarettes, and Medical Metaphors in Contemporary Recordings," Popular Music and Society, XVII (Winter 1993), pp. 105-124.

"The Drifters: From Gospel Glory to Rock Royalty," Popular Music and Society, XVII (Winter 1993), pp. 125-128.

1994

"Examining the Medical Profession Through Musical Metaphors," International Journal of Instructional Media, XXI, No. 2 (1994), pp. 155-163.

"Smokin' Songs: Examining Tobacco Use as an American Cultural Phenomenon Through Contemporary Lyrics," International Journal of Instructional Media, XXI, No. 3 (1994), pp. 261-268.

"Sex, Songs, and Censorship: A Thematic Taxonomy of Popular Recordings for Music Librarians and Sound Recording Archivists," Popular Culture in Libraries, II, No. 4 (1994), pp. 11-47.

1995

Baseball and American Culture: A Thematic Bibliography of Over 4,500 Works (Jefferson, North Carolina: McFarland and Company, 1995), 257 pp. (with Donald E. Walker).

The Literature of Rock III, 1984-1990 (Metuchen, New Jersey: Scarecrow Press, 1995), 1,003 pp. (with Frank Hoffmann).

Rock Music in American Popular Culture: Rock 'N' Roll Resources (New York: Haworth Press, 1995), 386 pp. (with Wayne S. Haney).

"From Johnny Ace to Frank Zappa: Debating the Meaning of Death in Rock Music – A Review Essay," Popular Culture in Libraries, III, No. 1 (1995), pp. 51-75.

"Popular Music in Print," Popular Music and Society, XIX, No. 4 (Winter 1995), pp. 105-112.

1996

"Reveille, Riveting, and Romance Remembered: Popular Recordings of the World War II Era," in Proceedings of the University of Great Falls World War II Symposium (October 2-6, 1995), edited by William Furdell (Great Falls, Montana: University of Great Falls, 1996), pp. 43-73.

"Please Mr. Postman: Images of Written Communication in Contemporary Lyrics," International Journal of Instructional Media, XXIII, No. 1 (1996), pp. 79-89.

"Popular Music During World War II: Patriotism and Personal Communications," International Journal of Instructional Media, XXIII, No. 2 (1996), pp. 181-192.

"Cover Recordings by Dot Artists," Popular Music and Society, XX, No. 2 (Summer 1996), pp. 119-204.

"A Taxonomy of Tributes on Compact Disc," Popular Music and Society, XX, No. 2 (Summer 1996), pp. 204-217.

"Revisiting Rhythm 'N' Blues Royalty: A Review Essay," Popular Music and Society, XX, No. 3 (Fall 1996), pp. 119-122.

"Booklist," Popular Music, XV (October 1996), pp. 371-396 (with Simon Frith, Bernhard Hefele, Dave Lang, and Toru Mitsui).

"From 'Love Letters' to 'Miss You': Popular Recordings, Epistolary Imagery, and Romance During War Time, 1941-1945," Journal of American Culture, XIX, No. 4 (Winter 1996), pp. 15-27.

1997

Rock Music in American Popular Culture II: More Rock 'N' Roll Resources (New York: Haworth Press, 1997), 404 pp. (with Wayne S. Haney).

"What Kind of Fool Am I? Audio Imagery, Personal Identity, and Social Relationships," International Journal of Instructional Media, XXIV, No. 3 (1997), pp. 253-267.

"It's Still Rock and Roll to Me: Reflections on the Evolution of Popular Music and Rock Scholarship," Popular Music and Society, XXI, No. 1 (Spring 1997), pp. 101-108.

"Wise Men Never Try: A Discography of Fool Songs, 1945-1995," Popular Music and Society, XXI, No. 2 (Summer 1997), pp. 115-131.

"Terror Translated into Comedy: The Popular Music Metamorphosis of Film and Television Horror, 1956-1991," Journal of American Culture, XX, No. 3 (Fall 1997), pp. 31-42.

"Booklist," Popular Music, XVI, No. 3 (October 1997), pp. 327-351 (with Bernhard Hefele, Dave Laing, and Toru Mitsui).

"A Telephone Song Discography," Popular Music and Society, XXI, No. 4 (Winter 1997), pp. 111-122.

1998

"Teaching with Popular Music Resources: A Bibliography of Interdisciplinary Instructional Approaches," Popular Music and Society, XXII, No. 2 (Summer 1998), pp. 85-115.

"Booklist," Popular Music, XVIII, No. 3 (October 1998), pp. 359-383 (with Bernhard Hefele, Dave Laing, Toru Mitsui, and Christophe Pirenne).

"The Life of the Mind: A Personal Perspective," Delta Epsilon Sigma Journal, XLIII, No. 1 (Winter 1998), pp. 32-33.

"It's Still Rock and Roll to Me: Reflections on the Evolution of Popular Music and Rock Scholarship," Rock and Blues News, No. 1 (December 1998-January 1999), pp. 19-21.

1999

Rock Music in American Popular Culture III: More Rock 'N' Roll Resources (New York: Haworth Press, 1999), 337 pp. (with Wayne S. Haney).

"Revising 'Oldies But Goodies' Playlists: Radio Programming, Market Expansion, and America's Musical Heritage," Rock and Blues News, No. 2 (February-March 1999), pp. 19-20.

"There's a Surfeit of Java in Rio: Coffee Songs as Teaching Resources," International Journal of Instructional Media, XXVI, No. 2 (1999), pp. 231-236 (with William L. Schurk).

"My Vote's on Jerry Lee…" Rock and Blues News, No. 3 (April-May 1999), pp. 35-37.

"Squeezing Sugar From the Phone: Rock, Blues, and Pop Telephone Songs," Rock and Blues News, No. 4 (May-June 1999), pp. 26-28.

"The Great Falls Higher Education Center: A Public-Private Partnership," Great Falls Business Journal, I, No. 1 (July-August-September 1999), pp. 14-15.

"You're the Cream in My Coffee: A Discography of Java Jive," Popular Music and Society, XXIII, No. 2 (Summer 1999), pp. 91-100.

"From Lady Day to Lady Di: Images of Women in Contemporary Recordings, 1938-1998," International Journal of Instructional Media, XXVI, No. 3 (1999), pp. 353-358.

"Booklist," Popular Music, XIX, No. 3 (October 1999), pp. 425-446 (with Bernhard Hefele, Dave Laing, Toru Mitsui, and Christophe Pirenne).

"Singing, Smoking, and Sentimentality: Cigarette Imagery in Contemporary Recordings," Popular Music and Society, XXIII, No. 3 (Fall 1999), pp. 79-88.

"Audio Musicology: A Discography of Tributes to Musical Styles and Recording Artists," International Journal of Instructional Media, XXVI, No. 4 (1999), pp. 459-467.
"Women's Studies and Popular Music Stereotypes," Popular Music and Society, XXIII, No. 4 (Winter 1999), pp. 31-43.

"Bibliography of Popular Music Teaching Resources," Popular Music and Society, XXIII, No. 4 (Winter 1999), pp. 123-129.

2000

"Answer Songs: Comedy, Parody, and Social Commentary," Rock and Blues News, No. 8 (February-March 2000), pp. 29-31.

"The Bridge as Metaphor in Modern Popular Music," Rock and Blues News, No. 9 (April-May 2000), pp. 25-27.

"Sultry Songs and Censorship," Rock and Blues News, No. 10 (June-July 2000), pp. 33-35.

"Building, Burning, Crossing…and Feelin' Groovy: Examining the Human Condition Through Bridge Songs," International Journal of Instructional Media, XXVII, No. 3 (2000), pp. 315-326.

"Why Don't You Write Me? A Letter Song Discography, 1945-1995," Rock and Blues News, No. 12 (October/November 2000), pp. 37-39.

"Popular Music's Dilemma During the Vietnam War: Presumed Patriotism Versus Democratic Dissent," in Proceedings of the University of Great Falls Vietnam Symposium (April 3-7, 2000), edited by William Furdell (Great Falls, Montana: University of Great Falls Press, 2000), pp. 79-107.

"Booklist," Popular Music, XIX, No. 3 (October 2000), pp. 403-434 (with Bernhard Hefele, Dave Laing, Toru Mitsui, and Christophe Pirenne).

American Culture Interpreted Through Popular Music: Interdisciplinary Teaching Approaches (Bowling Green, Ohio: Popular Music and Society/Bowling Green State University Popular Press, 2000), 129 pp.

"Women and P.M.S. (Popular Music Stereotypes): A Politically Incorrect Analysis," in Women are Not From Venus Anymore: A Conference Exploring the Changing Role of Women in Society, edited by Roger P. Snow and Judith D. Snow (Great Falls, Montana: University of Great Falls Press, 2000), pp. 41-66.

2001

"Rock 'N' Roll Royalty: Jerry Lee Lewis and Little Richard," Rock and Blues News, No. 13 (December 2000-January 2001), pp. 27-28.

"From Piccolo Pete to The Piano Man: Music Instruments Referenced in Sound Recordings," International Journal of Instructional Media, XXVIII, No. 3 (2001), pp. 319-326 (with Patty Falk and William L. Schurk).

"Formal Education as a Lyrical Target: Images of Schooling in Popular Music, 1955-1980," in Images of Youth: Popular Culture as Educational Ideology, compiled by Michael A. Oliker and Walter P. Krolikowski (New York: Peter Lang, 2001), pp. 73-95.

"Booklist," Popular Music, XX, No. 3 (October 2001), pp. 453-477 (with Bernhard Hefele, Dave Laing, Toru Mitsui, and Christophe Pirenne).

2002

"Teardrops in the Night: A Discography of Crying Theme Recordings, 1950-2000," International Journal of Instructional Media, XXIX, No. 3 (2002), pp. 345-354.

2003

"The Pendulum of Cultural Imperialism: Popular Music Interchanges Between the United Stated and Britain, 1943-1967," in The American Impact on European Popular Culture Since 1945, edited by Sabrina P. Ramet and Gordana P. Crnkovic (Lanham, Maryland: Rowman and Littlefield, 2003), pp. 69-82 (with Laura E. Cooper).

"'A' - You're Adorable: Abbreviations, Acronyms, and Other Alphabetical Arrangements in Popular Recordings, 1920-2000," International Journal of Instructional Media, XXX, No. 3 (2003), pp. 1-8.

"Accordions, Banjos, Cornets…and Zithers: Sound Recordings Archives and Musical Instruments," Popular Music and Society, XXVI, No. 3 (October 2003), pp. 387-398 (with Patty Falk and William L. Schurk).

2004

The Popular Music Teaching Handbook: An Educator's Guide to Music-Related Print Resources (Westport, Connecticut: Libraries Unlimited, 2004), 371 pp. (with Rebecca A. Condon).

"The Sky is Crying: Tales Told in Tearful Tunes," Popular Music and Society, XXVII, No. 1 (Winter 2004), pp. 107-115.

"Sam Phillips (1923-2003): Reflections on Legends," Popular Music and Society, XXVII, No. 2 (June 2004), pp. 241-242.

2005

"Ray Charles (1930-2004): Reflections on Legends," Popular Music and Society, XXVIII, No. 1 (February 2005), pp. 107-108.

"Music, Popular," in Tobacco in History and Culture: An Encyclopedia, edited by Jordan Goodman (Detroit: Charles Scribner's Sons/Thomson Gale, 2005), pp. 369-373.

"Tribute Discs, Career Development, and Death: Perfecting the Celebrity Product from Elvis Presley to Stevie Ray Vaughan," Popular Music and Society, XXVIII, No. 2 (May 2005), pp. 229-248.

"Bibliographies," in The B.B. King Reader: Six Decades of Commentary, edited by Richard Kostelanetz (Milwaukee, Wisconsin: Hal Leonard Corporation, 2005), pp. 307-319.

2006

"From 'Mystery Train' to 'Cyberspace Sadie': References to Technology in Blues Recordings, 1923-2003," International Journal of Instructional Media, XXXIII, No. 3 (2006), pp. 1-9.

"Record Labels as Gateways to Popular Music Teaching: A Bibliography and Discography, Popular Music and Society, XXIX, No. 5 (December 2006), pp. 585-617.

"In Memoriam: Wilson Pickett, 1941-2005," Popular Music and Society, XXIX, No. 3 (July 2006), pp. 387-388.

2007

"Good Timin': Searching for Meaning in Clock Songs," Popular Music and Society, XXX, No. 1 (February 2007), pp. 93-106.

"Tribute Recordings As Teaching Tools: Recommended Audio Resources," International Journal of Instructional Media XXXIV, No. 2 (2007), pp. 223-233.

"Before The Beatles: International Influences on American Popular Recordings, 1940-1963," Popular Music and Society, XXX, No. 2 (May 2007), pp. 227-266 (with William L. Schurk and Julie Cooper).

"American Disc Jockeys, 1945-1975: A Bibliographic and Discographic Survey," Popular Music and Society, XXX, No. 3 (July 2007), pp. 401-423.

"Apple and Atlantic, Stax and Sun: Teaching About Contemporary Music From a Record Label Perspective," International Journal of Instructional Media, XXXIV, No. 4, (2007), pp. 457-467.

"From the Bunny Hop to the Funky Chicken: An American Dance Song Discography, 1945-1975," Popular Music and Society, XXX, No. 5 (December 2007), pp. 651-666.

-- 2008 --

"Record Label Resources Revisited: A Teaching Discography," International Journal of Instructional Media, XXXV, No. 1 (2008), pp. 1-12.

" 'Do You Know What it Means to Miss New Orleans?' Discovery, Dominance, and Decline of the Crescent City's Popular Music Influence, 1946-2006," Popular Music and Society, XXXI, No. 2 (May 2008), pp. 151-190.

"Architects of the New Orleans Sound, 1946-2006: A Bio-Bibliography," Popular Music and Society, XXXI, No. 2 (May 2008), pp. 221-261.

"Right Place, Wrong Time: Discography of a Disaster," Popular Music and Society, XXXI, No. 2 (May 2008), pp. 263-268.

"Honky Tonks, Jukeboxes, and Wild, Wild Women: Audio Images of Blue Collar Night Life – A Selected Discography," Popular Music and Society, XXXI, No. 5 (December 2008), pp. 663-683.

2009

"Review of Johnny B. Goode: His Complete '50s Chess Recordings by Chuck Berry, "Popular Music and Society, XXXII, No. 1 (February 2009), pp. 127-128.

"Review of The Cosimo Matassa Story," Popular Music and Society, XXXII, No. 1 (February 2009), pp. 125-127.

"Review of Son of Skip James by Dion," Popular Music and Society, XXXII, No. 1 (February 2009), pp. 128-129.

"Review of Respect: Aretha's Influences and Inspiration Featuring Various Artists," Blue Suede News, No. 87 (Summer 2009), pp. 48-49.

"Review of Holy Mackerel! Pretenders to Little Richard's Throne Featuring Various Artists," Blue Suede News, No. 87 (Summer 2009), p. 49.

"Review of Night Work by Billy Price and Fred Chapellier, Blue Suede News, No. 88 (Fall 2009), p. 36.

"Review of The Dirty Dozen by George Thorogood and the Destroyers," Blue Suede News, No. 89 (Winter 2009/2010), p. 46.

2010

"Rock Journalists and Music Critics: A Selected Bibliography," Popular Music and Society, XXXIII, No. 1 (February 2010), pp. 75-101.

"Charting the Success of Male Recording Duos: Billboard Recognition of Country, Pop, and R&B/Rap Pairs, 1944 - 2004," Popular Music and Society, XXXIII, No. 2 (May 2010), pp. 237-257.

"Contemporary Blueswomen: A Bibliography of Female Blues Singers, Composers, and Instrumentalists, 1955 – 2005," Popular Music and Society, XXXIII, No. 3 (July 2010), pp. 395-414.

"Blue-Eyed Soul Performers Before and After the Wicked Pickett and Lady Soul: A Bibliography and Discography," Popular Music and Society, XXXIII, No. 5 (December 2010), pp. 663-693.

"Charting Cultural Change, 1953-1957: Song Assimilation Through Cover Recording," in Play It Again: Cover Songs in Popular Music, edited by George Plasketes (Burlington, Vermont: Ashgate Publishing Company, 2010), pp. 43-76.

2011

"Odes to Obesity: Images of Overweight Men and Women in Commercial Sound Recordings – A Discography," Popular Music and Society, XXXIV, No. 2 (May 2011), pp. 237-246.

"Bumble Boogie: 100 Years of Bee Imagery in American Sound Recordings – A Discography," Popular Music and Society, XXXIV, No. 4 (July 2011), pp. 493-502. (With William L. Schurk.)

"Killer Bees: The Bountiful B-Side Bonanzas of the '50s," Blue Suede News, No. 95 (Fall 2011), p. 27.

"Review of Next Stop is Vietnam: The War on Record, 1961-2008 by Various Artists," Popular Music and Society, XXXIV, No. 4 (October 2011), pp. 507-511.

"Seasonal Music: Heat Up the Holidays With This Playlist," Goldmine, No. 808 (November 2011), pp. 11-15.

2012

"Review of Blues and Chaos: The Music Writing of Robert Palmer by Anthony DeCurtis," Popular Music and Society, XXXV, No. 1 (February 2012), pp. 131-132.

"Review of Diana Ross Presents The Jackson 5 by The Jackson 5," Popular Music and Society, XXXV, No. 2 (May 2012), pp. 317-319.

"Review of The Chitlin' Circuit: The Road to Rock 'N' Roll by Preston Lauterbach," Popular Music and Society, XXXV, No. 3 (July 2012), pp. 458-460.

"Review of A Whole Lotta' Shakin' Goin' On by Various Artists," Blue Suede News, No. 98 (Summer/Fall 2012), p. 46.

"Review of The Killer Live, 1964-1970 by Jerry Lee Lewis," Blue Suede News, No. 99 (Winter 2012/2013), p. 39.

"Review of Screaming and Crying: 75 Masterpieces by 35 Blues Guitar Heroes by Various Artists," Blue Suede News, No. 99 (Winter 2012-2013), p. 41.

2013

"Contemporary Christmas Recordings", "Fools and Foolish Behavior", "Halloween and Horror Recordings", "Matrimony in Music", "Nonsense Lyrics", "Obesity in Song", "Personal Appearance and Clothing Styles on Disc", and "Technology in Lyrics" in Music in American Life: An Encyclopedia of the Songs, Styles, Stars, and Stories That have shaped our Culture, edited by Jacqueline Edmondson (Santa Barbara, California: ABC/CLIO Publishers, 2013), pp. 215-217, 231-233, 462-463, 536-537, 695-696, 807-809, 815-816, and 1132-1137.

"Good Time Rollers: Little Richard and Huey 'Piano' Smith" and "Midnight in Memphis with the Wicked Pickett," in Please Allow Me to Introduce Myself: Essays on Debut Discs, edited by George Plasketes (Burlington, Vermont: Ashgate Publishing Company, 2013), pp. 29-34 and 49-52 (with William L. Schurk).

"John Fogerty and America's Three Rock Generations," in Finding Fogerty: Interdisciplinary Readings of John Fogerty and Creedence Clearwater Revival, edited by Thomas M. Kitts (Lanham, Maryland: Lexington Books/Rowman and

Littlefield Publishing Company, 2013), pp. 151-173 (with William L. Schurk). "From Cement Mixers to Personal Computers: Images of Technology in Commercial Recordings, 1910-2010," Popular Music and Society, 36 (February 2013), pp. 40-75.

"Review of Hall of Fame (2012), The Fame Studios Story (2011), Take Me to the River (2008), and The Muscle Shoals Sound (1993) by Various Artists," Popular Music and Society, 36 (May 2013), pp. 293-295.

"My Music, Not Yours: Ravings of a Rock-and-Roll Fanatic," Popular Music and Society, 36 (July 2013), pp. 397-410.

"Review of 45 RPM Answer/Parody Songs: A Reference Guide to Response Songs by Ron Davis and Brenda Davis," Popular Music and Society, 36 (July 2013), pp. 417-420.

"Review of Love Me Do (2010), Beatles Beginnings (2009, 2010, 2011), and The Hamburg List (2010) by Various Artists," Popular Music and Society, 36 (October 2013), pp. 550-554.

"Review of This Could Be the One (2013), Secret Agent Man (2006), Last Train to Memphis (1998), and The Memphis Sun Recordings (1991) by Johnny Rivers," Popular Music and Society, 36 (December 2013), pp. 715-718.

2014

"Review of Before Elvis: The Prehistory of Rock 'N' Roll by Larry Birnbaum," Rock Music Studies, I (February 2014), pp. 97-99.

"Review of Midnight at the Barrelhouse and On With the Show by Johnny Otis and Rocks by Chuck Berry," Rock Music Studies, I (February 2014), pp. 106-109.

"Review of Greatest Hits From Outer Space by Various Artists," Rock Music Studies, I (May 2014), pp. 203-205.

"Review of Cadillac Cuties and Hot Rod Heroes by Various Artists," Popular Music and Society, 37 (July 2014), pp. 389-391.

"Review of The Road to Rock and Roll – Volume One: Jitterbug Jive by Various Artists," Rock Music Studies, I (May 2014), pp. 200-203.

"Review of Doo-Wop: The R&B Vocal Group Sound, 1950-1960 and Doo-Wop: The Rock & Roll Vocal Group Sound, 1957-1961 by various artists," Popular Music and Society, 37 (October 2014), pp. 513-516.

"Review of Sleigh Rides, Jingle Bells, and Silent Nights: A Cultural History of American Christmas Songs by Ronald D. Lankford, Jr.," Rock Music Studies, I (October 2014), pp. 299-302.

"Review of Hidden in the Mix: The African American Presence in Country Music by Diane Pecknold," Popular Music and Society, 37 (December 2014), pp. 680-682.

2015

Academic Reviews of Rock Writings: A Topical Presentation of Critical Commentaries (Charleston, South Carolina: Paw Paw Press, 2015), 136 pp. (with Frank W. Hoffmann).

Answer Songs: A Reference Guide to Response Recordings, 1900-2015 – Two Volumes (Charleston, South Carolina: Paw Paw Press, 2015), 614 pp. (with Frank W. Hoffmann, Stephen D. Briggs, David A. Milberg, and William L. Schurk, with assistance from Debbie Edens).

Dawn of the Sing-Song Writer Era, 1944-1963: Bibliographic Profiles of the Performer-Composers (Charleston, South Carolina: Paw Paw Press, 2015), 451 pp. (with Frank W. Hoffmann).

Discs of Distinction: Essays on Remarkable Recordings by Exceptional Artists (Charleston, South Carolina: Paw Paw Press, 2015), 164 pp. (with Frank W. Hoffmann and Debbie Edens).

The Keyboard Kingdom: A Resource Guide to Rock, Pop, Blues and Country Keyboard Players and Their Music (San Bernardino, California: Paw Paw Press, 2015), 126 pp. (with Michael L. Cooper, Frank W. Hoffmann, Debbie Edens, and William L. Schurk).

Lyrical Legacies: Essays on Topics in Rock, Pop, and Blues Lyrics…and Beyond (Charleston, South Carolina: Paw Paw Press, 2015), 171 pp. (with Frank W. Hoffmann and Debbie Edens).

More Discs of Distinction: Additional Essays on Remarkable Recordings by Exceptional Artists (Charleston, South Carolina: Paw Paw Press, 2015), 220 pp. (with Frank W. Hoffmann and Debbie Edens).

More Than Just the Music: Essays in Lyrical Analysis and Topical Identification (Charleston, South Carolina: Paw Paw Press, 2015), 260 pp. (with Frank W. Hoffmann, Stephen D. Briggs, William L. Schurk, and Debbie Edens).

Novelty Records: Selected Subjects and Artists (Charleston, South Carolina: Paw Paw Press, 2015), 257 pp. (with Frank Hoffmann and Debbie Edens).

Novelty Records: A Topical Discography, 1900-2015 (Charleston, South Carolina: Paw Paw Press, 2015), 497 pp. (with Frank W. Hoffmann).

Popular Music Research: Answer Songs, Blue-Eyed Soul, Cover Recordings…and Beyond (Charleston, South Carolina: Paw Paw Press, 2015), 284 pp. (with Frank W. Hoffmann and Debbie Edens).

Popular Music Scholarship: Articles, Bibliographies, Book/CD Reviews, and Discographies (San Bernardino, California: Paw Paw Press, 2015), 323 pp. (with Frank W.Hoffmann, Debbie Edens, and William L. Schurk).

Prominent Themes in Popular Songs: An Exploration of 54 Persistent Lyrical Themes (Charleston, South Carolina: Paw Paw Press, 2015), 392 pp. (with Frank W. Hoffmann, Debbie Edens, Matthew J. Masters, and William L. Schurk).

Three of a Kind: The Rolling Stones, John Fogerty, and Male/Female Recording Duos (Charleston, South Carolina: Paw Paw Press, 2015), 137 pp. (edited by Frank W. Hoffmann). Visions of Axemen: A Resource Guide to Guitarists and Their Recordings (Charleston, South Carolina: Paw Paw Press, 2015), 196 pp. (with Michael L. Cooper, Frank W. Hoffmann, and William L. Schurk).

"The Hyperbolic Hit Parade: A Discographic Study of Extravagant Lyrical Assertions in Romantic Recordings," Popular Music and Society, XXXVIII, No. 5 (December 2015), pp. 611-624.

"Review of Encyclopedia of Great Popular Song Recordings by Steve Sullivan," Rock Music Studies, II, No 3 (October 2015), pp. 315-318.

"Review of 'Live at the BBC'" and " 'On the Air - Live at the BBC' by The Beatles," Rock Music Studies, II (February 2015), pp. 100-102.

"Review of The Republic of Rock: Music and Citizenship in the Sixties Counterculture by Michael J. Kramer," Rock Music Studies, II (February 2015), pp. 91-93.

"Review of Understanding Fandom: An Introduction to the Study of Media Fan Culture by Mark Duffett," Popular Music and Society, 38 (February 2015), pp. 109-111.

"Review of Who Did It First? Great Rhythm and Blues Cover Songs and Their Original Artists by Bob Leszczak," Rock Music Studies, II (May 2015), pp. 208-211.

2016

Cover Recordings, 1900-2016 (Charleston, South Carolina: Paw Paw Press, 2016), 378 pp. (with Frank W. Hoffmann)

Persistent Themes in Sound Recordings - Seven Volumes (Charleston, South Carolina: Paw Paw Press, 2016) (with Frank W. Hoffmann).

The Rise of Rock 'n' Roll, 1950-1959 (Charleston, South Carolina: Paw Paw Press, 2016), 363 pp. (with Frank W. Hoffmann)

Rockabilly - The Artists, The Music, The Heritage: A Literary Resource Guide (Charleston, South Carolina: Paw Paw Press, 2016), 342 pp. (with Frank W. Hoffmann)

"My Music, Not Yours: Ravings of a Rock 'n' Roll Fanatic," in Fan Identities and Practices in Context: Dedicated to Music, edited by Mark Duffett (Oxford, England: Routledge, 2016), pp. 99-112.

"Review of Country Soul by Charles L. Hughes," Popular Music and Society, XXXIX, No. 4 (October 2016), pp. 469-471.

"Review of R&B No. 1 Hits of the '50s by various artists," Rock Music Studies, III, No. 3 (October 2016)), pp. 331-333.

"Review of Wade in the Water by various artists and Get Your Soul Right by Various Artists," Popular Music and Society, XXIX, No. 2 (May 2016), pp. 279-281.

2017

America in Transition, 1945-1975: A Musical Perspective on Historical Change (Charleston, South Carolina: Paw Paw Press, 2017), 581 pp. (with Frank W. Hoffmann)

Cover Recordings, 1900-2016 – Volume Two (Charleston, South Carolina: Paw Paw Press, 2017), 443 pp. (with Frank W. Hoffmann)

The Doo-Wop Decades, 1945-1965 (Columbia, South Carolina: Paw Paw Press, 2017), 354 pp. (with Frank W. Hoffmann)

New Orleans Rhythm & Blues: A Resource Guide to Crescent City Artists and Their Recordings, 1945-1975 (Columbia, South Carolina: Paw Paw Press, 2017), 223 pp. (with Debbie Edens and Frank W. Hoffmann)

Revisiting Rock's "Lost Years", 1959-1963 (Middleton, Delaware: Paw Paw Press, 2017), 378 pp. (with Frank W. Hoffmann)

Soul Music Ascending, 1961-1970 (Columbia, South Carolina: Paw Paw Press, 2017), 492 pp. (with Frank W. Hoffmann)

The Triumph of Rhythm & Blues, 1945-1960 (Columbia, South Carolina: Paw Paw Press, 2017), 385 pp. (with Frank W. Hoffmann)

"Review of Directly From My Heart by Little Richard," Rock Music Studies, IV, No. 1 (February 2017), pp. 80-81.

"Review of Jerry Lee Lewis by Rick Bragg and Elvis Presley by Joel Williamson," Rock Music Studies, IV, No. 2 (May 2017), pp. 157-159.

"Review of Just Around Midnight: Rock and Roll and the Racial Imagination by Jack Hamilton," Popular Music and Society, XL, No. 2 (May 2017), pp. 239-240.

"Review of Love for Sale: Pop Music in America by David Hajdu," Popular Music and Society, XL, No. 3 (July 2017), pp. 363-364.

"Review of Politically Incorrect by Various Artists," Popular Music and Society, XL, No. 1 (February 2017), pp. 122-123.

"Review of The Beatles and The Historians: An Analysis of Writings About the Fab Four by Erin Torkelson Weber," Rock Music Studies, IV, No. 1 (February 2017), pp. 78-79.

2018

Music-Making Giants of the Rockin' 50s: A Bio-Bibliography (Columbia, South Carolina: Paw Paw Press, 2018) (with Frank W. Hoffmann).

Cover of an early B. Lee Cooper rock music guidebook

OLLI CLASSES TAKEN AT UNC-ASHEVILLE BY JILL AND LEE COOPER (2008-2018)
(Alphabetical Listing of Courses by Instructor Names)

Dave Bates (davebates95@yahoo.com)	"History of Broadway Sing-Along"
Cynthia Berryman-Fink (berrymanfink@gmail.com)	"Men and Women Communicating"
Bill Britain (britt4@charter.net)	"Early Alfred Hitchcock Films"
Robert Busey (unreported)	"Niebuhr, Graham, Peale - Three 20th Century Religious Voices"
Jacob Cohen (jacobwoodworker@gmail.com)	"Scrabble: Become A Family Champ and Beyond"
B. Lee Cooper (ashevillecats1@charter.net)	"America in Transition, 1945-1975: Recordings That Reflect These Changing Times"
B. Lee Cooper (ashevillecats1@charter.net)	"America in Transition, 1945-1975: Recordings That Reflect These Changing Times 2.0"
B. Lee Cooper (ashevillecats1@charter.net)	"America in Transition, 1945-1975: Recordings That Reflect These Changing Times 3.0"
B. Lee Cooper (ashevillecats1@charter.net)	"America in Transition, 1945-1975: Recordings That Reflect These Changing Times 4.0"
B. Lee Cooper (ashevillecats1@charter.net)	"Black Music Goes Mainstream: Cover Recordings As Catalysts, 1940-1990"
B. Lee Cooper (ashevillecats1@charter.net)	"Changing Times, Changing Music: Recordings as History, 1945-1975"
B. Lee Cooper (ashevillecats1@charter.net)	"Novelty Recordings, 1940-1990"
B. Lee Cooper (ashevillecats1@charter.net)	"Persistent Themes in Popular Music"

B. Lee Cooper (ashevillecats1@charter.net)	"Persistent Themes in Popular Music 2.0"
B. Lee Cooper (ashevillecats1@charter.net)	"Persistent Themes in Popular Music 3.0"
B. Lee Cooper (ashevillecats1@charter.net)	"Persistent Themes in Popular Music 4.0"
B. Lee Cooper (ashevillecats1@charter.net)	"Persistent Themes in Popular Music 5.0"
B. Lee Cooper (ashevillecats1@charter.net)	"Persistent Themes in Popular Music 6.0"
Alice Doner (adoner@verizon.net)	"Heroes and Villains on Film"
Chuck Fink (charlesfink1@gmail.com)	"Marxism: The Marx Brothers' Films"
Catherine Frank and others	"A Change Is Gonna Come: The Civil Rights Movement and American Culture"
Leslie Gaspar (lgaspar@me.com)	"Running Wild II: Genres in Pre-code Movies"
Larry Griswold (si54guy@gmail.com)	"The 1919 Black Sox, the 1969 Miracle Mets, And 96 Other World Series Championships"
Dick Hansley (hansleym@aol.com)	"Architectural History of Asheville"
Jay Jacoby (jbjacoby@uncc.edu)	"Philip Roth at The Movies"
RoseLynn Katz (rosecarol@charter.net)	"The Joys of Children's Literature: Sharing Books With Kids"
Chip Kaufmann (jjk44@bellsouth.net)	"If I Had A 'Hammer' Film"
Chip Kaufmann (jjk44@bellsouth.net)	"Lon Chaney: The Man of A Thousand Faces"

Jim Kehoe (jkehoe11@charter.net)	"The Civil War: A Film Series by Ken Burns"
Mary Lasher (mlelasher.avl@gmail.com)	"Meaning of Life"
Jim Lenburg (leroynitny@aol.com)	"America in The Cold War Era"
Jim Lenburg (jlenburg@mhc.edu)	"Idealism, Pragmatism, And Realism in The Foreign Policies of Three Democratic Presidents"
Cleve Mathews (clevem@mich.edu)	"Issues of The Day, In and Out of The Media"
Rene Melchiorre (rdm10and11@gmail.com)	"The American Home Front in World War II"
Rene Melchiorre (reneeclio@yahoo.com)	"Postwar American Society in The Years of Confidence, 1945-1960"
Rene Melchiorre (reneeclio@yahoo.com)	"Profiles Of The 35th President: John Fitzgerald Kennedy"
Bob Mellor (BM.OLLI@Charter.net)	"Folk Music's Transformation into Folk-Rock"
Bob Mellor (bm.ncccr@charter.net)	"Frank Lloyd Wright: America's Most Famous Architect"
Bob Mellor (BM.OLLI@Charter.net)	"Rock Music's Evolution, 1966-1970s"
William Moore (unreported)	"Frank Lloyd Wright: An American Architect"
Morgan Phillips (mlphilli@charter.net)	"The Dead Sea Scrolls in Historical Context"
Morgan Phillips (mlphilli@charter.net)	"The Female Image in Biblical Thought"
Morgan Phillips (mlphilli@charter.net)	"The Five Faces of God"

Morgan Phillips (mlphilli@charter.net)	"The History of Anti-Semitism"
Morgan Phillips and RoseLynn Katz (RoseCarol@charter.net)	"The Holocaust: A Perspective from Film, History, and Religion"
Morgan Phillips (mlphilli@charter.net)	"Separation of Church and State in American History"
Carl Ricciardelli (cfr666@bellsouth.net)	"Studies in Skepticism"
Michael Ruiz (ruiz@unca.edu)	"Piano Lecture Recitals: Classical, Jazz, And Popular Music"
Michael Ruiz (mjtruiz@gmail.com)	"Popular Music of The 1960s"
Michael Ruiz (ruiz@unca.edu)	"Romantic Music"
Michael Ruiz (mjtruiz@gmail.com)	"Stephen Sondheim: His Life and Music"
Michael Ruiz (ruiz@unca.edu)	"Tin Pan Alley, Jazz, And Swing"
Joe Sasfy (jsasfy@gmail.com)	"The '50s Rock 'N' Roll Revolution"
Joe Sasfy (jsasfy@gmail.com)	"Rock 'N' Roll's Lost Years, 1958-1963"
Joe Sasfy (jsasfy@google.com)	"The '60s Rock And Soul Revolution"
Farley Snell (snellfarleyw@netscape.net)	"Chicago: Before and Between the Fairs"
Farley Snell (snellfarleyw@netscape.net)	"1500 Years of Christian Thought"
Farley Snell (snellfarleyw@netscape.net)	"Gnosticism -- or Not"

Farley Snell (snellfarleyw@netscape.net)	"God in The Hands of An Ageing Theologian"
Farley Snell (snellfarleyw@netscape.net)	"H. Richard Niebuhr's THE RESPONSIBLE SELF"
Farley Snell (snellfarley@netscape.net)	"Niebuhr, Niebuhr, And Tillich"
Farley Snell (snellfarley@netscape.net)	"Varieties of Christianity"
Barbara S. Weitz (weitzb@fiu.edu)	"New American Cinema: How the Rock 'N' Roll Generation Saved Hollywood"
Wayne Wheeler (wswheeler3@yahoo.com)	"History of Lighthouses And aids To Navigation"
Lewis Wills (lewiswillls2011@gmail.com)	"The Folk Music Revival in America"
Lewis Wills (lewis and katie@chater.net)	"Jack the Ripper and The Victorian Age"
Doug Wingeier (dcwing@att.net)	"Seeing Ourselves in The Movies"
Doug Wingeier (dcwing@att.net)	"Seeing Ourselves in The Movies"
Paula Withrow (pvwithrow@aolcom)	"History's Mysteries"
Paula Withrow (pvwithrow@aol.com)	"Monuments Men: Art and Architectural Heroes"
George Yates (gcyates104@gmail.com)	"America's Foreign Policy Since 1940"
Catharine Frank, Larry Griswold, Jim Lenburg, Joe Sasfy, and others	"A Change Is Gonna Come: The Civil Rights Movement and American Culture"

Peter, Paul and Mary

A COURSE OUTLINE FOR "AMERICA IN TRANSITION" (2016)

Course Title: "America in Transition, 1945-1975: Recordings That Reflect Changing Times"

Instructor: B. Lee Cooper, Ph.D.

Course Description:

A survey of popular recordings that address three decades (1945-1975) of changes in American life. General areas covered include teenage culture, economic circumstances, international diplomacy/warfare, and political, social, and technological/scientific changes. Specific topics examined will include atomic energy, baseball, civil rights, radio/TV, railroading, space exploration, the Vietnam War, and more. Students will listen to a variety of recordings from the period, suggest additional songs that relate to specific topics, and reflect on their own life experiences at the intersection of social change and popular music.

Course Objectives:

1. To assist students to identify and analyze selected topics contained in the lyrics of 20th Century recordings

2. To acquaint students with a spectrum of recorded songs and performing artists found in several musical genres

3. To stimulate student recollections of recorded song lyrics

4. To enhance student listening skills in respect to recorded lyrics, with special attention to identifying key words and specific topics embedded in musical contexts

5. To review several ideas, characters, and events that dominated American history from 1945-1975

Supplementary Readings (most of these texts are available at the UNC-Asheville Campus Library):

Richard D. Barnet, Bruce Nemerov, and Mayo R. Taylor. THE STORY BEHIND THE SONG: 150 SONGS THAT CHRONICLE THE 20TH CENTURY. Westport, Connecticut: Greenwood Press, 2004.

B. Lee Cooper. IMAGES OF AMERICAN SOCIETY IN POPULAR MUSIC. Chicago: Nelson-Hall, 1982.

B. Lee Cooper. A RESOURCE GUIDE TO THEMES IN CONTEMPORARY SONG LYRICS, 1950-1985. Westport, Connecticut: Greenwood Press, 1986.

B. Lee Cooper. POPULAR MUSIC PERSPECTIVES: IDEAS, THEMES, AND PATTERNS IN CONTEMPORARY LYRICS. Bowling Green, Ohio: Bowling Green State University Popular Press, 1991.

B. Lee Cooper and Wayne S. Haney. ROCK MUSIC IN AMERICAN POPULAR CULTURE (Three Volumes). New York: Haworth Press, 1995, 1997, and 1999.

B. Lee Cooper and Rebecca A. Condon. THE POPULAR MUSIC TEACHING HANDBOOK. Westport, Connecticut: Libraries Unlimited, 2004.

Paul Dickson. TIMELINES. Reading, Massachusetts: Addison-Wesley, 1990.

Mary Ellison. LYRICAL PROTEST: BLACK MUSIC'S STRUGGLE AGAINST DISCRIMINATION. New York: Praeger Books, 1989.

Philip H. Ennis. THE SEVENTH STREAM: THE EMERGENCE OF ROCK 'N' ROLL IN AMERICAN POPULAR MUSIC. Hanover, New Hampshire: Wesleyan University Press/ University Press of New England, 1992.

Reebee Garofalo. ROCKIN' OUT: POPULAR MUSIC IN THE U.S.A. Boston: Allyn and Bacon, 1997.

Lois Gordon and Alan Gordon. AMERICAN CHRONICLE: SIX DECADES IN AMERICAN LIFE, 1920-1980. New York: Atheneum Books, 1987.

Bernard Grun. THE TIMETABLES OF HISTORY: A HORIZONTAL LINKAGE OF PEOPLE AND EVENTS (Revised Edition). New York: Touchstone Books/Simon and Schuster, 1982.

S.I. Hayakawa. "Popular Songs vs. The Facts Of Life." ETC: A REVIEW OF GENERAL SEMANTICS, 12 (Winter 1955): 83-95.

Herb Hendler. YEAR BY YEAR IN THE ROCK ERA: EVENTS AND CONDITIONS SHAPING THE ROCK GENERATIONS THAT RESHAPED AMERICA. Westport, Connecticut: Greenwood Press, 1983.

Kevin Hillstrom and Laurie Collier Hillstrom. THE VIETNAM EXPERIENCE: A CONCISE ENCYCLOPEDIA OF AMERICAN LITERATURE, SONGS, AND FILMS. Westport, Connecticut: Greenwood Press, 1998.

George Lipsitz. TIME PASSAGES: COLLECTIVE MEMORY AND AMERICAN POPULAR CULTURE. Minneapolis, Minnesota: University of Minnesota Press, 1990.

Linda Martin and Kerry Segrave. ANTI-ROCK: THE OPPOSITION TO ROCK 'N' ROLL. Hamden, Connecticut: Archon Books, 1988.

John Paxton and Sheila Fairfield (comps.). CHRONOLOGY OF CULTURE: A CHRONOLOGY OF LITERATURE, DRAMATIC ARTS, MUSIC, ARCHITECTURE, THREE-DIMENSIONAL ART, AND VISUAL ARTS FROM 3,000 B.C. TO THE PRESENT. New York: Van Nostrand Reinhold, 1984 (c. 1979).

James E. Perone. MUSIC OF THE COUNTERCULTURE ERA. Westport, Connecticut: Greenwood Press, 2004.

James E. Perone. SONGS OF THE VIETNAM CONFLICT. Westport, Connecticut: Greenwood Press, 2001.

David Pichaske. A GENERATION IN MOTION: POPULAR MUSIC AND CULTURE IN THE SIXTIES. New York: Schirmer Books, 1979.

Laurence Urdang (editor). THE TIMETABLES OF AMERICAN HISTORY. New York: Touchstone Books/Simon and Schuster, 1981.

Craig Werner. A CHANGE IS GONNA COME: MUSIC, RACE, AND SOUL IN AMERICA. New York: Plume/Penguin Putnam, 1999.

Introduction

1. "Rock Island Line"
   Lonnie Donegan
2. "Hey Porter"
   Johnny Cash
3. "City of New Orleans"
   Arlo Guthrie
4. "People Get Ready"
   The Impressions
5. "Love Train"
   The O'Jays

Processing A Hybrid Course
1. History
2. Memory
3. Music

A. Typical History Lesson
1. "We Didn't Start The Fire"
Billy Joel (1989)

B. Anthems From Our Memories
1. "The Times They Are A-Changin'"
Bob Dylan (1964)
2. "Blowin' In The Wind"
Bob Dylan (1963)
3. "Blowin' In The Wind"
Peter, Paul, and Mary (1963)
4. "We Shall Overcome"
Mahalia Jackson (1963)
5. "If I Had A Hammer (The Hammer Song)"
Peter, Paul, and Mary (1962)
6. "A Change Is Gonna Come"
Sam Cooke (1965)
7. "Abraham, Martin, and John"
Dion (1968)

C. Hair As A Historical Trope
1. "G. I. Haircut"
Spike Jones and His City Slickers (1943)
2. "(You Dyed Your Hair) Chartreuse"
Louis Jordan and his Tympany Five (1950)
3. "My Boy Flat Top"
Boyd Bennett and His Rockets (1955
4. "Ducktail"
Joe Clay (1956)
5. "My Beatle Haircut"
The Twiliters (1964)
6. "I Don't Want You Cuttin' Off Your Hair"
B.B. King (1967)
7. "San Francisco (Be Sure to Wear Some Flowers In Your Hair)"
Scott McKenzie (1967)
8. "How You Gonna Get Respect (You Haven't Cut Your Process Yet)"
Hank Ballard (1968)
9. "Hair"
The Cowsills (1969)
10. "I Almost Cut My Hair"
Crosby, Stills, Nash, and Young (1970)
11. "Signs"
The Five Man Electrical Band" (1971)
12. "The Haircut Song"
Ray Stevens (1985)
13. "Get A Haircut"
George Thorogood and the Destroyers (1993)

D. Warnings About Atomic Energy
-- recorded Civil Defense Nuclear Warning announcements (1953)

1. "Fallout Shelter"
Peter Scott Peters (1961)
2. "Atom And Evil"
Golden Gate Quartet (1946)
3. "We Almost Lost Detroit"
Gil Scott-Heron (1979)
4. "Three Mile Island"
Pinkard and Bowden (1984)

(E-Mail essays on "Space", "Cover Recording", and "The Twist" To All Class Members)

E. Fads, Distractions, and Singular Events
1. "The Mickey Mouse Club March"
Jimmie Dodd and The Mouseketeers (1955)
2. "Satellite Rock"
Joe Tate and The Hi-Fives (1958)
3. "The Hula Hoop Song"
Teresa Brewer (1958)
4. "The Twist"
Hank Ballard (1959)
5. "The Twist"
Chubby Checker (1960, 1961)
6. "Woodstock"
Crosby, Stills, Nash & Young (1970)
7. "The Streak"
Ray Stevens (1974)
8. "Convoy"
C.W. McCall (1975)

F. Soldiers, Duty, and Patriotism
1. "Gallant Men"
Senator Everett McKinley Dirkensen (1966)
2. "Billy And Sue"
B.J. Thomas (1966)
3. "War"
Edwin Starr (1970)
4. "I-Feel-Like-I'm-Fixin'-To-Die Rag"
Country Joe McDonald and The Fish (1969)
5. "Fortunate Son"
Creedence Clearwater Revival (1969)

G. Teenage Demographic -- Personal Testimony
1. "At Seventeen"
Janis Ian (1975)

2. "I'm Eighteen"
Alice Cooper (1971)
3. "Society's Child (Baby I've Been Thinking)"
Janis Ian (1967)

(Administer "Teen Idols" Quiz)

H. Baseball In History
1. "Take Me Out To The Ballgame"
Carly Simon (1994)
2. "Who's On First"
Bud Abbott and Lou Costello (1945)
3. "Did You See Jackie Robinson Hit That Ball?"
Count Basie and His Orchestra (1949)
4. "The Robbie-Doby Boogie"
Brownie McGhee (1948)
5. "Let's Keep The Dodgers In Brooklyn"
Phil Foster (1957?)
6. "Baseball, Baseball"
Jane Morgan (1954)
7. "The Ball Game"
Sister Wynona Carr (1953)
8. "Jackie Robinson Eulogy"
Rev. Jesse Jackson (1972)
9. Move Over Babe (Here Comes Henry)"
Bill Slayback (1973)
10. "Mrs. Robinson"
Simon and Garfunkel (1968)
11. "Talkin' Baseball (Willie, Mickey, and The Duke)"
Terry Cashman (1995)
12. "A Dying Cub Fan's Last Request"
Steve Goodman (1981)
13. "Centerfield"
John Fogerty (1985)

I. Automobiles and Highways
1. "Rev Off"
1951 Mercury Custom & 1960 Chevrolet Impala
2. "See The U.S.A. In Your Chevrolet"
Dinah Shore (19)
3. "Maybelline"
Chuck Berry (1955)
4. "The Ballad Of Thunder Road"
Robert Mitchum (1958, 1962)
5. "Transfusion"
Nervous Norvus (1956)

(E-mail Essay on "Automobiles" to All Class Members)

J. Metropolitan Memories, Myths, and Images
1. "Detroit City"
Bobby Bare (1963)
2. "Living for The City"
Ray Charles (1975)
3. "My Kind Of Town (Chicago Is)"
Frank Sinatra (1964)
4. "Chicago"
Frank Sinatra (1957)
5. "Sweet Home Chicago"
Little Junior Parker (19)
6. "Dead End Street"
Lou Rawls (1967)
7. "Street Corner Hustler's Blues"
Lou Rawls (196)
8. "World Of Trouble"
Lou Rawls (196)
9. "Born In Chicago"
Paul Butterfield Blues Band (1965)
10. "Chicago"
Graham Nash (1971)
11. "A Dying Cub Fan's Last Request"
Steve Goodman (1981)
12. "Take Me To Chicago"
Dave Hole (2003)

(Introduce Optional Assignment for All Class Members to Create a 3-to-5 Song Lyrical Topic)

Lonnie Donegan

A COURSE OUTLINE FOR "PERSISTENT THEMES IN POPULAR MUSIC" (2015)

Course Title: "Persistent Themes in Popular Music"

Instructor: B. Lee Cooper, Ph.D.

Course Description:

A survey of prominent themes that appear in the lyrics of 20th century popular recordings. Topics examined will include answer songs, couples, murders and suicides, nicknames, railroads and trains, tribute tunes, weddings, and more. Students will identify and analyze topics in songs, explore various musical genres and recorded performances, reflect on personal musical experiences, and develop listening skills by identifying key words and phrases embedded within musical contexts.

Course Objectives:

1. To assist students to identify and analyze selected topics and themes contained in the lyrics of 20th century recordings

2. To acquaint students with a spectrum of recorded songs and performing artists from several musical genres

3. To stimulate student recollctions of song titles and recorded lyrics

4. To enhance student listening skills, with particular attention to identifying key words and specific topics embedded in lyrical phrases

Supplementary Readings Available at the UNC-Asheville Ramsey Library:

B. Lee Cooper. IMAGES OF AMERICAN SOCIETY IN POPULAR MUSIC. Chicago: Nelson-Hall, 1982.

B. Lee Cooper. A RESOURCE GUIDE TO THEMES IN CONTEMPORARY SONG LYRICS. Westport, Connecticut: Greenwood Press, 1986.

B. Lee Cooper. POPULAR MUSIC PERSPECTIVES: IDEAS, THEMES, AND PATTERNS IN CONTEMPORARY LYRICS. Bowling Green, Ohio: Bowling Green State University Popular Press, 1991.

B. Lee Cooper and Wayne S. Haney. ROCK MUSIC IN AMERICAN POPULAR CULTURE - Three Volumes. New York: Haworth Press, 1995, 1997, and 1999.

B. Lee Cooper and Rebecca A. Condon. THE POPULAR MUSIC TEACHING HANDBOOK. Westport, Connecticut: Libraries Unlimited, 2004.

Instructor Profile:

B. Lee Cooper (ashevillecats1@charter.net) is an experienced teacher, former university administrator, and award-winning author. He has published 15 books and numerous articles and reviews about popular music. He is currently President/CEO of Popular Music Research, Ltd., a newtwork of scholars who provide assistance to students and colleagues studying various music-related topics.

Class Introduction
--identifying persistent themes
--examining various musical styles
--recognizing the romantic emphasis in popular recordings
--highlighting names in song titles and recorded lyrics

1. "Toot, Toot, Tootsie (Goo'bye)"
   by Al Jolson (1922)

Railroads, Trains, and Rail Travel Themes

1. "Take The 'A' Train" (jazz)
   by Duke Ellington Orchestra (1966)
2. "Sentimental Journey" (pop)
   by Doris Day, with Les Brown and His Orchestra (1945)
3. "Golden Gate Gospel Train" (gospel)
   by Golden Gate Gospel Quartet (1937)
4. "Rock Island Line" (folk)
   by Lonnie Donegan (1956)
5. "I'm Movin' On" (country)
   by Hank Snow (1950)
6. "King's Special" (blues)
   by B.B. King (1970)
7. "Love Train" (R&B/soul)
   by O'Jays (1973)
8. "Train, Train" (rock)
   by Blackfoot (1979)

Names Related To Railroads, Trains, and Rail Travel

9. "John Henry"
   by Lonnie Donegan (1956)
10. "Railroad Bill"
    by Walt Robertson (1959)
11. "Zack, The Mormon Engineer"
    by L. M. Hilton (1951)

What's Your Name?

1. "Who Are You"
   by Who (1978)
2. "What's Your Name"
   by Lynyrd Skynyrd (1977)
3. "What's Your Name"
   by Don and Juan (1962)

(Ask students to identify names from song titles or lyrics of recordings issued between 1900 and 1950.)

(Ask students to identify names from song titles or lyrics of recordings issued between 1950 and 2000.)

(Ask students to suggest the most frequently mentioned boys names in recordings issued between 1900 and 2000.)

(Ask students to suggest the most frequently mentioned girls names in recordings issued between 1900 and 2000.)

(Ask students to identify any nicknames utilized in recordings between 1950 and 2000.)

Nicknames

1. "Lollipop"
   by Chordettes (1958)
2. "Speedoo"
   by Cadillacs (1955)
3. "Dr. Feelgood (Love Is Serious Business)"
   by Aretha Franklin (1967)

Peculiar Names

1. "Be-Bop-A-Lula"
   by Gene Vincent (1956)
2. "My Names Is Bocephus"
   by Hank Williams, Jr. (1986)
3. "Rama Lama Ding Dong"
   by Edsels (1961)

Mean, Mean Men

1. "Ringo"
   by Lorne Greene (1964)
2. "Bad, Bad Leroy Brown"
   by Jim Croce (1973)

3. "You Don't Mess Around With Jim"
     by Jim Croce (1972)

Wild, Wild Women

  1. "Cyberspace Sadie"
     by Big Al Jano's Blues Mafia Show (2002)
  2. "Lady Marmalade"
     by LaBelle (1975)
  3. "Hard Hearted Hannah"
     by Ray Charles (1960)

(Ask students to identify songs that related to marriage and weddings.)

Wedding Themes

  1. "Love And Marriage"
     by Dinah Shore (1955)
  2. "At Last"
     by Ray Anthony and His Orchestra (1952)
  3. "At Last"
     by Etta James (1961)
  4. "At Last"
     by Beyonce (2009)
  5. "To The Aisle"
     by Five Satins (1957)
  6. "If You Wanna Be Happy"
     by Jimmy Soul (1963)

Names Related to Wedding Songs

  7. "Daisy Bell"
     by Don Quinn (1893)
  8. "Betty And Dupree"
     by Chuck Willis (1958)
  9. "Hey Paula"
     by Paul and Paula (1962)
 10. "Big Bopper's Wedding"
     by Big Bopper (1958)
 11. "I'm Henry VIII, I Am"
     by Herman's Hermits (1965)
 12. "Wedding Bell Blues"
     by The Fifth Dimension (1969)

Ilustrations of Names In Various Musical Styles

1. "Lucille" (blues)
   by B.B. King (1968)
2. "Sweet Lorraine" (jazz)
   by Ella Fitzgerald, with Count Basie and His Orchestra (1982)
3. "Norman" (pop)
   by Sue Thompson (1962)
4. "Michael" (folk)
   by Highwaymen (1961)
5. "Elvira" (country)
   by Oak Ridge Boys (1981)
6. "Mona (I Need You Baby)" (R&B/soul)
   by Bo Diddley (1957) The Swan Silvertones (1959)
7. "Francene" (rock)
   by ZZ Top (1972)
8. "The Trouble With Harry" (novelty/humor)
   by Alfi and Harry" (1956)
9. "Mary Don't You Weep" (gospel)
   By The Caravans (1958)

Answer Songs, Cover Recordings, and Continuing Sagas

1. "Work With Me Annie"
   by Hank Ballard and The Midnighters (1954)
2. "Annie Had A Baby"
   by Hank Ballard and The Midnighters (1954)
3. "A Boy Named Sue"
   by Johnny Cash (1969)
4. "A Girl Named Johnny Cash"
   by Jane Morgan (1970)
5. "A Girl Named Harry"
   by Joni Credit
6. "Are You Lonesome Tonight"
   by Elvis Presley (1960)
7. "Yes, I'm Lonesome Tonight"
   by Thelma Carpenter
8. "Runaround Sue"
   by Dion (1961)
9. "I'm No Run Around"
   by Ginger Davis

Behind Closed Doors

1. "Open The Door, Richard"
   by Count Basie aand His Orchestra (1947)

2. "Hernando's Hideaway"
   by Archie Bleyer and His Orchestra (1954)
3. "Green Door"
   by Jim Lowe (1956)
4. "Let Me In"
   by Sensations (1962)

(Ask students to identify songs that feature the telephone as a topic or means of communication.)

Telephone Themes

1. "Beechwood 4-5789"
   by Marvelettes (1962)
2. "634-5789 (Soulsville, U.S.A.)"
   by Wilson Pickett (1966)
3. "He'll Have To Go"
   by Jim Reeves (1959)

Names Related To Telephone Songs

4. "Hello, This Is Joannie (The Telephone Answering Machine Song)"
   by Paul Evans (1978)

(Ask students to identify songs that address topics of murder or suicide.)

Names Related To Murder or Suicide Themes

1. "Richard Cory"
   by Simon and Garfunkel (19)
2. "Running Bear"
   by Johnny Preston (1959)
3. "Ode To Billie Joe"
   by Bobbie Gentry (1967)
4. "Miss Otis Regrets"
   by Linda Ronstadt (2007)
5. "Smackwater Jack"
   by Carole King (1971)
6. "Stagger Lee"
   by Lloyd Price (1958)

(Ask students to identify songs that address occupations or workplace situations.)

Names Related to Occupations

1. "Lovely Rita"
   by Beatles (1967)

2. "Abigail Beecher"
     by Freddy Cannon (1964)
  3. "Big Bad John"
     by Jimmy Dean (1961)
  4. "Clap For The Wolfman"
     by Guess Who (1974)

(Ask students to identify songs that honor the memories of historical or musical figures.)

Names Mentioned In Tributes or Remembrances

   1. "The Late, Great Johnny Ace"
      by Paul Simon (1983)
   2. "Abraham, Martin, and John"
      by Dion (1968)
   3. "Bob Wills Is Still The King"
      by Waylon Jennings (1975)
   4. "Candle In The Wind"
      by Elton John (1987)
   5. "Candle In The Wind 1997"
      by Elton John (1997)
   6. "Gene And Eddie"
      by Stray Cats (1996)
   7. "R.O.C.K. In The U.S.A."
      by John Mellencamp (1986)
   8. "Rock And Roll Heaven"
      by Righteous Brothers (1974)
   9. "Sir Duke"
      by Stevie Wonder (1977)
  10. "Sister Rosa"
      by Neville Brothers (1989)

(Ask students to identify couples mentioned in song titles.)

Names Of Couples And Their Stories

  1. "My True Story"
     by Jive Five (1961)
  2. "Love Theme From Romeo And Juliet"
     by Henry Mancini (1969)
  3. "(Just Like) Romeo And Juliet"
     by Reflections (1964)
  4. "Frankie And Johnny"
     by Lonnie Donegan (197)
  5. "Billy And Sue"
     by B. J. Thomas and The Triumphs (1966)

6. "Jack And Diane"
   by John Cougar (1982)
7. "Me And Bobby McGee"
   by Janis Joplin (1971)

POPULAR MUSIC RESEARCH, LTD.
MEMBERSHIP LIST (2019)

Friends,

Last year we celebrated our 10th anniversary of Popular Music Research, Ltd. service to students and scholars. In 2019 we launch our second decade of voluntary research assistance. Congratulations and well done! Many of you were present at the creation; others have joined our consulting ranks over the past decade. It has been a pleasure to work with all of you. I look forward to many more years of aiding music researchers.

I am attaching the 2019 Popular Music Research, Ltd. membership list. You will note that no new fields of musical study were added during the past twelve months. When necessary, we'll seek additional members. But as of now we are fully capable of fielding queries across a wide range of music-related specialties. Have a healthy, prosperous, productive, and happy 2019. Thanks again for your generous contributions of time and expertise. Later, friends...

Lee

B. Lee Cooper, Ph.D.
President and CEO
Popular Music Research, Ltd.
4 Grey Goose Court
Biltmore Lake, North Carolina 28715
U. S. A.
ashevillecats1@charter.net
(828) 633-6150

Popular Music Research, Ltd. Purpose Statement

Popular Music Research, Ltd. is a voluntary association of authors, broadcasters, editors, journalists, librarians, musicians, and teachers. This network of popular music enthusiasts is a source of consulting expertise for persons seeking information related to preparing academic manuscripts or dissertations, assembling music-related anthologies, exploring discographic or bibliographic resources, or creating music-oriented radio or television programming. Each member of PMRL serves on the Board of Advisors. The areas of consulting competence for each member are delineated below. This information, along with individual names and e-mail addresses, is circulated among the full Board membership. Specific research requests and general popular music inquiries may be fielded individually or circulated among several PMRL members for group consultation. All responses from PMRL members will be provided promptly and without charge in the hope of advancing popular music scholarship.

B. Lee Cooper, Ph.D.
President and CEO

Popular Music Research, Ltd. Board Of Advisors (February 1, 2019)

Patrick Argent, MCSD
patrickargent@googlemail.com

--British New Wave/Alternative (1977-1985)
--British Punk Rock (1976-1981)

Justin Brummer, Ph.D.
justinbrummer@hotmail.com

--Gov. George Wallace songs
--John F. Kennedy songs
--Lyndon B. Johnson songs
--Martin Luther King, Jr. songs
--Richard M. Nixon/Watergate scandal songs
--Vietnam War songs

Gary Burns, Ph.D.
gburns@niu.edu

--editorial issues related to music articles
--music magazines
--rock music, 1960-1970
--scholarly music journals

B. Lee Cooper, Ph.D.
ashevillecats1@charter.net

--audio reviews
--book reviews
--cover recordings
--dance music and dancing styles
--instrumental recordings
--persistent themes in popular lyrics
--teaching with popular music resources

Michael L. Cooper
mcooper33@hotmail.com

--audio recording equipment
--heavy metal
--record collecting
--re-conditioning instruments (drums, guitars)

Brenda A. Davis
BD71bug@aol.com

--answer songs and oddities
--45 rpm records
--record collecting
--record label art

Ronald D. Davis
RonOR45rpm@aol.com

--answer songs and novelty records
--country, doo-wop, and rock 'n' roll
--record collecting
--record label histories

Howard A. DeWitt, Ph.D.
Howard217@aol.com

--biographical studies (The Beatles, Chuck Berry, Van Morrison, Elvis Presley, Del Shannon)
--record collecting
--rock music bibliography
--teaching the history of rock 'n' roll

Matt Donohue, Ph.D.
md1210@yahoo.com

--heavy metal music
--popular culture
--punk music
--rap music
--reggae music
--rock 'n' roll history

Mark Duffett, Ph.D.
m.duffett@chester.ac.uk

--music fandom
--Elvis Presley

Jacqueline Edmondson, Ph.D.
jxe117@psu.edu

--cultural issues in recorded music
--music-related encyclopedia entries and biography
--political activism in recorded music
--social concerns in recorded music

Eldon R. Edwards, M.A.
eldonedw@gmail.com

--American popular music
--classic country
--1950s & 1960s music
--Elvis Presley

Steve Hamelman, Ph.D.
steveh@coastal.edu

--alt rock
--popular music
--sixties rock

Nyalls Hartman, M.F.A.
Nyalls@yahoo.com

--American standards
--female vocalists, 1990 to the present
--live musical performance
--motion picture soundtracks
--selected musical genres (blues, R&B, rock, zydeco)

Frank W. Hoffmann, Ph.D.
hoffmannfrank49@yahoo.com

--academic journals and music magazines
--censorship in lyrics and sound recordings
--music chartography
--music-related biography and bibliography
--record collecting
--sound recordings archives
--20th Century sound recordings

Hugo Keesing, Ph.D.
musicdoc@erols.com

--Keesing Musical Archive
--Korean War-related music

--music cards and comic books
--record collecting
--rock bibliography
--topical songs
--teaching the history of popular music
--Vietnam War-related music
--World War II songs

Thomas M. Kitts, Ph.D.
tomkitts@aol.com

--British Invasion music and performers
--editorial issues related to music articles
--selected musical genres (alternative rock, blues, folk, punk rock)

Andy Leach, M.S.
aleach@rockhall.org

--history of popular music
--Library and Archives of the Rock and Roll Hall of Fame and Museum
--music business
--sound recordings

Matthew J. Masters
mattmasters@myninestar.net

--The Beatles and British Invasion Music
--blues, country, doo-wop, jazz, novelty, R&B, rock 'n' roll, and rockabilly music, 1945-1965
--Halloween and Christmas recordings
--lyrical themes in recorded music
--radio broadcasting

David A. Milberg, J.D.
recordman48@gmail.com

--baseball records
--Billboard-charted recordings
--Christmas records
--discography development
--history of American popular music
--intellectual property and copyrights
--radio broadcasting

Gillian A. M. Mitchell, Ph.D.
gamm2@st-andrews.ac.uk

--folk music revival in Canada, 1945-1975
--folk music revival in U. S. A., 1945-1975
--popular music in Great Britain, 1955-1965
--rock 'n' roll in Great Britain, 1955-1965

Gregory P. Moss, Ed.D.
mossg@cox.net

--The Beatles
--British Invasion
--1960's rock and roll

Neil Nehring, Ph.D.
neilnehring@sbcglobal.net

--Avant-garde influences in rock music
--Blues and rhythm 'n' blues
--British culture and history (1945 - present)
--Glam rock and punk rock (British and American)
--History of rock 'n' roll

Barbara B. Newman
barbara@blues.org

--blues artists
--The Blues Foundation in Memphis, Tennessee
--blues heritage
--blues performance
--blues recordings

George Plasketes, Ph.D.
plaskgm@mail.auburn.edu

--cover recordings
--music personalities in American popular culture
--tribute songs

David W. Robb
audiosaurus@me.com

--audio systems design for theaters and amphitheaters
--growth and development of the professional audio industry
--hearing conservation
--live music performance, technology, and logistics
--touring with popular musicians (1960-2000)

Jerry Rodnitzky, Ph.D.
jerry.rodnitzky@uta.edu

--folk music
--protest songs
--women in popular music

Michael J. Ruiz, Ph.D.
mjtruiz@gmail.com

--Broadway musicals
--history of American popular music
--history of jazz
--Hollywood musicals
--piano performance
--popular music, jazz, classical
--Tin Pan Alley

Ben Sandmel
hotbiscuits@att.net
bsandmel@tulane.edu

--biography (Ernie K-Doe)
--blues
--Cajun/zydeco
--jazz
--Mardi Gras Indians
--R&B and soul
--rockabilly

Joe Sasfy, Ph.D.
jsasfy@comcast.net

--bluegrass
--country and western music
--early rock 'n' roll
--R&B and soul music

Timothy E. Scheurer, Ph.D.
tscheurer@shawnee.edu

--Broadway musicals
--film music
--folk/rock music, 1950-1970
--history of American popular music
--history of jazz
--popular/cabaret singers
--sheet music
--Tin Pan Alley

William L. Schurk, M.S.L.S.
wschurk@bgsu.edu

--cataloging records
--history of sound recordings
--musical genres (bluegrass, blues, comedy/novelty, country, ethnic/foreign, folk,
  heavy metal, hip-hop, jazz, old-time, pop, R&B, rock, soul, zydeco, and more)
--record collecting
--The Bill Schurk Sound Recordings Archives at Bowling Green State University

George W. Sistrunk, D.M.A.
sistrunkg@bellsouth.net

--classical music
--conducting
--professional music training
--traditional church music
--vocal pedagogy

Erin Torkelson Weber, M.A.
adxwebere@newmanu.edu

--Beatles bibliographies
--Beatles historiography
--historical methods in mass media
--historical methods in popular culture

Chas "Dr. Rock" White
drrock27@gmail.com

--radio broadcasting
--R&B and rock 'n' roll music
--rock biography (Jerry Lee Lewis, Little Richard)

PRINT RESOURCES ON POPULAR MUSIC

Glenn C. Altschuler. ALL SHOOK UP: HOW ROCK 'N' ROLL CHANGED AMERICA. New York: Oxford University Press, 2003.

Richard Aquila. LET'S ROCK: HOW 1950s AMERICA CREATED ELVIS AND THE ROCK AND ROLL CRAZE. Lanham, Maryland: Rowman and Littlefield, 2017.

Richard Aquila. THAT OLD TIME ROCK AND ROLL: A CHRONICLE OF AN ERA, 1954-1963. New York: Schirmer Books, 1989.

Michael Bane. WHITE BOY SINGIN' THE BLUES: THE BLACK ROOTS OF WHITE ROCK. New York: Da Capo Books, 1992 (c1982).

Jason Berry, Jonathan Foose, and Tad Jones. UP FROM THE CRADLE OF JAZZ. Athens, Georgia: University of Georgia Press, 1986.

Michael T. Bertrand. RACE, ROCK, AND ELVIS. Urbana, Illinois: University of Illinois Press, 2005 (c2000).

Kenneth J. Bindas (ed.). AMERICA'S MUSICAL PULSE: POPULAR MUSIC IN TWENTIETH-CENTURY SOCIETY. Westport, Connecticut: Praeger Books, 1992.

Larry Birnbaum. BEFORE ELVIS: THE PREHISTORY OF ROCK 'N' ROLL. Lanham, Maryland: Scarecrow Press, 2013.

Stanley Booth. RYTHM OIL: A JOURNEY THROUGH THE MUSIC OF THE AMERICAN SOUTH. New York: Da Capo Press, 2000 (c1991).

Rob Bowman. SOULSVILLE U.S.A.: THE STORY OF STAX RECORDS. New York: Schirmer Books/Simon and Schuster, 1997.

David Brackett (ed.). THE POP, ROCK, AND SOUL READER: HISTORIES AND DEBATES. New York: Oxford University Press, 2005.

Fred Bronson. THE BILLBOARD BOOK OF NUMBER ONE HITS (Fourth Edition). New York: Billboard Books, 1997.

John Broven. RECORD MAKERS AND BREAKERS: VOICES OF THE INDEPENDENT ROCK 'N' ROLL PIONEERS. Urbana: University of Illinois Press, 2009.

Louis Cantor. WHEELIN' ON BEALE: HOW WDIA-MEMPHIS BECAME THE NATION'S FIRST ALL-BLACK RADIO STATION AND CREATED THE SOUND THAT CHANGED AMERICA. New York: Pharos Books, 1992.

Bill Carroll. RANKING THE ROCK WRITERS: A COMPLETE CATALOG OF ALL THE WRITERS APPEARING ON THE MAJOR POP SINGLES CHARTS, 1955-1991. Dallas, Texas" Carroll Applied Science, LLC, 2018.

Theo Cateforis (ed.). THE ROCK HISTORY READER. New York: Routledge, 2007.

Jim Cogan and William Clark. TEMPLES OF SOUND: INSIDE THE GREAT RECORDING STUDIOS. San Francisco, California: Chronicle Books, 2003.

Rich Cohen. MACHERS AND ROCKERS: CHESS RECORDS AND THE BUSINESS OF ROCK AND ROLL. New York: Atlas Books / W. W. Norton and Company, 2004.

Rick Coleman. BLUE MONDAY: FATS DOMINO AND THE LOST DAWN OF ROCK 'N' ROLL. Cambridge, Massachusetts: Da Capo Press, 2006.

Stuart Colman. THEY KEPT ON ROCKIN': THE GIANTS OF ROCK 'N' ROLL. Poole, Dorset, England: Blandford Press, 1982.

B. Lee Cooper and Frank W. Hoffmann. AMERICA IN TRANSITION, 1945-1975: A MUSICAL PERSPECTIVE ON HISTORICAL CHANGE. Charleston, South Carolina: Paw Paw Press, 2017.

B. Lee Cooper, Frank W. Hoffmann, and Debbie Edens. GALLANT MEN, FORTUNATE SONS, AND DRAFT RESISTERS: A SURVEY OF 20th CENTURY POPULAR MUSIC RESPONSES TO AMERICAN MILITARY ENGAGEMENTS. Columbia, South Carolina: Paw Paw Press, 2020.

B. Lee Cooper. IMAGES OF AMERICAN SOCIETY IN POPULAR MUSIC: A GUIDE TO REFLECTIVE TEACHING. Chicago: Nelson-Hall Publishing, 1982.

B. Lee Cooper. POPULAR MUSIC PERSPECTIVES: IDEAS, THEMES, AND PATTERNS IN CONTEMPORARY LYRICS. Bowling Green, Ohio: Bowling Green State University Popular Press, 1991.

B. Lee Cooper and Frank W. Hoffmann. PROMINENT THEMES IN POPULAR SONGS. Charleston, South Carolina: Paw Paw Press, 2015.

B. Lee Cooper. A RESOURCE GUIDE TO THEMES IN CONTEMPORARY AMERICAN SONG LYRICS, 1950-1985. Westport, Connecticut: Greenwood Press, 1986.

B. Lee Cooper and Wayne S. Haney. ROCK MUSIC IN AMERICAN POPULAR CULTURE: ROCK 'N' ROLL RESOURCES. New York: Haworth Press, 1995.

B. Lee Cooper and Wayne S. Haney. ROCK MUSIC IN AMERICAN POPULAR CULTURE II: MORE ROCK 'N' ROLL RESOURCES. New York: Haworth Press, 1997.

B. Lee Cooper and Wayne S. Haney. ROCK MUSIC IN AMERICAN POPULAR CULTURE III: MORE ROCK 'N' ROLL RESOURCES. New York: Haworth Press, 1999.

B. Lee Cooper and Frank W Hoffmann. THE ROCK 'N' ROLL BOOKSHELF: COMMENTARIES ON LITERARY INVESTIGATIONS OF AMERICA'S MUSICAL CULTURE (Second Edition). Columbia, South Carolina: Paw Paw Press, 2018.

B. Lee Cooper and Frank W. Hoffmann. TOPICAL TUNES AND HOLIDAY HITS: PERSISTENT IMAGERY AND COMMON THEMES IN POPULAR RECORDINGS. Monee, Illinois: Paw Paw Press, 2022.

B. Lee Cooper and Frank W. Hoffmann. ROCKERS! FROM CHUCK BERRY TO ZZ TOP - A REFERENCE GUIDE. Monee, Illinois: Paw Paw Press, 2022.

Lee Cotten. SHAKE, RATTLE, AND ROLL: THE GOLDEN AGE OF ROCK 'N' ROLL - VOLUME ONE, 1952-1955. Ann Arbor, Michigan: Pierian Press, 1989.

Lee Cotten. REELIN' AND ROCKIN': THE GOLDEN AGE OF ROCK 'N' ROLL - VOLUME TWO, 1956-1959. Ann Arbor, Michigan: Popular Culture, Ink., 1995.

Lee Cotten. TWIST AND SHOUT: THE GOLDEN AGE OF ROCK 'N' ROLL - VOLUME THREE, 1960-1963. Sacramento, California: High Sierra Books, 2002.

Jim Dawson and Steve Propes. WHAT WAS THE FIRST ROCK 'N' ROLL RECORD? Boston: Faber and Faber, 1992.

Anthony DeCurtis and James Henke, with Holly George-Warren (eds.). THE ROLLING STONE ILLUSTRATED HISTORY OF ROCK AND ROLL (Second Edition). New York: Random House, 1992.

R. Serge Denisoff and William D. Romanowski. RISKY BUSINESS: ROCK IN FILM. New Brunswick, New Jersey: Transaction Books, 1991.

Howard A. DeWitt. ELVIS - THE SUN YEARS: THE STORY OF ELVIS PRESLEY IN THE FIFTIES. Ann Arbor, Michigan: Popular Culture, Ink., 1993.

David Dicaire. BLUES SINGERS: BIOGRAPHIES OF 50 LEGENDARY ARTISTS OF THE EARLY 20th CENTURY. Jefferson: North Carolina: McFarland and Company, 1999.

David Dicaire. MORE BLUES SINGERS: BIOGRAPHIES OF 50 ARTISTS FROM THE LATER 20th CENTURY. Jefferson, North Carolina: McFarland and Company, 2002.

James Dickerson. MOJO TRIANGLE: BIRTHPLACE OF COUNTRY, BLUES, JAZZ, AND ROCK 'N' ROLL. New York: Schirmer Books, 2005.

Dave DiMartino. SINGER-SONGWRITERS: POP MUSIC'S PERFORMER COMPOSERS, FROM A TO ZEVON. New York: Billboard Books, 1994.

Mark Duffett. COUNTING DOWN ELVIS: HIS 100 FINEST HITS. Lanham, Maryland: Rowman and Littlefield, 2018.

Mark Duffett. ELVIS: ROOTS, IMAGE, COMEBACK, PHENOMENON. Sheffield, South Yorkshire, United Kingdom: Equinox Publishing, 2020.

Mark Duffett (ed.). FAN IDENTITIES AND PRACTICES IN CONTEXT: DEDICATED TO MUSIC. Oxford, England: Routledge, 2016.

Mark Duffett. POPULAR MUSIC FANDOM: IDENTITIES, ROLES, AND PRACTICES. Oxford, England: Routledge, 2014.

Jacqueline Edmondson (ed.). MUSIC IN AMERICAN LIFE: AN ENCYCLOPEDIA OF THE SONGS, STYLES, STARS, AND STORIES THAT HAVE SHAPED OUR CULTURE. Santa Barbara, California: Green Press/ABC-CLIO Publishers, 2013.

Howard Elson. EARLY ROCKERS. New York: Proteus Books, 1982.

Philip H. Ennis. THE SEVENTH STREAM: THE EMERGENCE OF ROCK 'N' ROLL IN AMERICAN POPULAR MUSIC. Hanover, New Hampshire: Wesleyan University Press, 1992.

Colin Escott. ALL ROOTS LEAD TO ROCK: LEGENDS OF EARLY ROCK 'N' ROLL. New York: Schirmer Books, 1999.

Colin Escott, with Martin Hawkins. GOOD ROCKIN' TONIGHT: SUN RECORDS AND THE BIRTH OF ROCK 'N' ROLL. New York: St. Martin's Press, 1991.

Colin Escott. ROADKILL ON THE THREE-CHORD HIGHWAY: ART AND TRASH IN AMERICAN POPULAR MUSIC. New York: Routledge, 2002.

Colin Escott. TATTOOED ON THEIR TONGUES: A JOURNEY THROUGH THE BACKROOMS OF AMERICAN MUSIC. New York: Schirmer Books, 1996.

Ben Fong-Torres. THE HITS JUST KEEP ON COMING: THE HISTORY OF TOP 40 RADIO. San Francisco, California: Miller-Freeman Books, 1998.

Jon Hartley Fox. KING OF THE QUEEN CITY: THE STORY OF KING RECORDS. Urbana, Illinois: University of Illinois Press, 2009.

Pete Frame. THE RESTLESS GENERATION: HOW ROCK MUSIC CHANGED THE FACE OF 1950s BRITAIN. London: Rogan House, 2007.

Simon Frith and Andrew Goodwin (ed.). ON RECORD: ROCK, POP, AND THE WRITTEN WORD. New York: Pantheon Press, 1990.

Simon Frith. PERFORMING RITES: ON THE VALUE OF POPULAR MUSIC. Cambridge, Massachusetts: Harvard University Press, 1996.

Simon Frith. SOUND EFFECTS: YOUTH, LEISURE, AND THE POLITICS OF ROCK 'N' ROLL. New York: Pantheon Books, 1981.

Gillian G. Gaar. SHE'S A REBEL: THE HISTORY OF WOMEN IN ROCK & ROLL (Second Edition). New York: Seal Press, 2002 (c. 1992).

Charlie Gillett. THE SOUND OF THE CITY: THE RISE OF ROCK AND ROLL. New York: Da Capo Press, 1996 (c1970).

Robert Gordon. RESPECT YOURSELF: STAX RECORDS AND THE SOUL EXPLOSION. New York: Bloomsbury, 2013.

Jennifer Greenburg. THE ROCKABILLIES. Chicago: Center Books on American Places, 2009.

Robert Greenfield. THE LAST SULTAN: THE LIFE AND TIMES OF AHMET ERTEGUN. New York: Simon and Schuster, 2011.

Anthony J. Gribin and Matthew M. Schiff. DOO-WOP: THE FORGOTTEN THIRD OF ROCK 'N' ROLL. Iola, Wisconsin: Krause Publications, 1992.

Peter Guralnick. CARELESS LOVE: THE UNMAKING OF ELVIS PRESLEY. Boston: Little, Brown and Company, 1999.

Peter Guralnick. LAST TRAIN TO MEMPHIS: THE RISE OF ELVIS PRESLEY. Boston: Little, Brown, and Company, 1994.

Peter Guralnick. SAM PHILLIPS: THE MAN WHO INVENTED ROCK 'N' ROLL. New York: Little, Brown and Company, 2015.

Peter Guralnick. SWEET SOUL MUSIC: RHYTHM AND BLUES AND THE SOUTHERN DREAM OF FREEDOM. Boston: Back Bay Books/Little, Brown and Company, 1999 (c1986).

Adam Gussow. WHOSE BLUES? FACING UP TO RACE AND THE FUTURE OF THE MUSIC. Chapel Hill, North Carolina: University of North Carolina Press, 2020.

David Hajdu. LOVE FOR SALE: POP MUSIC IN AMERICA. New York: Farrar, Straus, and Giroux, 2016.

Jack Hamilton. JUST AROUND MIDNIGHT: ROCK AND ROLL AND THE RACIAL IMAGINATION. Cambridge, Massachusetts: Harvard University Press, 2016.

Jeff Hannusch. I HEAR YOU KNOCKIN': THE SOUND OF NEW ORLEANS RHYTHM AND BLUES. Ville Platte, Louisiana: Swallow Publications, 1985.

Jeff Hannusch. THE SOUL OF NEW ORLEANS: A LEGACY OF RHYTHM AND BLUES. Ville Platte, Louisiana: Swallow Publications, 2001.

Nigel Harrison. SONGWRITERS: A BIOGRAPHICAL DICTIONARY WITH DISCOGRAPHIES. Jefferson, North Carolina: McFarland and Company, 1998.

Herb Hendler. YEAR BY YEAR IN THE ROCK ERA: EVENTS AND CONDITIONS SHAPING THE ROCK GENERATIONS THAT RESHAPED AMERICA. Westport, Connecticut: Greenwood Press, 1983.

Clinton Heylin (ed.). THE PENGUIN BOOK OF ROCK AND ROLL WRITING. New York: Penguin Books, 1992.

Charles L. Hughes. COUNTRY SOUL: MAKING MUSIC AND MAKING RACE IN THE AMERICAN SOUTH. Chapel Hill, North Carolina: University of North Carolina Press, 2015.

Bruce Iglauer and Patrick A. Roberts. BITTEN BY THE BLUES: THE ALLIGATOR RECORDS STORY. Chicago: University of Chicago Press, 2018.

Andrew Grant Jackson. 1965: THE MOST REVOLUTIONARY YEAR IN MUSIC. Thomas Dunne Books/St. Martin's Press, 2015.

John A. Jackson. AMERICAN BANDSTAND: DICK CLARK AND THE MAKING OF A ROCK 'N' ROLL EMPIRE. New York: Oxford University Press, 1997.

John A. Jackson. BIG BEAT HEAT: ALAN FREED AND THE EARLY YEARS OF ROCK AND ROLL. New York: Schirmer Books, 1991.

David E. James. ROCK 'N' FILM: CINEMA'S DANCE WITH POPULAR MUSIC. New York: Oxford University Press, 2016.

Wayne Jancik. THE BILLBOARD BOOK OF ONE-HIT WONDERS (Revised Edition). New York: Billboard Books, 1998.

Joli Jensen. THE NASHVILLE SOUND: AUTHENTICITY, COMMERCIALIZATION, AND COUNTRY MUSIC. Nashville, Tennessee: The Country Music Foundation Press/ Vanderbilt University Press, 1998.

Preston Lauterbach. THE CHITLIN' CIRCUIT AND THE ROAD TO ROCK 'N' ROLL. New York: W.W. Norton and Company, 2011.

Jennifer C. Lena and Richard A. Peterson. "Classification As Culture: Types And Trajectories Of Music Genres," AMERICAN SOCIOLOGICAL REVIEW, 73 (October 2008): 697-718.

Bob Leszczak. WHO DID IT FIRST? GREAT POP COVER SONGS AND THEIR ORIGINAL ARTISTS. Lanham, Maryland: Rowman and Littlefield, 2014.

Bob Leszczak. WHO DID IT FIRST? GREAT RHYTHM AND BLUES COVER SONGS AND THEIR ORIGINAL ARTISTS. Lanham, Maryland: Scarecrow Press, 2013.

Bob Leszczak. WHO DID IT FIRST? GREAT ROCK AND ROLL COVER SONGS AND THEIR ORIGINAL ARTISTS. Lanham, Maryland: Rowman and Littlefield, 2014.

Mark Lewisohn. TUNE IN: THE BEATLES - ALL THESE YEARS: VOLUME ONE. New York: Crown Publishing/Penguin Random House. 2013.

Grace Lichtenstein and Laura Dankner. MUSICAL GUMBO: THE MUSIC OF NEW ORLEANS. New York: W.W. Norton and Company, 1993.

Michael Lydon and Ellen Mandel. BOOGIE LIGHTNING: HOW THE MUSIC BECAME ELECTRIC. New York: Da Capo Press, 1980.

Michael Lydon. ROCK FOLK: PORTRAITS FROM THE ROCK 'N' ROLL PANTHEON. New York: Dial Press, 1971.

Ian MacDonald. REVOLUTION IN THE HEAD: THE BEATLES' RECORDS AND THE SIXTIES (Third Edition). Chicago: Chicago Review Press, 2007 (c1994).

Bill C. Malone and Tracey E.W. Laird. COUNTRY MUSIC USA: 50th ANNIVERSARY EDITION. Austin, Texas: University of Texas Press, 2018.

Greil Marcus. MYSTERY TRAIN: IMAGES OF AMERICA IN ROCK 'N' ROLL MUSIC (Third Edition). New York: Plume/Penguin Books, 1990.

Greil Marcus (ed.). STRANDED: MUSIC FOR A DESERT ISLAND. New York: Da Capo Press, 1996 (c1979).

Dave Marsh. THE HEART OF ROCK AND SOUL: THE 1001 GREATEST SINGLES EVER MADE. New York: Da Capo Press, 1999 (c1989).

Linda Martin and Kerry Segrave. ANTI-ROCK: THE OPPOSITION TO ROCK 'N' ROLL. New York: Da Capo Press, 1993.

Randy McNutt. GUITAR TOWNS: A JOURNEY TO THE CROSSROADS OF ROCK 'N' ROLL. Bloomington, Indiana: Indiana University Press, 2002.

Randy McNutt. KING RECORDS OF CINCINNATI. San Francisco, California: Arcadia Publishing, 2009.

Randy McNutt. TOO HOT TO HANDLE: AN ILLUSTRATED ENCYCLOPEDIA OF AMERICAN RECORDING STUDIOS OF THE 20th CENTURY. Fairfield, Ohio: Hamilton Hobby Press, 2001.

Robert McParland. SINGER-SONGWRITERS OF THE 1970s: 150+ PROFILES. Jefferson, North Carolina: McFarland and Company, 2022.

Jim Miller (ed.). THE ROLLING STONE ILLUSTRATED HISTORY OF ROCK AND ROLL (Updated Edition). New York: Random House/Rolling Stone Press, 1980.

Craig Morrison. GO CAT GO! ROCKABILLY MUSIC AND ITS MAKERS. Urbana, Illinois: University of Illinois Press, 1996.

Craig Morrison. ROLL & ROLL. New York: Facts on File, 2006.

David Neale. ROOTS OF ELVIS. Lincoln, Nebraska: iUniverse Press, 2003.

Jas Obrecht (ed.). BLUES GUITAR: THE MEN WHO MADE THE MUSIC. San Francisco, California: G.P.I. Books, 1990.

Jas Obrecht (ed.). ROLLIN' AND TUMBLIN': THE POSTWAR BLUES GUITARISTS. San Francisco, California: Miller Freeman Books, 2000.

Steve O'Brien (ed.). THE ROCK 'N' ROLL YEARS - VOLUME ONE, 1950-1954. London: Vintage Rock/Anthem Publishing, 2021.

Steve O'Brien (ed.). THE ROCK 'N' ROLL YEARS - VOLUME TWO, 1955-1959. London: Vintage Rock/Anthem Publishing, 2021.

Steve O'Brien (ed.). THE ROCK 'N' ROLL YEARS - VOLUME THREE, 1960-1964. London: Vintage Rock, Anthem Publishing, 2022.

Jim O'Neal and Amy Van Singel (eds.). THE VOICE OF THE BLUES: INTERVIEWS FROM LIVING BLUES MAGAZINE. New York: Routledge, 2002.

Steve Otfinoski. THE GOLDEN AGE OF ROCK INSTRUMENTALS. New York: Billboard Books, 1997.

Ray Padgett. COVER ME: THE STORIES BEHIND THE GREATEST COVER SONGS OF ALL TIMES. New York: Sterling Books, 2017.

Robert Palmer (edited by Anthony DeCurtis). BLUES & CHAOS: THE MUSIC WRITING OF ROBERT PALMER. New York: Scribner, 2009.

Robert Palmer. DEEP BLUES. New York: Viking Press, 1981.

Richard A. Peterson. CREATING COUNTRY MUSIC: FABRICATING AUTHENICITY. Chicago: University of Chicago Press, 1997.

Richard A. Peterson. "Why 1955? Explaining The Advent of Rock Music," POPULAR MUSIC, 9:1 (January 1990): 97-116.

David R. Pichaske. A GENERATION IN MOTION: POPULAR MUSIC AND CULTURE IN THE SIXTIES. Granite Falls, Minnesota: Ellis Press, 1989 (c1979).

Robert G. Pielke. ROCK MUSIC IN AMERICAN CULTURE: THE SOUNDS OF REVOLUTION (Secong Edition). Jefferson, North Carolina: McFarland and Company, 2012.

George Plasketes (ed.). PLAY IT AGAIN: COVER SONGS IN POPULAR MUSIC. Burlington, Vermont: Ashgate Publishing Company, 2010.

Robert Pruter. CHICAGO SOUL. Urbana, Illinois: University of Illinois Press, 1991.

Robert Pruter. DOO-WOP: THE CHICAGO SCENE. Urbana, Illinois: University of Illinois Press, 1996.

Mitch Rosalsky. ENCYCLOPEDIA OF RHYTHM & BLUES AND DOO-WOP VOCAL GROUPS. Lanham, Maryland: Scarecrow Press, 2000.

Scott Rowley (ed.). THE BLUES COLLECTION: CLASSIC STORIES OF THE BLUES GREATS (Sixth Edition). London: Future Publishing Limited, 2022.

William Ruhlmann. BREAKING RECORDS: 100 YEARS OF HITS. New York: Routledge, 2004.

Robert Santelli, Holly George-Warren, and Jim Brown (eds.). AMERICAN ROOTS MUSIC. New York: Harry N. Abrams/rolling Stone Press Book, 2001.

Timothy E. Scheurer (ed.). AMERICAN POPULAR MUSIC - VOLUME ONE: THE NINETEENTH CENTURY TO TIN PAN ALLEY. Bowling Green, Ohio: Bowling Green State University Popular Press, 1989.

Timothy E. Scheurer (ed.). AMERICAN POPULAR MUSIC - VOLUME TWO: THE AGE OF ROCK. Bowling Green, Ohio: Bowling Green State University Popular Press, 1989.

Roberta Freund Schwartz. HOW BRITAIN GOT HE BLUES: THE TRANSMISSION AND RECEPTION OF AMERICAN BLUES STYLE IN THE UNITED KINGDOM. Aldershot, United Kingdom: Ashgate Publishing, 2007.

Lisa Scrivani-Tidd, Rhonda Markowitz, Chris Smith, Maryann Janosik, and Bob Gulla (comps.). THE GREENWOOD ENCYCLOPEDIA OF ROCK HISTORY, 1951-2005 (Six Volumes). Westport, Connecticut: Greenwood Press, 2006.

Nat Shapiro and Bruce Pollock (eds.). POPULAR MUSIC, 1920-1979 - A REVISED COMPILATION (Three Volumes). Detroit, Michigan: Gale Research, 1985.

Arnold Shaw. HONKERS AND SHOUTERS: THE GOLDEN YEARS OF RHYTHM AND BLUES. New York: Collier Books/Macmillan Publishing, 1978.

Arnold Shaw. THE ROCKIN' FIFTIES: THE DECADE THAT TRANSFORMED THE POP MUSIC SCENE. New York: Hawthorn Books, 1974.

R.J. Smith. CHUCK BERRY: AN AMERICAN LIFE. New York: Hachette Books, 2022.

R.J. Smith. THE ONE: THE LIFE AND TIMES OF JAMES BROWN. New York: Gotham Books, 2012.

Wes Smith. THE PIED PIPERS OF ROCK 'N' ROLL: RADIO DEEJAYS OF THE '50s AND '60s. Marietta, Georgia: Longstreet Press, 1989.

Bob Stanley. LET'S DO IT: THE BIRTH OF POP. London: Faber and Faber, 2022.

Bob Stanley. YEAH! YEAH! YEAH! THE STORY OF POP MUSIC FROM BILL HALEY TO BEYONCE. New York: W.W. Norton and Company, 2014 (c. 2013).

James Sullivan. WHICH SIDE ARE YOU ON? 20th CENTURY AMERICAN HISTORY IN 100 PROTEST SONGS. New York: Oxford University Press, 2019.

Steve Sullivan. ENCYCLOPEDIA OF GREAT POPULAR SONG RECORDINGS (Two Volumes). Lanham, Maryland: Scarecrow Press, 2013.

Harry Sumrall. PIONEERS OF ROCK AND ROLL: 100 ARTISTS WHO CHANGED THE FACE OF ROCK. New York: Billboard Books, 1994.

Nick Talevski. THE UNOFFICIAL ENCYCLOPEDIA OF THE ROCK AND ROLL HALL OF FAME. Westport, Connecticut: Greenwood Press, 1998.

Art Tipaldi. CHILDREN OF THE BLUES: 49 MUSICIANS SHAPING A NEW BLUES TRADITION. San Francisco, California: Backbeat Books, 2002.

Gary Tipp (ed.). ROCKABILLY: SPECIAL EDITION. London: Vintage Rock/Anthem Publishing, 2019.

Gary Tipp (ed.). SUN RECORDS: SPECIAL EDITION. London: Vintage Rock/Anthem Publishing, 2019.

Brad Tolinski and Alan di Perna. PLAY IT LOUD: AN EPIC HISTORY OF THE STYLE, SOUND, AND REVOLUTION OF THE ELECTRIC GUITAR. New York: Doubleday, 2016.

Nick Tosches. UNSUNG HEROES OF ROCK 'N' ROLL: THE BIRTH OF ROCK IN THE WILD YEARS BEFORE ELVIS (Revised Edition). New York: Harmony Books, 1991.

Steven C. Tracy (ed.). WRITE ME A FEW OF YOUR LINES: A BLUES READER. Amherst, Massachusetts: University of Massachusetts Press, 1999.

Don Tyler. HIT SONGS, 1900-1955: AMERICAN POPULAR MUSIC OF THE PRE-ROCK ERA. Jefferson, North Carolina: McFarland and Company. 2007.

Richie Unterberger. TURN! TURN! TURN! THE '60s FOLK-ROCK REVOLUTION. San Francisco, California: Backbeat Books, 2002.

Dorothy Wade and Justine Picardie. MUSIC MAN: AHMET ERTEGUN, ATLANTIC RECORDS, AND THE TRIUMPH OF ROCK 'N' ROLL New York: W.W. Norton and Company, 1990.

Steve Waksman. INSTRUMENTS OF DESIRE: THE ELECTRIC GUITAR AND THE SHAPING OF MUSICAL EXPERIENCE. Cambridge, Massachusetts: Harvard University Press, 1999.

Brian Ward. JUST MY SOUL RESPONDING: RHYTHM AND BLUES, BLACK CONSCIOUSNESS, AND RACE RELATIONS. Berkeley, California: University of California Press, 1998.

Ed Ward. THE HISTORY OF ROCK & ROLL - VOLUME ONE, 1920-1963. New York: Flatiron Books, 2016.

Ed Ward. THE HISTORY OF ROCK & ROLL - VOLUME TWO, 1964-1977: THE BEATLES, THE STONES, AND THE RISE OF CLASSIC ROCK. New York: Flatiron Books, 2019.

Jay Warner. THE BILLBOARD BOOK OF AMERICAN SINGING GROUPS: A HISTORY, 1940-1990. New York: Billboard Books, 1992.

Erin Torkelson Weber. THE BEATLES AND THE HISTORIANS: AN ANALYSIS OF WRITINGS ABOUT THE FAB FOUR. Jefferson, North Carolina: McFarland and Company, 2016.

Marc Weingarten. STATION TO STATION: THE HISTORY OF ROCK 'N' ROLL ON TELEVISION New York: Pocket Books/Simon and Schuster, 2000.

Pete Welding and Toby Byron (eds.). BLUESLAND: PORTRAITS OF TWELVE MAJOR AMERICAN BLUES MASTERS. New York: Dutton/Penguin Books, 1991.

Craig Werner. A CHANGE IS GONNA COME: MUSIC, RACE, AND THE SOUL OF AMERICA. New York: Plume/Penguin Putnam Books, 1999.

Joel Whitburn (comp.). AMERICA'S GREATEST ALBUMS, 1956-2018. Menomonee Falls, Wisconsin: Record Research, 2019.

Joel Whitburn (comp.). BILLBOARD POP HITS: SINGLES AND ALBUMS, 1940-1954. Menomonee Falls, Wisconsin: Record Research, 2002.

Joel Whitburn (comp.) A CENTURY OF POP MUSIC: YEAR-BY-YEAR TOP 40 RANKINGS OF THE SONGS AND ARTISTS THAT SHAPED A CENTURY. Menomonee Falls, Wisconsin: Record Research, 1999.

Joel Whitburn (comp.). POP MEMORIES, 1890-1954: THE HISTORY OF AMERICAN POPULAR MUSIC. Menomonee Falls, Wisconsin: Record Research, 1986.

Joel Whitburn (comp.). POP MEMORIES: THE HISTORY OF AMERICAN POPULAR MUSIC, 1900-1940. Menomonee Falls, Wisconsin: Record Research, 2015.

Joel Whitburn (comp.). TOP COUNTRY SINGLES, 1944-2017. Menomonee Falls, Wisconsin: Record Research, 2018.

Joel Whitburn (comp.). TOP POP SINGLES, 1955-2018. Menomonee Falls, Wisconsin: Record Research, 2019.

Joel Whitburn (comp.). TOP RHYTHM & BLUES SINGLES, 1942-2016. Menomonee Falls, Wisconsin: Record Research, 2017.

Adam White and Fred Bronson. THE BILLBOARD BOOK OF NUMBER ONE RHYTHM & BLUES HITS. New York: Billboard Books, 1993.

Timothy White. ROCK LIVES: PROFILES AND INTERVIEWS. New York: Henry Holt and Company, 1990.

James Wierzbicki. MUSIC IN THE AGE OF ANXIETY: AMERICAN MUSIC IN THE FIFTIES. Urbana, Illinois: University of Illinois Press, 2016.

James Brown

AUTHOR/EDITOR PROFILES

B. Lee Cooper is a freelance writer and popular music analyst. He has been a professor of history and American culture, a dean of students, a provost and vice president for academic affairs, and a university president. He holds degrees from Bowling Green State University (B.S., 1964), Michigan State University (M.A., 1965), Ohio State University (Ph.D., 1971), and Newman University (D.H.L., 2009). He also studied at the Institute for Educational Management (I.E.M., 1980) at Harvard University. Dr. Cooper has an avid interest in 20th Century American popular music. He collects blues, doo-wop, rockabilly, and rock 'n' roll CDs. His scholarly pursuits in popular music include bibliography, discography, song theme identification, and biographical studies. Dr. Cooper has authored more than 600 book and record reviews and over 175 articles. He has also published 50 books, including A RESOURCE GUIDE TO THEMES IN CONTEMPORARY SONG LYRICS, 1950-1985 (Greenwood Press, 1986), ROCK MUSIC IN AMERICAN POPULAR CULTURE - 3 Volumes (Haworth, 1995, 1997, 1999), THE POPULAR MUSIC HANDBOOK (Libraries Unlimited, 2004), NEW ORLEANS MUSIC: LEGACY AND SURVIVAL (Routledge, 2008), and GUITAR BOOGIE SHUFFLE (Paw Paw Press, 2019). In 1983 he received the ASCAP-Deems Taylor Award for excellence in music research after the publication of IMAGES OF AMERICAN SOCIETY IN POPULAR MUSIC (Nelson-Hall, 1982). Dr. Cooper is currently President and CEO of Popular Music Research, Ltd., a voluntary association of scholars and teachers who assist young writers who are investigating music-related projects. He also teaches for The Osher Lifelong Learning Institute (OLLI) at the University of North Carolina (UNC) - Asheville.

Frank Hoffmann served as a Professor of Library & Information Science, as well as Music, from 1979 through 2015. He has written more than fifty trade books (publishers include Routledge, Haworth, Scarecrow, Shoe String and Libraries Unlimited) and thirty e-books (available from NetLibrary and Amazon.com). He has won the Choice Magazine Best Academic Books award for both THE LITERATURE OF ROCK and INTELLECTUAL FREEDOM AND CENSORSHIP.

Dick Clark hosting AMERICAN BANDSTAND in early 1958

THE PAW PAW PRESS

Frank W. Hoffmann, Ph.D.
Founder and Executive Editor
P.O. Box 8313
Bloomington, Indiana 47407
U. S. A.

B. Lee Cooper, Ph.D.
Associate Editor and Chief Acquisitions Officer
4 Grey Goose Court
Biltmore Lake, North Carolina 28715
U. S. A.

Recent publications in the "POPULAR MUSIC AND AMERICAN CULTURE" series:

ACADEMIC REVIEWS OF ROCK WRITINGS: A TOPICAL PRESENTATION OF CRITICAL COMMENTARIES (2015)
B. Lee Cooper and Frank W. Hoffmann

ADDICTIONS AND VICES, HEROES AND VILLAINS: FINDING MEANING IN THE LYRICS OF COMMERICAL RECORDINGS - VOLUME TWO (2020)
B. Lee Cooper and Frank W. Hoffmann

AIN'T THAT PECULIAR: ANSWER SONGS, NOVELTY NUMBERS, ONE-HIT WONDERS, AND MORE (2020)
B. Lee Cooper and Frank W. Hoffmann

AMERICA IN TRANSITION, 1945-1975: A MUSICAL PERSPECTIVE ON HISTORICAL CHANGE (2017)
B. Lee Cooper and Frank W. Hoffmann

AMERICAN RECORD LABELS, RECORDING ARTISTS, AND THE PURSUIT OF HIT SONGS (2022)
B. Lee Cooper and Frank W. Hoffmann

ANSWER SONGS: A REFERENCE GUIDE TO RESPONSE RECORDINGS, 1910 TO THE PRESENT - TWO VOLUMES (2015)
B. Lee Cooper, Frank W. Hoffmann, Stephen Briggs, David Milberg, and William L. Schurk, with assistance from Debbie Edens

ANTHEMS AND AUTOMOBILES, PATRIOTISM AND PROTEST: FINDING MEANING IN THE LYRICS OF COMMERCIAL RECORDINGS - VOLUME ONE (2020)
B. Lee Cooper and Frank W. Hoffmann

ARTISTIC INGENUITY, POLITICAL UPHEAVAL, AND SOCIAL CHANGE REFLECTED IN AMERICAN POPULAR MUSIC, 1945-1985 (2022)
B. Lee Cooper and Frank W. Hoffmann

ASSESSING THE SONIC CULTURE: REVELATIONS THROUGH RECORD REVIEWS (2018)
B. Lee Cooper and Frank W. Hoffmann

ASSESSING THE SONIC CULTURE: REVELATIONS THROUGH RECORD REVIEWS - VOLUME TWO (2020)
B. Lee Cooper and Frank W. Hoffmann

BLACK MUSIC MATTERS: AFRO-AMERICAN RECORDING ARTISTRY AND U.S. POP CHART INTEGRATION, 1945-1975 (2020)
B. Lee Cooper and Frank W. Hoffmann

BLACK RECORDINGS: ARTISTIC CREATIVITY, U.S. POP CHART SUCCESS, AND WORLDWIDE MUSICAL INFLUENCE, 1945-1975 (2022)
B. Lee Cooper and Frank W. Hoffmann

BLUE-EYED SOUL: MYTHS AND REALITY IN AMERICAN POPULAR MUSIC (2018)
B. Lee Cooper and Frank W. Hoffmann

BLUES POWER: INFLUENTIAL BLUES ARTISTS AND THEIR MUSIC - A REFERENCE GUIDE (2023)
B. Lee Cooper and Frank W. Hoffmann

BLUESWOMEN, COUNTRY QUEENS, GIRL GROUPS, GOSPEL GIANTS, JAZZ SINGERS, POP DIVAS, ROCKABILLY REBELS, AND SOUL SISTERS: A BIO-BIBLIOGRAPHY OF FEMALE RECORDING ARTISTS, 1945-1975 (2019)
B. Lee Cooper and Frank W. Hoffmann

BRIGHT LIGHTS, BIG CITY: AMERICAN METROPOLITAN MUSIC AND URBAN MUSICIANS, 1945-1975 (2020)
B. Lee Cooper and Frank W. Hoffmann

CELEBRATING SOUL SINGERS AND BLUE-EYED SOUL/FUNK RECORDINGS (2023)
B. Lee Cooper and Frank W. Hoffmann

CHRISTMAS RECORDINGS: A RESOURCE GUIDE TO TRADITIONAL HYMNS, SANTA CLAUS SONGS, AND OTHER HOLIDAY NOVELTY NUMBERS (2019)
B. Lee Cooper and Frank W. Hoffmann, with research assistance from David A. Milberg

THE COLORFUL PALETTE OF POPULAR RECORDING ARTISTS: TOPICS AND THEMES ILLUMINATED IN SONG TITLES AND LYRICS (2021)
B. Lee Cooper and Frank W. Hoffmann

COVER RECORDINGS, 1900-2016: TWELVE DECADES OF SIGNIFICANT SONG REVIVALS - VOLUME ONE (2016)
B. Lee Cooper and Frank W. Hoffmann

COVER RECORDINGS, 1900-2016: TWELVE DECADES OF SIGNIFICANT SONG REVIVALS - VOLUME TWO (2017)
B. Lee Cooper and Frank W. Hoffmann

COVERING NEW RECORDINGS AND REVIVING FORMER HITS: USING PREVIOUSLY RECORDED SONGS TO ACHIEVE MUSIC CHART RECOGNITION (2021)
B. Lee Cooper and Frank W. Hoffmann

DAWN OF THE SING-SONGWRITER ERA, 1944-1963: BIBLIOGRAPHIC PROFILES OF THE PERFORMER-COMPOSERS (2015)
B. Lee Cooper and Frank W. Hoffmann

DISCS OF DISTINCTION: ESSAYS ON REMARKABLE RECORDINGS BY EXCEPTIONAL ARTISTS (2015)
B. Lee Cooper and Frank W. Hoffmann, with assistance from Debbie Edens

DOCUMENTING THE BLUES: PRINT RESOURCES ON KEY ARTISTS, INFLUENTIAL RECORDINGS, AND MUSICAL CHANGE, 1960-2020 (2019)
B. Lee Cooper and Frank W. Hoffmann

THE DOO-WOP DECADES, 1945-1965: A RESOURCE GUIDE TO VOCAL GROUPS AND THEIR RECORDINGS (2017)
B. Lee Cooper and Frank W. Hoffmann

THE DOO-WOP PHENOMENON (2021)
Frank W. Hoffmann and B. Lee Cooper

DREAMS AND NIGHTMARES, GHOSTS AND MONSTERS: FINDING MEANING IN THE LYRICS OF COMMERCIAL RECORDINGS - VOLUME THREE (2020)
B. Lee Cooper and Frank W. Hoffmann

EVEN MORE SONIC CHOICES: EVALUATING RECORDING ARTISTS, MUSICAL STYLES, AND LYRICAL TOPICS (2019)
B. Lee Cooper and Frank W. Hoffmann

EXPANDING THE ROCK 'N' ROLL FOOTPRINT, 1960-1965: INFLUENCING OTHER AMERICAN MUSICAL GENRES AND CONVERTING THE BRITISH POP MUSIC SCENE (2021)
B. Lee Cooper and Frank W. Hoffmann

GALLANT MEN, FORTUNATE SONS, AND DRAFT RESISTERS: POPULAR MUSIC REACTIONS TO 20th CENTURY AMERICAN MILITARY ENGAGEMENTS (2020)
B. Lee Cooper, Frank W. Hoffmann, and Debbie Edens

THE GREAT AMERICAN WALL OF SOUND (2022)
B. Lee Cooper and Frank W. Hoffmann

GUITAR BOOGIE SHUFFLE: WHEN INSTRUMENTAL PERFORMERS AND THEIR RECORDINGS RULED AMERICA'S POP CHARTS, 1945-1975 (2019)
B. Lee Cooper, Michael L. Cooper, and Frank W. Hoffmann

HALLOWEEN SONGS AND HORROR RECORDINGS, 1920-2020: A CENTURY OF SCARY LYRICS AND SPOOKY MELODIES (2019)
B. Lee Cooper, Julie Cooper, and Frank W. Hoffmann

HUNDREDS OF HITS: NOTEWORTHY RECORDINGS FROM A VARIETY OF MUSICAL GENRES (2020)
B. Lee Cooper and Frank W. Hoffmann

JUKEBOX REVOLUTIONS: CULTURAL TRADITIONS, SOCIAL CHANGE, AND POPULAR MUSIC, 1950-1975 (2020)
B. Lee Cooper and Frank W. Hoffmann

JUKEBOX REVOLUTIONS: CULTURAL TRADITIONS, SOCIAL CHANGE, AND POPULAR MUSIC, 1950-1975 - VOLUME TWO (2020)
B. Lee Cooper and Frank W, Hoffmann

THE KEYBOARD KINGDOM: A RESOURCES GUIDE TO ROCK, POP, BLUES, AND COUNTRY KEYBOARD PLAYERS AND THEIR MUSIC (2015)
B. Lee Cooper, Michael L. Cooper, and Frank W. Hoffmann, with research assistance from William L. Schurk

LEGENDARY BLACK RECORDING ARTISTS: PIVOTAL PERFORMERS OF BLUES, JAZZ, POP, R&B, AND SOUL, 1945-1975 (2019)
B. Lee Cooper and Frank W. Hoffmann

LISTEN TO ME! ANALYZING VOCAL ARTISTS, LYRICISTS, AND COMPOSERS, 1950-2020 (2021)
B. Lee Cooper and Frank W. Hoffmann

LYRICAL LEGACIES: ESSAYS ON TOPICS IN ROCK, POP, AND BLUES LYRICS... AND BEYOND (2015)
B. Lee Cooper and Frank W, Hoffmann, with assistance from Debbie Edens

MORE DISCS OF DISTINCTION: ADDITIONAL ESSAYS ON REMARKABLE RECORDINGSBY EXCEPTIONAL ARTISTS (2015)
B. Lee Cooper and Frank W. Hoffmann, with assistance from Debbie Edens

MORE ROCKERS! FROM AC/DC TO STEVIE RAY VAUGHAN - A REFERENCE GUIDE (2022)
B. Lee Cooper and Frank W. Hoffmann

MORE SONIC CHOICES: EVALUATING RECORDING ARTISTS, MUSICAL STYLES, AND LYRICAL TOPICS (2019)
B. Lee Cooper and Frank W. Hoffmann

MORE THAN JUST THE MUSIC: ESSAYS IN LYRICAL ANALYSIS AND TOPICAL IDENTIFICATION (2015)
B. Lee Cooper, Frank W. Hoffmann, Stephen D. Briggs, and William L. Schurk, with assistance from Debbie Edens

MUSIC-MAKING LEGENDS OF THE ROCKIN' '50s: A REFERENCE GUIDE (2018)
B. Lee Cooper and Frank W. Hoffmann

A MUSICAL MEMOIR: REFLECTIONS ON LIFE, DEATH, AND AMERICAN CULTURE, 1942-2022 (2023)
B. Lee Cooper

NEW ORLEANS RHYTHM & BLUES: A RESOURCE GUIDE TO CRESCENT CITY ARTISTS AND THEIR RECORDINGS, 1945-1975 (2017)
B. Lee Cooper, Frank. W. Hoffmann, and Debbie Edens

THE 1950s: A DISTINCTIVE DECADE DEPICTED IN POPULAR MUSIC (2020)
B. Lee Cooper and Frank W. Hoffmann

THE 1960s: A TURBULENT DECADE DEPICTED IN POPULAR MUSIC (2020)
B. Lee Cooper and Frank W. Hoffmann

NOVELTY RECORDS: A TOPICAL DISCOGRAPHY, 1900-2015 (2015)
B. Lee Cooper and Frank W. Hoffmann

NOVELTY RECORDS: SELECTED SUBJECTS AND ARTISTS (2015)
B. Lee Cooper and Frank W. Hoffmann, with assistance from Debbie Edens

PERSISTENT THEMES IN SOUND RECORDINGS: TOPICAL DISCOGRAPHIES ON ADDICTIONS, CHRISTMAS, DEATH, AND RELIGION (2016)
B. Lee Cooper and Frank W. Hoffmann

PERSISTENT THEMES IN SOUND RECORDINGS: TOPICAL DISCOGRAPHIES ON ANIMALS, DANCE, HALLOWEEN, AND MILITARY CONFLICTS (2016)
B. Lee Cooper and Frank W. Hoffmann

PERSISTENT THEMES IN SOUND RECORDINGS: TOPICAL DISCOGRAPHIES ON COMMUNICATIONS, METROPOLITAN CENTERS, TRANSPORTATION VEHICLES, AND WEDDINGS (2016)
B. Lee Cooper and Frank W. Hoffmann

PERSISTENT THEMES IN SOUND RECORDINGS: TOPICAL DISCOGRAPHIES ON BASEBALL, EDUCATION, PHYSICAL APPEARANCE, AND THE ROMANTIC CYCLE (2016)
B. Lee Cooper and Frank W. Hoffmann

PERSISTENT THEMES IN SOUND RECORDINGS: TOPICAL DISCOGRAPHIES ON NOVELTY RECORDINGS, TECHNOLOGY, TIME, AND WEATHER (2016)
B. Lee Cooper and Frank W. Hoffmann

PERSISTENT THEMES IN SOUND RECORDINGS: TOPICAL DISCOGRAPHIES ON ANSWER SONGS, FOOD & DRINK, MEDICAL IMAGERY, AND NURSERY RHYMES (2016)
B. Lee Cooper and Frank W. Hoffmann

PERSISTENT THEMES IN SOUND RECORDINGS: TOPICAL DISCOGRAPHIES ON COVER RECORDS, MUSICAL INSTRUMENTS, NONSENSE LYRICS, AND TRIBUTE TUNES (2016)
B. Lee Cooper and Frank W. Hoffmann

PERSONAL PERSPECTIVES, POLITICAL ISSUES, AND SOCIAL CONCERNS REFLECTED IN AMERICAN POPULAR MUSIC, 1945-1985 (2022)
B. Lee Cooper and Frank W. Hoffmann

PLAYING FAVORITES: HOW RECORD COMPANIES ATTRACTED CROSS-GENERATIONAL LISTENERS TO OLD MUSIC, 1980-2022 (2022)
B. Lee Cooper and Frank W. Hoffmann

POPULAR MUSIC RESEARCH: ANSWER SONGS, BLUE-EYED SOUL, COVER RECORDINGS...AND BEYOND (2015)
B. Lee Cooper and Frank W, Hoffmann, with assistance from Debbie Edens

POPULAR MUSIC SCHOLARSHIP: ARTICLES, BIBLIOGRAPHIES, BOOK/CD REVIEWS, AND DISCOGRAPHIES (2015)

B. Lee Cooper and Frank W. Hoffmann, with assistance from Debbie Edens and William L. Schurk

POPULAR SONGS AS ORAL HISTORY: ADDICTIONS AND CRIMINALITY, HALLOWEEN HITS, INTERNATIONAL WARFARE, CHRISTMAS TUNES, AND TRIBUTE RECORDINGS (2021)
B. Lee Cooper and Frank W. Hoffmann

POPULAR SONGS AS ORAL HISTORY: COVER RECORDINGS, DOO-WOP HARMONY GROUPS, INSTRUMENTAL HITS & SESSION PLAYERS, MEMPHIS MUSIC, AND SINGING THE BLUES (2021)
B. Lee Cooper and Frank W. Hoffmann

POPULAR SONGS AS ORAL HISTORY: MOTIVATIONAL MUSIC, TECHNOLOGICAL CHANGE, TEENAGE CULTURE, MUSIC CITIES, AND IMAGES OF WOMEN, 1950-1975 (2021)
B. Lee Cooper and Frank W. Hoffmann

POPULAR SONGS AS ORAL HISTORY: NOVELTY RECORDINGS, POPULAR MUIC CHART INTEGRATION, EXTRATERRESTRIAL IMAGERY, NEW ORLEANS MUSIC, AND ROCK 'N' ROLL HEROES (2021)
B. Lee Cooper and Frank W. Hoffmann

POPULAR SONGS AS ORAL HISTORY: THE ROCK 'N' ROLL LEGACY, EUROPEAN INHERITORS OF BLUES & ROCK, SECOND GENERATION AMERICAN & BRITISH ROCKERS, THE TRIUMPH OF SOUL MUSIC, AND ROMANCE & SEX (2021)
B. Lee Cooper and Frank W. Hoffmann

PROFILING POPULAR MUSIC: ESSAYS OF ARTISTS, LYRICS, RECORDINGS, AND FANS (2018)
B. Lee Cooper and Frank W. Hoffmann

PROMINENT THEMES IN POPULAR SONGS: AN EXPLORATION OF 54 PERSISTENT LYRICAL THEMES (2015)
B. Lee Cooper and Frank W. Hoffmann, with research assistance from Debbie Edens, Matthew J. Masters, and William L. Schurk

RECORD LABELS: GATEWAYS TO MUSICAL DIVERSITY IN THE UNITED STATES (2020)
B. Lee Cooper and Frank W. Hoffmann

REFLECTION, RESISTANCE, RACISM, AND REBELLION: LYRICAL RESPONSES TO CULTURAL CHANGE (2019)
B. Lee Cooper and Frank W. Hoffmann

REVISTING ROCK'S "LOST YEARS", 1959-1963: DEMONSTRATING CONTINUITY, ORIGINALITY, AND DEVELOPMENT IN AMERICAN POPULAR RECORDINGS (2017)
B. Lee Cooper and Frank W. Hoffmann

THE RISE OF ROCK 'N' ROLL, 1950-1959: A LITERARY GUIDE TO THE MOST INFLUENTIAL RECORDING ARTISTS, COMPOSERS, DISC JOCKEYS, AND RECORD COMPANIES OF THIS TRANSFORMATIVE DECADE (2016)
B. Lee Cooper and Frank W. Hoffmann

ROCK LIVES: VOCALISTS AND SINGING GROUPS, INSTRUMENTALISTS AND OTHER RECORD WORLD PROFESSIONALS (2021)
B. Lee Cooper and Frank W. Hoffmann

THE ROCK 'N' ROLL BOOKSHELF: COMMENTARIES ON LITERARY INVESTIGATIONS OF AMERICA'S MUSICAL CULTURE (Second Edition) (2020)
B. Lee Cooper and Frank W. Hoffmann

THE ROCK 'N' ROLL SOUNDSCAPE, 1954-1959: KEY RECORDING ARTISTS, INFLUENTIAL SONGWRITERS, AND OTHER CONTRIBUTING FACTORS (2021)
B. Lee Cooper and Frank W. Hoffmann

ROCKABILLY REBELS RULE: A REFERENCE GUIDE FROM CARL PERKINS TO BRIAN SETZER (2023)
B. Lee Cooper and Frank W. Hoffmann

ROCKABILLY! - THE ARTISTS, THE MUSIC, THE HERITAGE: A LITERARY RESOURCE GUIDE (2016)
B. Lee Cooper and Frank W. Hoffmann

ROCKERS! FROM CHUCK BERRY TO ZZ TOP - A REFERENCE GUIDE (2022)
B. Lee Cooper and Frank W. Hoffmann

SONGS, SONGWRITERS, AND LYRICAL TOPICS: UNEARTHING THE ROOTS OF AMERICAN POPULAR MUSI C, 1950-1964 (2018)
B. Lee Cooper and Frank W. Hoffmann

SONIC CHOICES: EVALUATING RECORDING ARTISTS, MUSICAL STYLES, AND LYRICAL TOPICS (2019)
B. Lee Cooper and Frank W. Hoffmann

SOUL MUSIC ASCENDING, 1961-1970: FROM THE GOSPEL/R&B ROOTS TO THE PINNACLE OF THE POP CHARTS - A REFERENCE GUIDE TO SOULFUL ARTISTS AND THEIR RECORDINGS (2017)
B. Lee Cooper and Frank W. Hoffmann

SOUTHERN ROOTS/NATIONAL POP HITS, 1945-1975: DIVERSITY WITHIN AMERICAN MUSIC FUELED BY RECORDING ARTISTS BORN BELOW THE MASON-DIXON LINE (2020)
B. Lee Cooper and Frank W. Hoffmann

THREE OF A KIND: THE ROLLING STONES, JOHN FOGERTY, AND MALE/FEMALE RECORDING DUOS (2015)
B. Lee Cooper (edited by Frank W. Hoffmann)

TOPICAL TUNES AND HOLIDAY HITS: PERSISTENT IMAGERY AND COMMON THEMES IN POPULAR RECORDINGS (2022)
B. Lee Cooper and Frank W. Hoffmann

TRACKING THE TRANSFORMATION OF AMERICAN POPULAR MUSIC: YEAR-TO-YEAR, DECADE-TO-DECADE, 1945-1922 (2022)
B. Lee Cooper and Frank W. Hoffmann

TRACKING TOPICAL TUNES: IDENTIFYING SONG LYRICS THAT FOCUS ON SPECIFIC THEMES IN AMERICAN POPULAR RECORDINGS (2019)
B. Lee Cooper and Frank W. Hoffmann

THE TRIUMPH OF RHYTHM & BLUES, 1945-1960: FROM MARGINALIZED MUSIC TO MAINSTREAM HITS - A REFERENCE GUIDE TO ARTISTS AND RECORDINGS (2017)
B. Lee Cooper and Frank W. Hoffmann

VISIONS OF AXEMEN: A RESOURCE GUIDE TO GUITARISTS AND THEIR RECORDINGS (2015)
B. Lee Cooper, Michael L. Cooper, and Frank W. Hoffmann, with research assistance from William L. Schurk

WHEN MEMPHIS RULED THE POPULAR MUSIC AIRWAVES: FROM BLUES, R&B, AND ROCKABILLY TO POP, ROCK, AND SOUL (2021)
B. Lee Cooper and Frank W. Hoffmann

Made in the USA
Columbia, SC
22 March 2023

e0e8e92e-f035-45b5-8dbf-3f986ac0b4e2R01